Introduction to Computer Graphics with OpenGL ES

JungHyun Han

CRC Press

Taylor & Francis Group

Boca Raton London New York

CRC Press is an imprint of the
Taylor & Francis Group, an **informa** business

Dedication

To my wonderful boy, Jihoon, who is embarking on a new journey in his life.

Contents

Part II - Advanced Topics

Preface

OpenGL ES is the standard graphics API for mobile and embedded systems. Virtually every pixel on a smartphone's screen is generated by OpenGL ES. However, there exists no textbook on OpenGL ES which has a balance between theory and practicality. This book is written to answer that need and presents the must-know in real-time graphics with OpenGL ES. This book suits the advanced undergraduate and beginner graduate courses in computer graphics.

Another primary group of readers that this book may benefit includes mobile 3D app developers, who have experiences in OpenGL ES and shader programming but lack theoretical background in 3D graphics. A few excellent programming manuals on OpenGL ES can be found in bookstores, but they do not provide a sufficient level of mathematical background for developers. Assuming that the readers have a minimal understanding of vectors and matrices, this book provides an opportunity to combine their knowledge with the background theory of computer graphics.

This book is built upon the author's previous work *3D Graphics for Game Programming* published in 2011. Reusing roughly half of the contents from that book, several new topics and a considerable number of OpenGL ES and shader programs have been added. As OpenGL ES is a subset of OpenGL, this book is also suitable for beginner OpenGL programmers.

The organization and presentation of this book have been carefully designed so as to enable the readers to easily understand the key aspects of real-time graphics and OpenGL ES. Over the chapters, numerous 3D illustrations are provided to help the readers effortlessly grasp the complicated topics. An important organizational feature of this book is that "non-core" details are presented in separate notes (in shaded boxes) and in optional sections (marked by asterisks). They can be safely skipped without incurring any difficulty in understanding the subsequent topics of the book.

If the optional parts are excluded, the entire contents of this book can be covered in a 16-week semester for graduate classes. For undergraduate classes, however, this feat will be difficult. According to the author's experience, teaching Chapters 1 through 14 is a feasible goal.

The sample programs presented in this book are available on GitHub: https://github.com/medialab-ku/openGLESbook. The site also provides links to the full-length lecture notes as PowerPoint files and additional materials including video clips.

Acknowledgments

The author is deeply indebted to his students at the 3D Interactive Media Lab of Korea University. Virtually all visual illustrations were generated by Myoung Gon Kim and Seungjik Lee, who have exceptional talents in both programming and visual arts. Inbum Park performed a lot of 3ds Max works requested by the author, and JeongHyeon Ahn was in charge of all sample programs. HyeongYeop Kang consistently helped the author reorganize the chapters, and Paul C. Gloumeau proofread the beta version of this book. The other lab members, Seungho Baek, SungIk Cho, Sang-bin Kim, Seung-wook Kim, Jinwoo Choi, Geonsun Lee, Min Hyung Kee, Seongsu Kwon, and Sun Young Park, always took time out of their busy schedules to respond to my inquiries in real time. The content of this book has been gradually built through the courses offered at Korea University. The students of the classes provided the author with invaluable feedback with which the book was improved.

My greatest appreciation goes to the brightest faces I have met in my life, Kyung-Ok, Jeehee, and Jihoon. Thank you for always being with me. I love you so much.

JungHyun Han
Computer Science Department
Korea University
Seoul, Korea

Part I
Rendering Pipeline

Chapter 1

Introduction

Computer graphics refers to the process of generating images using computers. Three-dimensional (3D) computer graphics takes as input 3D representations of objects and performs various calculations on them to produce images. The last three decades have seen a profusion of 3D computer graphics in films and video games.

Computer-generated images are often called *frames*. An illusion of movement is generated on the screen by displaying a sequence of changing frames. The frames can be generated at real time. The best-known area of real-time graphics is video games, which typically produce more than 30 frames per second (fps). On the other hand, special effects in films often take as long as minutes or hours for a single frame. In return, we may obtain images that are hardly distinguishable from views of the real world. The algorithms and techniques adopted in real-time graphics are fairly different from those in off-line graphics. This book presents the essential components of real-time graphics.

1.1 Computer Graphics Production

Computer graphics production is often described in five steps shown in Fig. 1.1, where graphic artists and programmers are the key players. Modeling, rigging, and animation are off-line tasks performed by the artists. At run time, computer programs replay the animation and perform rendering and post-processing.

A model is referred to as a computer representation of an object, and modeling is the process of creating the objects comprising the virtual scenes. Con-

Fig. 1.1: The major steps in computer graphics production.

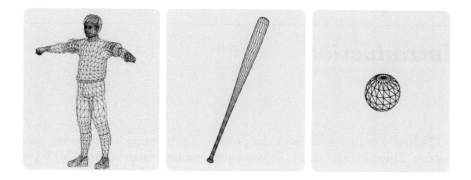

Fig. 1.2: Almost all 3D models in real-time graphics are represented in polygon meshes.

sider a baseball game. We need players, bats, balls, etc. They are usually represented in polygons, as shown in Fig. 1.2. Such polyhedral objects are named the *polygon meshes*.

The scope of modeling is not limited to constructing 3D models but includes creating *textures*. The simplest form of a texture is an image that is pasted on an object's surface. Fig. 1.3-(a) shows an image texture created for the baseball player model. The texture is pasted on the surface of the player at run time to produce the result shown in Fig. 1.3-(b).

The baseball player should be able to hit a ball, run, and slide into a base, i.e., we need to animate the player. For this purpose, we usually specify the *skeleton* or *rig* of the player. Fig. 1.4 shows a skeleton embedded in the polygon model. We then define how the skeletal motion deforms the player's polygon mesh such that, for example, the polygons of the arm are made to move when the arm bone is lifted. This process is often referred to as *rigging*.

The graphics artist creates a sequence of skeletal motions. At run time, the skeletal motions are replayed "per frame" and the polygon mesh is animated over frames. Fig. 1.5 shows a few snapshots of an animated player.

Rendering is the process of generating a 2D image from a 3D scene. The image makes up a frame. Fig. 1.6 shows the results of rendering the dynamic scene of Fig. 1.5. Realistic rendering is a complicated process, in which *lighting* as well as texturing is an essential component. For example, the shadow shown in Fig. 1.6 is a result of lighting.

The final step in the production of computer graphics, post-processing, is optional. It uses a set of special operations to give additional effects to the rendered images. An example is *motion blur* shown in Fig. 1.7. When a camera captures a scene, the resulting image represents the scene over a short period of time. Consequently, rapidly moving objects may result in motion

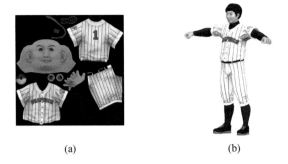

(a)   (b)

Fig. 1.3: Image texturing example: (a) This texture is a collection of small images, each of which is for a part of the baseball player's body. The texture may look weird at first glance, but Chapter 8 will present how such a texture is created and used. (b) The texture is pasted on the player's polygon mesh at run time.

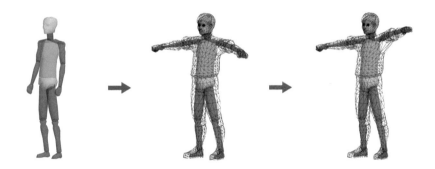

Fig. 1.4: A skeleton is composed of bones and is embedded in the polygon mesh for animation. This figure illustrates the bones as if they were solids, but the bones do not have explicit geometric representations. They are conceptual entities that are usually represented as matrices. This will be detailed in Chapter 13.

blur. It is a desirable effect in computer graphics, without which the moving objects would appear staggered or jerky. Another example is the depth-of-field effect, which makes objects outside of the camera's focus appear blurry.

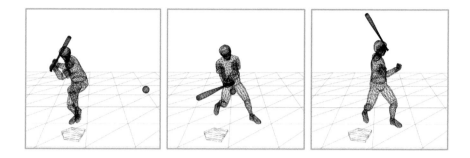

Fig. 1.5: The polygon mesh can be animated by controlling the skeleton embedded in it.

Fig. 1.6: Results of rendering the animated player.

Fig. 1.7: Motion blur effects.

1.2 Graphics API

The artists perform modeling, rigging, and animation in an off-line mode. Dedicated programs such as Autodesk 3ds Max and Autodesk Maya are popularly used. In contrast, run-time animation, rendering, and post-processing are executed by an application program. In games, the application is typically built upon a *game engine*. See Fig. 1.8. A game engine is a development tool that provides a suite of indispensable modules for animation, rendering, and post-processing. Modern game engines provide additional modules for physics-based simulation, sound, artificial intelligence, and so on. Well-known game engines include Unity Technologies' Unity and Epic Games' Unreal Engine.

In general, a game engine is built upon graphics APIs (Application Programming Interfaces). Two popular APIs are Direct3D [1] and OpenGL (Open Graphics Library) [2]. Direct3D is part of Microsoft's DirectX API and is available only for Microsoft platforms. OpenGL is a cross-platform API managed by a non-profit consortium for open standards, the Khronos Group. OpenGL ES (OpenGL for Embedded Systems) is a 3D API for handheld and embedded devices and is defined as a subset of OpenGL. It is widely used for mobile graphics programming.

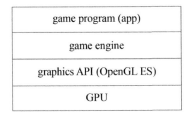

Fig. 1.8: Software and hardware hierarchy for mobile games.

Graphics APIs provide 3D applications or game engines with essential graphics functions. Today, such functions are implemented in GPU (Graphics Processing Unit). It is a processor specialized for graphics. A graphics API can be taken as the software interface of the GPU. The API translates the application's graphics commands to instructions that can be executed by the GPU.

Chapter 2

Mathematics: Basics

This chapter delivers an explicit presentation of the basic mathematical techniques, which are needed throughout this book. Matrices and vectors are indispensable tools in computer graphics and we start with them.

2.1 Matrices and Vectors

Shown below is a matrix with m rows and n columns:

$$
\begin{pmatrix}
a_{11} & a_{12} & \cdots & a_{1n} \\
a_{21} & a_{22} & \cdots & a_{2n} \\
\vdots & \vdots & \ddots & \vdots \\
a_{m1} & a_{m2} & \cdots & a_{mn}
\end{pmatrix}
\tag{2.1}
$$

Its dimensions are denoted as $m \times n$. If $m = n$, the matrix is called square. Two subscripts of an element specify where it is located. For instance, a_{12} is in the first row and second column. Two matrices A and B can be multiplied if the number of columns in A equals the number of rows in B. If A's dimensions are $l \times m$ and B's dimensions are $m \times n$, AB is an $l \times n$ matrix. See the example shown below:

$$
\begin{aligned}
AB &= \begin{pmatrix} a_{11} & a_{12} \\ a_{21} & a_{22} \\ a_{31} & a_{32} \end{pmatrix} \begin{pmatrix} b_{11} & b_{12} & b_{13} \\ b_{21} & b_{22} & b_{23} \end{pmatrix} \\
&= \begin{pmatrix}
a_{11}b_{11} + a_{12}b_{21} & a_{11}b_{12} + a_{12}b_{22} & a_{11}b_{13} + a_{12}b_{23} \\
a_{21}b_{11} + a_{22}b_{21} & a_{21}b_{12} + a_{22}b_{22} & a_{21}b_{13} + a_{22}b_{23} \\
a_{31}b_{11} + a_{32}b_{21} & a_{31}b_{12} + a_{32}b_{22} & a_{31}b_{13} + a_{32}b_{23}
\end{pmatrix}
\end{aligned}
\tag{2.2}
$$

A 2D vector is usually represented as (x, y) and a 3D vector as (x, y, z). They are often called the *row vectors*. Alternatively, we can use the *column vector* representation, e.g., a 2D column vector is written as

$$
\begin{pmatrix} x \\ y \end{pmatrix}
\tag{2.3}
$$

Vectors are special matrices. The above vector is a matrix with a single column and its dimensions are 2×1. Then, the method of matrix-matrix multiplication applies to matrix-vector multiplication. If M is a 3×2 matrix and v is a 2D column vector, for example, Mv is computed as follows:

$$Mv = \begin{pmatrix} a & b \\ c & d \\ e & f \end{pmatrix} \begin{pmatrix} x \\ y \end{pmatrix}$$
$$= \begin{pmatrix} ax + by \\ cx + dy \\ ex + fy \end{pmatrix} \quad (2.4)$$

Given a matrix M, its *transpose* denoted by M^T is obtained by interchanging the rows and columns of M. For example, the transpose of M given in Equation (2.4) is defined as

$$\begin{pmatrix} a & c & e \\ b & d & f \end{pmatrix} \quad (2.5)$$

The same applies to vectors. If v is a column vector, its transpose, v^T, is the row-vector counterpart.

The matrix-vector multiplication in Equation (2.4) can be represented in a different way. Instead of the column vector, v, we can use the row vector, v^T, and place it at the left of M^T:

$$v^T M^T = \begin{pmatrix} x & y \end{pmatrix} \begin{pmatrix} a & c & e \\ b & d & f \end{pmatrix}$$
$$= \begin{pmatrix} ax + by & cx + dy & ex + fy \end{pmatrix} \quad (2.6)$$

The result is the same as in Equation (2.4) but is represented in a row vector. (Whereas OpenGL uses the column vectors and the vector-on-the-right representation for matrix-vector multiplication, Direct3D uses the row vectors and the vector-on-the-left representation.)

The *identity matrix* is a square matrix with ones on the main diagonal (from the upper-left element to the lower-right element) and zeros everywhere else. It is denoted by I. For any matrix M, $MI = IM = M$, as shown in the following examples:

$$\begin{pmatrix} a_{11} & a_{12} & a_{13} \\ a_{21} & a_{22} & a_{23} \\ a_{31} & a_{32} & a_{33} \end{pmatrix} \begin{pmatrix} 1 & 0 & 0 \\ 0 & 1 & 0 \\ 0 & 0 & 1 \end{pmatrix} = \begin{pmatrix} a_{11} & a_{12} & a_{13} \\ a_{21} & a_{22} & a_{23} \\ a_{31} & a_{32} & a_{33} \end{pmatrix} \quad (2.7)$$

$$\begin{pmatrix} 1 & 0 & 0 \\ 0 & 1 & 0 \\ 0 & 0 & 1 \end{pmatrix} \begin{pmatrix} a_{11} & a_{12} & a_{13} \\ a_{21} & a_{22} & a_{23} \\ a_{31} & a_{32} & a_{33} \end{pmatrix} = \begin{pmatrix} a_{11} & a_{12} & a_{13} \\ a_{21} & a_{22} & a_{23} \\ a_{31} & a_{32} & a_{33} \end{pmatrix} \quad (2.8)$$

If two square matrices A and B are multiplied to return an identity matrix, i.e., if $AB = I$, B is called the *inverse* of A and is denoted by A^{-1}. By the same token, A is the inverse of B. Note that $(AB)^{-1} = B^{-1}A^{-1}$ as $(AB)(B^{-1}A^{-1}) = A(BB^{-1})A^{-1} = AIA^{-1} = AA^{-1} = I$. Similarly, $(AB)^T = B^T A^T$.

The coordinates of a 2D vector v are represented by (v_x, v_y). Its length denoted by $\|v\|$ is defined as $\sqrt{v_x^2 + v_y^2}$. If v is a 3D vector, its coordinates are (v_x, v_y, v_z) and $\|v\|$ is $\sqrt{v_x^2 + v_y^2 + v_z^2}$. Dividing a vector by its length is called *normalization*. The resulting vector, $v/\|v\|$, has the same direction as v. Such a normalized vector is called the *unit vector* since its length is one.

2.2 Coordinate System and Basis

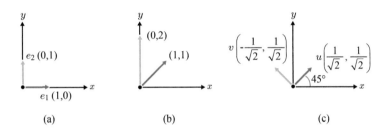

(a) (b) (c)

Fig. 2.1: Basis examples: (a) Standard basis. (b) A valid basis that is neither standard nor orthonormal. (c) An orthonormal basis that is not standard.

In the 2D coordinate system shown in Fig. 2.1-(a), $e_1 = (1, 0)$ along the x-axis and $e_2 = (0, 1)$ along the y-axis. (Throughout this book, we use the terms *coordinate system* and *space* interchangeably.) In the 2D space, every vector can be defined as a *linear combination*[1] of e_1 and e_2, e.g., $(3, 5) = 3e_1 + 5e_2$. In this sense, $\{e_1, e_2\}$ is a *basis*. Specifically, it is named the *standard* basis. Since e_1 and e_2 are unit vectors that are orthogonal to each other, they are also called *orthonormal*.

A different set of vectors may work as a basis. Consider $\{(1, 1), (0, 2)\}$ shown in Fig. 2.1-(b). Our example vector, $(3, 5)$, can be defined by linearly combining $(1, 1)$ and $(0, 2)$, i.e., $(3, 5) = 3(1, 1) + 1(0, 2)$. Observe that $\{(1, 1), (0, 2)\}$ is not an orthonormal basis. It is generally easier to work with an orthonormal basis rather than an arbitrary basis. Fig. 2.1-(c) shows an orthonormal basis, which is not standard. Note that $(3, 5) = 4\sqrt{2}u + \sqrt{2}v$.

---

[1] Given n vectors, $v_1, v_2, \ldots, v_n$, and n scalars, $c_1, c_2, \ldots, c_n$, the linear combination of the vectors with the scalars is $c_1 v_1 + c_2 v_2 + \cdots + c_n v_n$. It is also a vector.

Fig. 2.2: Standard basis for the 3D coordinate system.

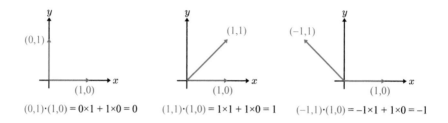

Fig. 2.3: Dot product of two vectors reveals their relative orientation.

As shown in Fig. 2.2, the standard basis in the 3D space is $\{e_1, e_2, e_3\}$, where $e_1 = (1, 0, 0)$, $e_2 = (0, 1, 0)$, and $e_3 = (0, 0, 1)$. It is an orthonormal basis. All 2D and 3D bases presented from now on will be orthonormal.

2.3　Dot Product

Consider two n-dimensional vectors, a and b. When their coordinates are represented by $(a_1, a_2, \ldots, a_n)$ and $(b_1, b_2, \ldots, b_n)$, respectively, their dot product, denoted by $a \cdot b$, is defined as follows:

$$a \cdot b = \sum_{i=1}^{n} a_i b_i = a_1 b_1 + a_2 b_2 + \ldots + a_n b_n \qquad (2.9)$$

When the angle between a and b is denoted as θ, $a \cdot b$ can be also defined as follows:

$$a \cdot b = \|a\|\|b\| cos\theta \qquad (2.10)$$

Fig. 2.4: Cross product and right-hand rule: (a) $a \times b$. (b) $b \times a$.

If a and b are orthogonal to each other, $\theta = 90°$ and $a \cdot b = 0$, as shown on the left of Fig. 2.3. See the other examples in Fig. 2.3. If θ is an acute angle, $a \cdot b$ is positive; if θ is an obtuse angle, $a \cdot b$ is negative. The same observation can be made when a and b are 3D vectors.

Equation (2.10) asserts that, if v is a unit vector, $v \cdot v = 1$. An orthonormal basis has an interesting and useful feature. Consider 2D and 3D standard bases. Given the 2D standard basis, $\{e_1, e_2\}$, $e_1 \cdot e_1 = e_2 \cdot e_2 = 1$ and $e_1 \cdot e_2 = e_2 \cdot e_1 = 0$. In the 3D standard basis, $\{e_1, e_2, e_3\}$, a similar observation is made, i.e., $e_i \cdot e_j = 1$ if $i = j$, and $e_i \cdot e_j = 0$ otherwise. This feature applies to every orthonormal basis.

2.4   Cross Product

The cross product takes two 3D vectors, a and b, and returns another 3D vector which is perpendicular to both a and b, as shown in Fig. 2.4-(a). The cross product is denoted by $a \times b$ and its direction is defined by the *right-hand rule*. The direction of $a \times b$ is indicated by the thumb of the right hand when the other fingers curl from a to b. The length of $a \times b$ equals the area of the parallelogram that a and b span:

$$\|a \times b\| = \|a\|\|b\| \sin \theta \tag{2.11}$$

The right-hand rule implies that the direction of $b \times a$ is opposite to that of $a \times b$, i.e., $b \times a = -(a \times b)$. However, their lengths are the same, as illustrated in Fig. 2.4-(b). In this sense, the cross product operation is called *anti-commutative*. When $a = (a_x, a_y, a_z)$ and $b = (b_x, b_y, b_z)$, $a \times b = (a_y b_z - a_z b_y, a_z b_x - a_x b_z, a_x b_y - a_y b_x)$. See [Note: Derivation of cross product][2].

---

[2]You can skip the notes in shaded boxes. No trouble will be encountered in further reading.

[Note: Derivation of cross product]

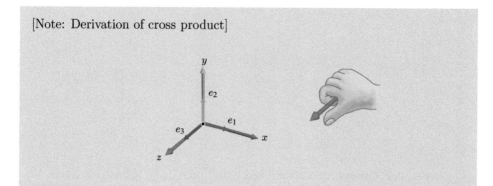

Fig. 2.5: Standard basis and right-hand rule: The thumb of the right hand points toward e_3 when the other four fingers curl from e_1 to e_2, i.e., $e_1 \times e_2 = e_3$. Similarly, $e_2 \times e_3 = e_1$ and $e_3 \times e_1 = e_2$.

In Fig. 2.5, the relative orientations among the basis vectors, e_1, e_2, and e_3, are described using the right-hand rule:

$$
\begin{aligned}
e_1 \times e_2 &= e_3 \\
e_2 \times e_3 &= e_1 \\
e_3 \times e_1 &= e_2
\end{aligned}
\tag{2.12}
$$

The anti-commutativity of the cross product leads to the following:

$$
\begin{aligned}
e_2 \times e_1 &= -e_3 \\
e_3 \times e_2 &= -e_1 \\
e_1 \times e_3 &= -e_2
\end{aligned}
\tag{2.13}
$$

Equation (2.11) also asserts that

$$
e_1 \times e_1 = e_2 \times e_2 = e_3 \times e_3 = \mathbf{0}
\tag{2.14}
$$

where $\mathbf{0}$ is the *zero vector*, $(0,0,0)$.

When $a = (a_x, a_y, a_z)$ and $b = (b_x, b_y, b_z)$, a is rewritten in terms of the standard basis as $a_x e_1 + a_y e_2 + a_z e_3$. Similarly, b is rewritten as $b_x e_1 + b_y e_2 + b_z e_3$. Then, $a \times b$ is derived as follows:

$$
\begin{aligned}
a \times b &= (a_x e_1 + a_y e_2 + a_z e_3) \times (b_x e_1 + b_y e_2 + b_z e_3) \\
&= a_x b_x (e_1 \times e_1) + a_x b_y (e_1 \times e_2) + a_x b_z (e_1 \times e_3) + \\
&\quad a_y b_x (e_2 \times e_1) + a_y b_y (e_2 \times e_2) + a_y b_z (e_2 \times e_3) + \\
&\quad a_z b_x (e_3 \times e_1) + a_z b_y (e_3 \times e_2) + a_z b_z (e_3 \times e_3) \\
&= a_x b_x \mathbf{0} + a_x b_y e_3 - a_x b_z e_2 \\
&\quad -a_y b_x e_3 + a_y b_y \mathbf{0} + a_y b_z e_1 \\
&\quad +a_z b_x e_2 - a_z b_y e_1 + a_z b_z \mathbf{0} \\
&= (a_y b_z - a_z b_y) e_1 + (a_z b_x - a_x b_z) e_2 + (a_x b_y - a_y b_x) e_3
\end{aligned}
\tag{2.15}
$$

The coordinates of $a \times b$ are $(a_y b_z - a_z b_y, a_z b_x - a_x b_z, a_x b_y - a_y b_x)$.

2.5 Line, Ray, and Linear Interpolation

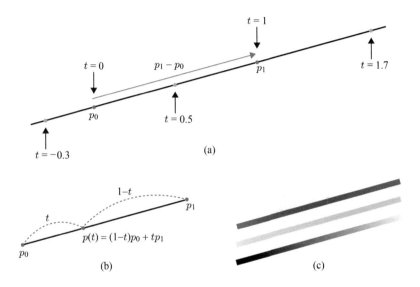

Fig. 2.6: Line and linear interpolation: (a) The infinite line connecting p_0 and p_1 is defined as $p_0 + t(p_1 - p_0)$. It is reduced to the line segment between p_0 and p_1 if t is restricted to $[0, 1]$. (b) The line segment is represented as the linear interpolation of p_0 and p_1. (c) Color interpolation examples.

A line is determined by two points. When p_0 and p_1 denote the points, the line is equivalently defined by p_0 and a vector, $p_1 - p_0$, which connects p_0 and p_1. Its parametric equation is given as follows:

$$p(t) = p_0 + t(p_1 - p_0) \tag{2.16}$$

As illustrated in Fig. 2.6-(a), the function $p(t)$ maps a scalar value of t to a specific point in the line. When $t = 1$, for example, $p(t) = p_1$. When $t = 0.5$, $p(t)$ represents the midpoint between p_0 and p_1. Fig. 2.6-(a) shows a few other instances of $p(t)$.

In Equation (2.16), t is in the range of $[-\infty, \infty]$ and $p(t)$ represents an infinite line. If t is limited to the range of $[0, \infty]$, $p(t)$ represents a *ray*. It starts from p_0 and is infinitely extended along the direction vector, $p_1 - p_0$. In contrast, when t is limited to a finite range, $p(t)$ represents a *line segment*. If the range is $[0, 1]$, $p(t)$ is a line segment connecting p_0 and p_1.

Equation (2.16) can be rephrased as follows:

$$p(t) = (1 - t)p_0 + tp_1 \qquad (2.17)$$

This represents a *weighted sum* of two points: the weight for p_0 is $(1 - t)$ and that for p_1 is t. If t is in the range $[0, 1]$, as illustrated in Fig. 2.6-(b), $p(t)$ is described as the *linear interpolation* of p_0 and p_1.

The function $p(t)$ is vector-valued, e.g., $p(t) = (x(t), y(t), z(t))$ in the 3D space. When $p_0 = (x_0, y_0, z_0)$ and $p_1 = (x_1, y_1, z_1)$, the linear interpolation is applied to each of the x-, y-, and z-coordinates:

$$p(t) = \begin{pmatrix} x(t) \\ y(t) \\ z(t) \end{pmatrix} = \begin{pmatrix} (1-t)x_0 + tx_1 \\ (1-t)y_0 + ty_1 \\ (1-t)z_0 + tz_1 \end{pmatrix} \qquad (2.18)$$

Whatever attributes are associated with the end points, they can be linearly interpolated. Suppose that the endpoints, p_0 and p_1, are associated with colors c_0 and c_1, respectively, where $c_0 = (R_0, G_0, B_0)$ and $c_1 = (R_1, G_1, B_1)$. In general, each RGB component is an integer in the range of $[0, 255]$ or a floating-point value in the normalized range of $[0, 1]$. The interpolated color $c(t)$ is defined as follows:

$$c(t) = (1-t)c_0 + tc_1 = \begin{pmatrix} (1-t)R_0 + tR_1 \\ (1-t)G_0 + tG_1 \\ (1-t)B_0 + tB_1 \end{pmatrix} \qquad (2.19)$$

Fig. 2.6-(c) shows examples of color interpolation. When $t = 0$, $c(t) = c_0$. As t increases, $c(t)$ becomes closer to c_1. When $t = 1$, $c(t) = c_1$.

Exercises

1. Construct a 3D orthonormal basis, where the first basis vector is along $(3, 4, 0)$, the second is along a principal axis, and the last is obtained by taking their cross product.

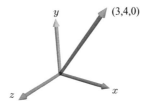

2. A line segment is defined by two end points, p_0 and p_1, where $p_0 = (2, 0)$ and $p_1 = (5, 0)$. Suppose that the vector assigned to p_0 is $(-1, 2)$ and that assigned to p_1 is $(2, 5)$. On the line segment, consider a point at $(4, 0)$. Compute the vector at the point by linearly interpolating the vectors at p_0 and p_1.

Chapter 3

Modeling

In computer graphics, various kinds of models are used to describe 3D objects, but the most preferred is the polygon mesh. This chapter presents how it is created, represented, and transferred to run-time applications such as game programs.

3.1   Polygon Mesh

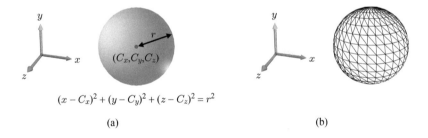

$$(x - C_x)^2 + (y - C_y)^2 + (z - C_z)^2 = r^2$$

(a)   (b)

Fig. 3.1: Two different representations of a sphere: (a) Smooth surface defined by the implicit function, $(x - C_x)^2 + (y - C_y)^2 + (z - C_z)^2 - r^2 = 0$. (b) Polygon mesh.

Consider a sphere with center (C_x, C_y, C_z) and radius r. The simplest way to describe the sphere is to use the equation presented in Fig. 3.1-(a). It is a compact representation but is not easy to draw on the screen. An alternative is to describe the surface in terms of its vertices and polygons, as shown in Fig. 3.1-(b). This is the polygon mesh representation. It is preferred in real-time applications because the GPU is optimized for processing polygons. Note that the mesh's vertices are the points that *sample* the smooth surface

Fig. 3.2: Triangle mesh versus quadrilateral mesh.

and therefore the polygon mesh is not an accurate representation but an approximate one.

A triangle is the simplest polygon and the *triangle mesh* is most popularly used. However, quadrilateral meshes (simply quad meshes) are often preferred especially for the modeling step, as can be observed in Section 3.1.1. Fig. 3.2 compares a triangle mesh and a quad mesh for the same object. A straightforward method to convert a quad mesh into a triangle mesh is to split each quad into two triangles.

In a typical closed triangle mesh, the number of triangles is approximately twice the number of vertices, e.g., given 100 vertices, we have about 200 triangles. See [Note: Vertex-triangle ratio in a triangle mesh].

[Note: Vertex-triangle ratio in a triangle mesh]

For a closed mesh with no hole, the Euler's polyhedron formula asserts

$$v - e + f = 2 \qquad (3.1)$$

where v, e, and f are respectively the numbers of vertices, edges, and faces of the mesh. In a closed triangle mesh, every edge is shared by two faces, and every face has three edges. Therefore, if we count two faces per edge, the counted number will be three times the number of faces of the mesh, i.e.,

$$2e = 3f \qquad (3.2)$$

As an example, consider a tetrahedron: e is 6 and f is 4. When we replace e in Equation (3.1) by $\frac{3}{2}f$ derived from Equation (3.2), we obtain the following:

$$f = 2v - 4 \qquad (3.3)$$

As the mesh's size increases, the number of faces converges to twice the number of vertices.

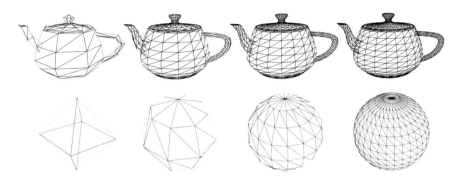

Fig. 3.3: Rendering a low-resolution mesh is fast but the model's polygonal nature is easily revealed. Rendering a high-resolution mesh is slow, but the rendering quality is improved in general.

When we approximate a smooth surface by a polygon mesh, the number of vertices matters, which is usually described as the *resolution* of the mesh. See Fig. 3.3. There is a trade-off between accuracy and efficiency. As the resolution increases, the shape of the mesh becomes closer to the original smooth surface, but the time needed for processing the mesh also increases.

3.1.1 Polygon Mesh Creation*

In general, the polygon mesh of an object is interactively created using graphics packages. The polygon mesh is stored in a file and is then input to the 3D application program which animates and renders it at run time. A programmer may not have to understand how a polygon mesh is created since it is the job of an artist. If you want, you can skip this subsection[1]. However, understanding the basics of modeling is often helpful for developing a 3D application as well as communicating with an artist. This section roughly sketches how a polygon mesh of a character is created.

Modeling packages provide the artist with various operations such as selection, translation, rotation, and scaling for manipulating the topological entities of a polygon mesh, i.e., vertices, edges, and faces. Furthermore, such topological entities can be cut, extruded, and connected. Consider modeling a character's head. There are many ways of creating its polygon mesh. In the example presented in this section, we choose to start with a box and modify its topology and geometry. Section 14.5 will present another way of creating the polygon mesh.

---

[1]The asterisk-marked sections can be skipped. No difficulty will be encountered in further reading.

(a) Edges are selected and then connected to refine the box mesh.

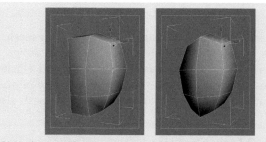

(b) Vertices are selected and moved to change the geometry of the mesh.

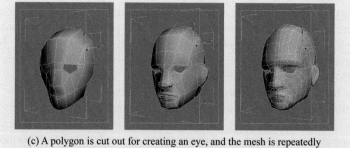

(c) A polygon is cut out for creating an eye, and the mesh is repeatedly refined.

Fig. 3.4: A polygon mesh is created by manual operations.

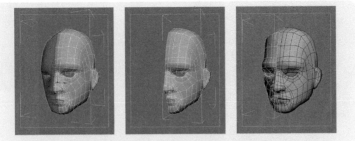

(d) The right half of the head is removed, and the left half is copied and
reflected to make the head symmetric.

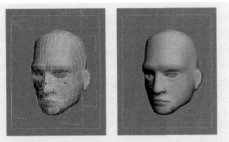

(e) Two separate meshes of the head are combined through
a welding operation to produce a single mesh.

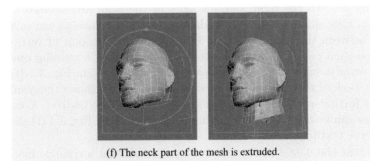

(f) The neck part of the mesh is extruded.

Fig. 3.4: A polygon mesh is created by manual operations (*continued*).

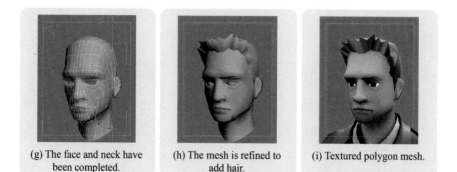

| (g) The face and neck have been completed. | (h) The mesh is refined to add hair. | (i) Textured polygon mesh. |

Fig. 3.4: A polygon mesh is created by manual operations (*continued*).

Fig. 3.4 shows the step-by-step process of editing a box mesh to generate a character's head. The box shown on the left of Fig. 3.4-(a) is empty and in fact a polygon mesh composed of six quads. The edges of the box are selected and connected using new edges to refine the coarse mesh, i.e., to produce a larger number of smaller polygons. In Fig. 3.4-(b), the vertices of the refined mesh are selected and moved to change the mesh's geometry. In Fig. 3.4-(c), a polygon is selected and cut out to make a hole for an eye, and then the mesh continues to be refined. Fig. 3.4-(d) shows that, for creating a symmetric object, one side of the mesh is copied, reflected, and pasted to the other side. In the modeling process, refining one side and copying it to the other side are often repeated to create a well-balanced object.

In Fig. 3.4-(d), the right and left sides of the head are separate meshes. However, they share the same boundary, and there are one-to-one correspondences between their vertices. Fig. 3.4-(e) shows that a pair of vertices at a single position can be combined into a vertex through a welding operation. Then, two adjacent meshes are combined into a single mesh. Fig. 3.4-(f) shows that the neck of the mesh is extruded, and Fig. 3.4-(g) shows the result. The mesh is further refined to add hair, as shown in Fig. 3.4-(h). A complete character can be created by continuing such operations. Fig. 3.4-(i) shows the bust of the textured mesh.

Note that the model in Fig. 3.4 is a quad mesh, not a triangle mesh. The quad mesh makes various operations easy. However, the modeling packages may output a triangle mesh of the same object, and therefore we can use it for rendering.

3.1.2 Polygon Mesh Representation

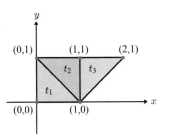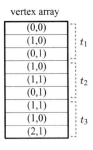

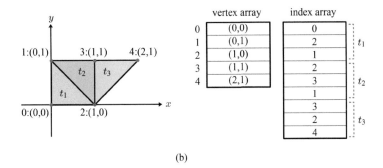

(b)

Fig. 3.5: Triangle mesh representations: (a) Non-indexed representation. (b) Indexed representation.

An obvious method to represent a triangle mesh is to enumerate its vertices such that three vertices are read in linear order to make up a triangle. See the example of a 2D triangle mesh in Fig. 3.5-(a). The memory space storing the vertices is named the *vertex array*.

The representation is quite intuitive. However, it is inefficient because the vertex array contains redundant data. In Fig. 3.5-(a), for example, the vertex at $(1,0)$ is shared by three triangles and appears three times in the vertex array.

The vertex array can be made compact by using a separate *index array*. The vertices are stored in the vertex array with no duplication, and their indices are stored in the index array, three per triangle. Fig. 3.5-(b) shows the vertex and index arrays for the same mesh of Fig. 3.5-(a).

The data stored in the vertex array are not restricted to vertex positions but include a lot of additional information. (All of these data will be presented one by one throughout this book.) Therefore, the vertex array storage saved by removing the duplicate data outweighs the additional storage needed for the index array. OpenGL ES supports both a non-indexed representation (illustrated in Fig. 3.5-(a)) and an indexed one (illustrated in Fig. 3.5-(b)), but the non-indexed representation is rarely used because there are very few cases where the indices are not preferred.

If a 16-bit index is used, we can represent 2^{16} (65,536) vertices. With a 32-bit index, 2^{32} (4,294,967,296) vertices can be represented. When fewer than 65,536 vertices are put into the vertex array, the 16-bit format is preferred because it results in a smaller index array.

3.2 Surface Normals

In rendering a 3D polygon mesh, its *surface normals* play a key role. They are classified into triangle normals and vertex normals.

3.2.1 Triangle Normals

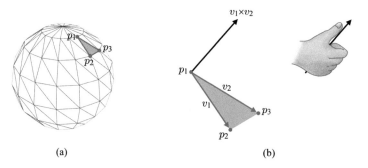

(a)   (b)

Fig. 3.6: Triangle normal: (a) The triangle is composed of three vertices, p_1, p_2, and p_3. (b) The cross product $v_1 \times v_2$ is normalized to define the triangle normal.

Consider the triangle $\langle p_1, p_2, p_3 \rangle$ in Fig. 3.6-(a). Its normal is obtained by taking the edges as vectors and calculating their cross product. Let v_1 denote

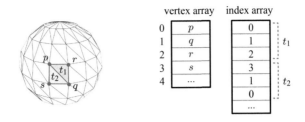

Fig. 3.7: In the indexed representation of a triangle mesh, the index array records the vertices in the CCW order.

the vector connecting the first vertex (p_1) and the second (p_2), as shown in Fig. 3.6-(b). Similarly, the vector connecting the first vertex (p_1) and the third (p_3) is denoted by v_2. Then, the triangle normal is computed as follows:

$$n_{12} = \frac{v_1 \times v_2}{\|v_1 \times v_2\|} \tag{3.4}$$

The cross product is divided by its length to make a unit vector. In computer graphics, every normal vector is a unit vector by default.

What if the vertices of the triangle are ordered as p_1, p_3, and p_2? The first vertex (p_1) and the second (p_3) are connected to generate v_2, the first (p_1) and the third (p_2) generate v_1, and finally v_2 and v_1 are combined using the cross product:

$$n_{21} = \frac{v_2 \times v_1}{\|v_2 \times v_1\|} \tag{3.5}$$

According to the right-hand rule, Equations (3.4) and (3.5) represent opposite directions. This shows that the normal of a triangle depends on its vertex order.

Observe that, in Fig. 3.6-(a), $\langle p_1, p_2, p_3 \rangle$ represents the counter-clockwise (CCW) order of vertices whereas $\langle p_1, p_3, p_2 \rangle$ represents the clockwise (CW) order. According to the right-hand rule, the CCW order makes the normal point out of the object whereas the CW order makes the normal point inward. The convention in computer graphics is to make the normal point outward, and therefore the triangle vertices are ordered CCW by default. Fig. 3.7 shows an example of the indexed mesh representation with the CCW vertex order.

3.2.2 Vertex Normals

We have so far discussed the triangle normals, but more important in computer graphics are the *vertex normals*. Recall that the mesh vertices are the points sampling the smooth surface, as illustrated in Fig. 3.8-(a). A normal can be assigned to a vertex such that the vertex normal approximates the normal of the smooth surface at the sampled point.

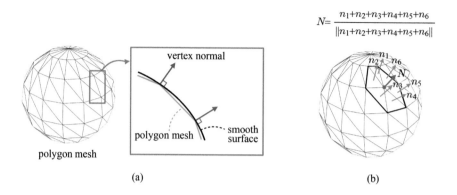

$$N= \frac{n_1+n_2+n_3+n_4+n_5+n_6}{\|n_1+n_2+n_3+n_4+n_5+n_6\|}$$

(a)   (b)

Fig. 3.8: Vertex normal estimation.

Given only a polygon mesh, computing the vertex normals is an underconstrained problem, and as such, rules of thumb and heuristics are often adopted. A simple method is to average the normals of all the triangles sharing a vertex, as shown in Fig. 3.8-(b). In general, the vertex normals are automatically computed by modeling packages such as 3ds Max. Vertex normals are crucial for lighting, which will be presented in Chapter 9, and are an indispensable component of the vertex array.

3.3 Polygon Mesh Export and Import

Polygon meshes and related data created using off-line graphics packages are stored in files and passed to the run-time 3D application program. The process is called *export*. On the other hand, taking such exported data is called *import*. For exporting and importing, simple scripts or programs are used. For example, 3ds Max provides MAXScript and an exporter can be written using MAXScript.

In 3ds Max, a lot of file formats are supported for export. Among the most popular is .obj. Fig. 3.9-(a) shows a low-resolution mesh of a unit sphere and some snippets of the .obj file for the mesh. The mesh is composed of 26 vertices and 48 triangles. The .obj file stores three topological entities: vertex positions (denoted by v), vertex normals (denoted by vn), and triangles (denoted by f which stands for face). In the .obj file, a line preceded by v contains three real values, which represent the 3D coordinates of a vertex position. Similarly, a line preceded by vn contains three coordinates of a vertex normal. In the

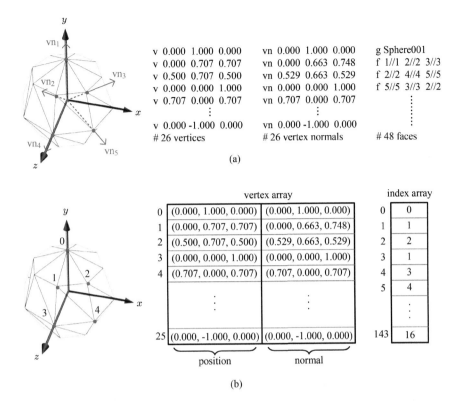

Fig. 3.9: A triangle mesh example: (a) The vertex positions and normals are indexed starting from 1. For clarity, the vertex normals on the mesh are illustrated with subscripts added. For example, vn_1 represents the first vertex normal, $(0, 1, 0)$. (b) The .obj file is imported into the vertex and index arrays.

sphere example of Fig. 3.9-(a), every vertex has a distinct normal, making the number of vertex normals equal that of vertex positions. In general, however, multiple vertices may share a single normal. Then, the number of vertex normals in the .obj file will be smaller than that of vertex positions.

A triangle is defined by three vertices, each described by its position and normal. In the .obj file, both positions and normals are indexed starting from 1, and a line preceded by f contains three position/normal index pairs, each separated by double slashes. For example, the first vertex of the first triangle in Fig. 3.9-(a) has the position $(0, 1, 0)$ and normal $(0, 1, 0)$ whereas the second vertex has the position $(0, 0.707, 0.707)$ and normal $(0, 0.663, 0.748)$.

The triangle mesh stored in a file is imported into the vertex and index arrays of the 3D application, as shown in Fig. 3.9-(b). As the mesh is composed of 48 triangles, the index array has 144 (48 times 3) elements.

Exercises

1. Consider the two triangles in the figure. Making sure that the triangle normals point out of the object, fill in the vertex and index arrays for the indexed mesh representation.

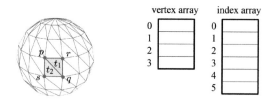

2. The simplest 3D closed mesh is a *tetrahedron*. Suppose that it is composed of four vertices, $(0,0,0)$, $(1,0,0)$, $(0,1,0)$, and $(0,0,1)$. Making sure that the triangle normals point out of the tetrahedron, draw the vertex and index arrays for the indexed mesh representation.

3. The triangle mesh shown below is composed of eight triangles. In the non-indexed mesh representation, the vertex array has (   ) elements. In the indexed representation, the vertex and index arrays have (   ) and (   ) elements, respectively. Fill in each blank with a number.

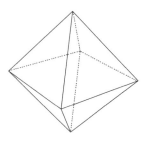

4. Consider a sphere, the center of which is located at the origin. Let us create a polygon mesh for the sphere by defining vertices at every 10 degrees along both latitude and longitude. How many vertices do we have?

5. Given the triangle mesh shown below, fill in the vertex and index arrays for its indexed mesh representation.

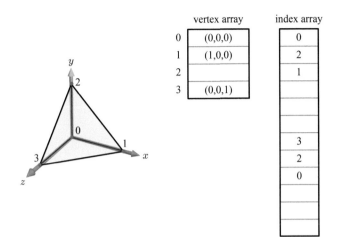

6. Let v, e, and f denote the numbers of vertices, edges and faces of a closed triangle mesh, respectively. In [Note: Vertex-triangle ratio in a triangle mesh], we have derived $f = 2v - 4$. Derive a similar relation between v and e.

Chapter 4

Spaces and Transforms

In general, a virtual 3D scene is composed of many objects. Each object has its own position and orientation in the scene, which are defined by translation and rotation, respectively. It may also be scaled larger or smaller. Such scaling, rotation, and translation are collectively called the *transforms*. In this chapter, we first present 2D transforms and their matrix representations. Then we extend them into 3D.

4.1   2D Transforms and Matrix Representations

4.1.1   Scaling

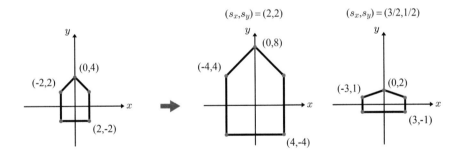

Fig. 4.1: 2D scaling examples: Every vertex of a polygon is multiplied by the same scaling matrix.

Two-dimensional scaling, denoted as S, is represented by a 2×2 matrix:

$$S = \begin{pmatrix} s_x & 0 \\ 0 & s_y \end{pmatrix} \tag{4.1}$$

where s_x and s_y are the *scaling factors* along the x-axis and y-axis, respectively. A 2D vector, (x, y), is scaled through *matrix-vector multiplication*:

$$\begin{pmatrix} s_x & 0 \\ 0 & s_y \end{pmatrix} \begin{pmatrix} x \\ y \end{pmatrix} = \begin{pmatrix} s_x x \\ s_y y \end{pmatrix} \tag{4.2}$$

When a polygon is scaled, all of its vertices are processed by Equation (4.2). Fig. 4.1 shows two examples of scaling.

4.1.2   Rotation

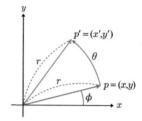

Fig. 4.2: A vector p is rotated by θ to define a new vector p'.

Fig. 4.2 illustrates 2D rotation of a vector, where p is rotated about the origin by θ to define p'. When p's length is r, its coordinates are defined as follows:

$$\begin{aligned} x &= r cos\phi \\ y &= r sin\phi \end{aligned} \tag{4.3}$$

The length of p' is also r, and its x-coordinate is computed as follows:

$$\begin{aligned} x' &= r cos(\phi + \theta) \\ &= r cos\phi cos\theta - r sin\phi sin\theta \\ &= x cos\theta - y sin\theta \end{aligned} \tag{4.4}$$

The y-coordinate is computed in a similar manner:

$$\begin{aligned} y' &= r sin(\phi + \theta) \\ &= r cos\phi sin\theta + r sin\phi cos\theta \\ &= x sin\theta + y cos\theta \end{aligned} \tag{4.5}$$

Equations (4.4) and (4.5) are combined into a matrix-vector multiplication form:

$$\begin{pmatrix} x' \\ y' \end{pmatrix} = \begin{pmatrix} cos\theta & -sin\theta \\ sin\theta & cos\theta \end{pmatrix} \begin{pmatrix} x \\ y \end{pmatrix} \tag{4.6}$$

The 2×2 matrix represents 2D rotation, which we denote by $R(\theta)$.

In Fig. 4.2, p is rotated counter-clockwise. The matrix for the clockwise rotation by θ is obtained by inserting $-\theta$ into the 2D rotation matrix. For example, the clockwise rotation by 90° is defined as follows:

$$R(-90°) = \begin{pmatrix} cos(-90°) & -sin(-90°) \\ sin(-90°) & cos(-90°) \end{pmatrix} = \begin{pmatrix} 0 & 1 \\ -1 & 0 \end{pmatrix} \qquad (4.7)$$

Note that rotation by $-\theta$ is equivalent to rotation by $(2\pi - \theta)$. For example, $R(-90°)$ in Equation (4.7) is identical to $R(270°)$:

$$R(270°) = \begin{pmatrix} cos270° & -sin270° \\ sin270° & cos270° \end{pmatrix} = \begin{pmatrix} 0 & 1 \\ -1 & 0 \end{pmatrix} \qquad (4.8)$$

4.1.3 Translation and Homogeneous Coordinates

As presented above, a vector is scaled or rotated through matrix multiplication. Scaling and rotation belong to a specific class of transforms named the *linear transforms*. Another transform frequently used in computer graphics is translation. It displaces a point at (x, y) to $(x + d_x, y + d_y)$. We call (d_x, d_y) the translation vector. Translation does not fall into the class of linear transforms and is expressed as vector addition:

$$\begin{pmatrix} x \\ y \end{pmatrix} + \begin{pmatrix} d_x \\ d_y \end{pmatrix} = \begin{pmatrix} x + d_x \\ y + d_y \end{pmatrix} \qquad (4.9)$$

We can describe translation as matrix multiplication if we use *homogeneous coordinates*. Given the 2D Cartesian coordinates (x, y) of a point, we can take the 3D vector $(x, y, 1)$ as its homogeneous coordinates. For now, the third component could be considered as a dummy. Then, the translation matrix is defined by inserting the translation vector, (d_x, d_y), into the third column of the 3×3 identity matrix:

$$\begin{pmatrix} 1 & 0 & d_x \\ 0 & 1 & d_y \\ 0 & 0 & 1 \end{pmatrix} \qquad (4.10)$$

The matrix is multiplied with the homogeneous coordinates of the point:

$$\begin{pmatrix} 1 & 0 & d_x \\ 0 & 1 & d_y \\ 0 & 0 & 1 \end{pmatrix} \begin{pmatrix} x \\ y \\ 1 \end{pmatrix} = \begin{pmatrix} x + d_x \\ y + d_y \\ 1 \end{pmatrix} \qquad (4.11)$$

Observe that Equations (4.9) and (4.11) return the same result, one in Cartesian coordinates and the other in homogeneous coordinates.

Given a 2D point, (x, y), its homogeneous coordinates are not necessarily $(x, y, 1)$ but generally (wx, wy, w) for any non-zero w. For example, the homogeneous coordinates for the Cartesian coordinates $(2, 3)$ can be not only

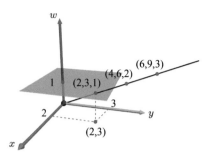

Fig. 4.3: The Cartesian coordinates, $(2, 3)$, are vertically displaced to the plane defined by the equation, $w = 1$. The 3D coordinates are $(2, 3, 1)$. The line connecting $(2, 3, 1)$ and the origin of the 3D space represents infinitely many points in homogeneous coordinates. Converting the homogeneous coordinates back to the Cartesian coordinates is often described as projecting a point on the line onto the plane.

$(2, 3, 1)$ but also $(4, 6, 2)$, $(6, 9, 3)$, or $(20, 30, 10)$. The concept of homogeneous coordinates is visualized in Fig. 4.3, where a 3D space is defined by the x-, y-, and w-axes. The 3D line consists of infinitely many points represented in homogeneous coordinates, which correspond to a single 2D point, $(2, 3)$.

Suppose that we are given the homogeneous coordinates, (X, Y, w). By dividing every coordinate by w, we obtain $(X/w, Y/w, 1)$. In Fig. 4.3, this corresponds to *projecting* a point on the line onto the plane, $w = 1$. We then take the first two components, $(X/w, Y/w)$, as the Cartesian coordinates.

In order to handle the homogeneous coordinates in a 3D vector form, the scaling matrix is extended to the 3×3 matrix:

$$\begin{pmatrix} s_x & 0 & 0 \\ 0 & s_y & 0 \\ 0 & 0 & 1 \end{pmatrix} \tag{4.12}$$

The 2×2 matrix in Equation (4.1) is copied into the upper-left sub-matrix whereas the third column and third row are filled with zeroes except the lower-right corner element, which is one. The same applies to the rotation matrix:

$$\begin{pmatrix} cos\theta & -sin\theta & 0 \\ sin\theta & cos\theta & 0 \\ 0 & 0 & 1 \end{pmatrix} \tag{4.13}$$

4.1.4 Composition of 2D Transforms

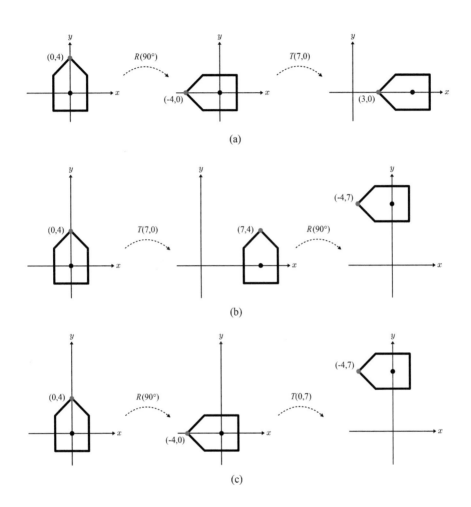

(a)

(b)

(c)

Fig. 4.4: Transform concatenation: (a) The polygon is rotated and then translated. (b) The polygon is translated and then rotated. Note that $R(90°)$ is "about the origin." (c) As presented in Equation (4.27), the affine matrix in (b) is conceptually decomposed into a linear transform (rotation) and a translation.

An object may go through multiple transforms. In the example of Fig. 4.4-(a), the polygon is rotated by $90°$ and then translated along the x-axis by seven units. We denote the rotation by $R(90°)$ and the translation by $T(7,0)$:

$$R(90°) = \begin{pmatrix} \cos90° & -\sin90° & 0 \\ \sin90° & \cos90° & 0 \\ 0 & 0 & 1 \end{pmatrix} = \begin{pmatrix} 0 & -1 & 0 \\ 1 & 0 & 0 \\ 0 & 0 & 1 \end{pmatrix} \qquad (4.14)$$

$$T(7,0) = \begin{pmatrix} 1 & 0 & 7 \\ 0 & 1 & 0 \\ 0 & 0 & 1 \end{pmatrix} \qquad (4.15)$$

Consider the vertex located at $(0,4)$. It is rotated to $(-4,0)$ by $R(90°)$:

$$\begin{pmatrix} 0 & -1 & 0 \\ 1 & 0 & 0 \\ 0 & 0 & 1 \end{pmatrix} \begin{pmatrix} 0 \\ 4 \\ 1 \end{pmatrix} = \begin{pmatrix} -4 \\ 0 \\ 1 \end{pmatrix} \qquad (4.16)$$

Then, the vertex at $(-4,0)$ is translated to $(3,0)$ by $T(7,0)$:

$$\begin{pmatrix} 1 & 0 & 7 \\ 0 & 1 & 0 \\ 0 & 0 & 1 \end{pmatrix} \begin{pmatrix} -4 \\ 0 \\ 1 \end{pmatrix} = \begin{pmatrix} 3 \\ 0 \\ 1 \end{pmatrix} \qquad (4.17)$$

As both $R(90°)$ and $T(7,0)$ are represented in $3{\times}3$ matrices, they can be concatenated to make a $3{\times}3$ matrix:

$$\begin{aligned} T(7,0)R(90°) &= \begin{pmatrix} 1 & 0 & 7 \\ 0 & 1 & 0 \\ 0 & 0 & 1 \end{pmatrix} \begin{pmatrix} 0 & -1 & 0 \\ 1 & 0 & 0 \\ 0 & 0 & 1 \end{pmatrix} \\ &= \begin{pmatrix} 0 & -1 & 7 \\ 1 & 0 & 0 \\ 0 & 0 & 1 \end{pmatrix} \end{aligned} \qquad (4.18)$$

The vertex originally located at $(0,4)$ is instantly transformed to $(3,0)$ by the combined matrix:

$$\begin{pmatrix} 0 & -1 & 7 \\ 1 & 0 & 0 \\ 0 & 0 & 1 \end{pmatrix} \begin{pmatrix} 0 \\ 4 \\ 1 \end{pmatrix} = \begin{pmatrix} 3 \\ 0 \\ 1 \end{pmatrix} \qquad (4.19)$$

The result is the same as in Equation (4.17).

It is important to note that matrix multiplication is not commutative. When a rotation (R) is followed by a translation (T), the general representation of the combination is given as follows:

$$\begin{aligned} TR &= \begin{pmatrix} 1 & 0 & d_x \\ 0 & 1 & d_y \\ 0 & 0 & 1 \end{pmatrix} \begin{pmatrix} \cos\theta & -\sin\theta & 0 \\ \sin\theta & \cos\theta & 0 \\ 0 & 0 & 1 \end{pmatrix} \\ &= \begin{pmatrix} \cos\theta & -\sin\theta & d_x \\ \sin\theta & \cos\theta & d_y \\ 0 & 0 & 1 \end{pmatrix} \end{aligned} \qquad (4.20)$$

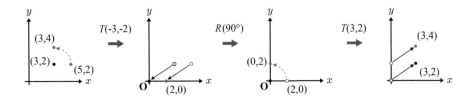

Fig. 4.5: Rotation about an arbitrary point.

If the order of R and T is reversed, we have a different result:

$$RT = \begin{pmatrix} cos\theta & -sin\theta & 0 \\ sin\theta & cos\theta & 0 \\ 0 & 0 & 1 \end{pmatrix} \begin{pmatrix} 1 & 0 & d_x \\ 0 & 1 & d_y \\ 0 & 0 & 1 \end{pmatrix}$$
$$= \begin{pmatrix} cos\theta & -sin\theta & d_x cos\theta - d_y sin\theta \\ sin\theta & cos\theta & d_x sin\theta + d_y cos\theta \\ 0 & 0 & 1 \end{pmatrix} \quad (4.21)$$

Compare Fig. 4.4-(a) and -(b).

The rotation presented in Section 4.1.2 is "about the origin." Now consider rotation about an arbitrary point, which is not the origin. An example is shown on the left of Fig. 4.5, where the point at $(5,2)$ is rotated about $(3,2)$ by $90°$. The rotated point will be at $(3,4)$. If we apply $R(90°)$ to $(5,2)$, we have an incorrect result:

$$\begin{pmatrix} 0 & -1 & 0 \\ 1 & 0 & 0 \\ 0 & 0 & 1 \end{pmatrix} \begin{pmatrix} 5 \\ 2 \\ 1 \end{pmatrix} = \begin{pmatrix} -2 \\ 5 \\ 1 \end{pmatrix} \quad (4.22)$$

The correct solution for the problem of rotating a point at (x,y) about an arbitrary point, (a,b), is obtained by concatenating three transforms: (1) translating (x,y) by $(-a,-b)$, (2) rotating the translated point about the origin, and (3) back-translating the rotated point by (a,b). Fig. 4.5 illustrates the three steps: (1) The point at $(5,2)$ is translated by $(-3,-2)$. This has the effect of translating the "center of rotation" to the origin. (2) The translated point at $(2,0)$ is rotated "about the origin." (3) The rotated point at $(0,2)$ is back-translated by $(3,2)$. The combined matrix is defined as follows:

$$\begin{pmatrix} 1 & 0 & 3 \\ 0 & 1 & 2 \\ 0 & 0 & 1 \end{pmatrix} \begin{pmatrix} 0 & -1 & 0 \\ 1 & 0 & 0 \\ 0 & 0 & 1 \end{pmatrix} \begin{pmatrix} 1 & 0 & -3 \\ 0 & 1 & -2 \\ 0 & 0 & 1 \end{pmatrix} = \begin{pmatrix} 0 & -1 & 5 \\ 1 & 0 & -1 \\ 0 & 0 & 1 \end{pmatrix} \quad (4.23)$$

This matrix produces the correct result:

$$\begin{pmatrix} 0 & -1 & 5 \\ 1 & 0 & -1 \\ 0 & 0 & 1 \end{pmatrix} \begin{pmatrix} 5 \\ 2 \\ 1 \end{pmatrix} = \begin{pmatrix} 3 \\ 4 \\ 1 \end{pmatrix} \tag{4.24}$$

4.2   Affine Transform

Recall that translation does not fall into the linear transform class, which encompasses scaling and rotation. The union of the translation and the linear transform is called the *affine transform*.

No matter how many affine matrices are given, they can be combined into a matrix. Equation (4.20) presents the general representation of a rotation (R) followed by a translation (T). It is denoted as TR. In contrast, Equation (4.21) presents the general representation of RT. Let us now combine RT and a scaling (denoted as S):

$$\begin{aligned} SRT &= \begin{pmatrix} s_x & 0 & 0 \\ 0 & s_y & 0 \\ 0 & 0 & 1 \end{pmatrix} \begin{pmatrix} cos\theta & -sin\theta & d_x cos\theta - d_y sin\theta \\ sin\theta & cos\theta & d_x sin\theta + d_y cos\theta \\ 0 & 0 & 1 \end{pmatrix} \\ &= \begin{pmatrix} s_x cos\theta & -s_x sin\theta & s_x d_x cos\theta - s_x d_y sin\theta \\ s_y sin\theta & s_y cos\theta & s_y d_x sin\theta + s_y d_y cos\theta \\ 0 & 0 & 1 \end{pmatrix} \end{aligned} \tag{4.25}$$

The examples in Equations (4.20), (4.21), and (4.25) show that, when a series of affine transforms is concatenated to make a single 3×3 matrix, the third row is always (0 0 1).

Ignoring the third row, we often denote the remaining 2×3 elements by $[L|t]$, where L is a 2×2 matrix and t is a 2D column vector. L represents the 'combined' linear transform. In Equations (4.20) and (4.21), L is identical to R because R is the only linear transform involved in the matrix composition. In contrast, L in Equation (4.25) is a combination of S and R. L does *not* include any terms from the input translations. Observe that, in Equations (4.20), (4.21), and (4.25), the translation terms, d_x and d_y, are not found in L. On the other hand, t in $[L|t]$ represents the 'combined' translation, which may contain the input linear-transform terms.

Consider the matrix composition in Fig. 4.4-(b):

$$\begin{aligned} R(90°)T(7,0) &= \begin{pmatrix} 0 & -1 & 0 \\ 1 & 0 & 0 \\ 0 & 0 & 1 \end{pmatrix} \begin{pmatrix} 1 & 0 & 7 \\ 0 & 1 & 0 \\ 0 & 0 & 1 \end{pmatrix} \\ &= \begin{pmatrix} 0 & -1 & 0 \\ 1 & 0 & 7 \\ 0 & 0 & 1 \end{pmatrix} \end{aligned} \tag{4.26}$$

The 2×2 sub-matrix colored in red is L, and the two elements in blue represent t. L equals $R(90°)$, which is the only linear transform involved in the matrix composition, but t is different from the translation vector stored in $T(7, 0)$.

Looking rather complicated, t in Equation (4.21) or (4.25) works as a translation vector. Transforming an object by $[L|t]$ is 'conceptually' decomposed into two steps: L is applied first and then the linearly transformed object is translated by t. In other words, $[L|t]p = Lp + t$, where p represents a vertex of the object's mesh. The combined matrix in Equation (4.26) is decomposed as follows:

$$\begin{pmatrix} 0 & -1 & 0 \\ 1 & 0 & 7 \\ 0 & 0 & 1 \end{pmatrix} = \begin{pmatrix} 1 & 0 & 0 \\ 0 & 1 & 7 \\ 0 & 0 & 1 \end{pmatrix} \begin{pmatrix} 0 & -1 & 0 \\ 1 & 0 & 0 \\ 0 & 0 & 1 \end{pmatrix} \tag{4.27}$$

Fig. 4.4-(c) shows the conceptual steps of applying L first and then t.

Consider a combination of only rotations and translations, i.e., no scaling is involved. When the combined affine matrix is applied to an object, the pose of the object is changed but its shape is not. In this sense, the transform is referred to as a *rigid-body motion* or simply a *rigid motion*. No matter how many rotations and translations are combined, the resulting matrix is of the structure, $[R|t]$, where R represents the 'combined' rotation, which does not include any translation terms, and t represents the 'combined' translation, which may contain the rotation terms. Transforming an object by $[R|t]$ is 'conceptually' decomposed into two steps: R is applied first and then the rotated object is translated by t.

4.3 3D Transforms and Matrix Representations

We have so far presented 2D affine transforms. It is straightforward to extend them into 3D.

4.3.1 Scaling

Three-dimensional scaling is represented by a 3×3 matrix:

$$\begin{pmatrix} s_x & 0 & 0 \\ 0 & s_y & 0 \\ 0 & 0 & s_z \end{pmatrix} \tag{4.28}$$

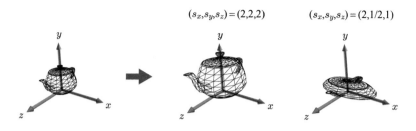

Fig. 4.6: 3D scaling examples: Every vertex of a polygon mesh is multiplied by the same scaling matrix.

where the new element, s_z, is the scaling factor along the z-axis. The scaling matrix is applied to a 3D vector:

$$\begin{pmatrix} s_x & 0 & 0 \\ 0 & s_y & 0 \\ 0 & 0 & s_z \end{pmatrix} \begin{pmatrix} x \\ y \\ z \end{pmatrix} = \begin{pmatrix} s_x x \\ s_y y \\ s_z z \end{pmatrix} \tag{4.29}$$

When a 3D mesh is scaled, all of its vertices are processed by Equation (4.29). Fig. 4.6 shows two examples of 3D scaling: The first is a *uniform* scaling in that all scaling factors are identical, and the second is a *non-uniform* scaling.

4.3.2 Rotation

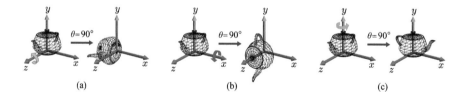

Fig. 4.7: Rotations about the principal axes: (a) $R_z(90°)$. (b) $R_x(90°)$. (c) $R_y(90°)$.

Unlike 2D rotation which requires a center of rotation, 3D rotation requires an *axis of rotation*. Consider rotation about the z-axis by θ, which we denote by $R_z(\theta)$. Suppose that it rotates (x, y, z) into (x', y', z'). Obviously, the z-coordinate is not changed by $R_z(\theta)$:

$$z' = z \tag{4.30}$$

On the other hand, Equations (4.4) and (4.5) hold for the x- and y-coordinates, respectively. Then, Equations (4.4), (4.5), and (4.30) are combined into a matrix-vector multiplication form:

$$\begin{pmatrix} x' \\ y' \\ z' \end{pmatrix} = \begin{pmatrix} cos\theta & -sin\theta & 0 \\ sin\theta & cos\theta & 0 \\ 0 & 0 & 1 \end{pmatrix} \begin{pmatrix} x \\ y \\ z \end{pmatrix} \tag{4.31}$$

All vertices of a polygon mesh are rotated by the same matrix of $R_z(\theta)$. In Fig. 4.7-(a), the teapot is rotated by $R_z(90°)$.

Now consider rotation about the x-axis, $R_x(\theta)$, shown in Fig. 4.7-(b). The x-coordinate is not changed by $R_x(\theta)$:

$$x' = x \tag{4.32}$$

When the thumb of the right hand is aligned with the rotation axis in Fig. 4.7-(b), the other fingers curl from the y-axis to the z-axis. Returning to Fig. 4.7-(a), observe that the fingers curl from the x-axis to the y-axis. Shifting from Fig. 4.7-(a) to -(b), the x-axis is replaced with the y-axis, and the y-axis is replaced with the z-axis. Then, by making such replacements in Equations (4.4) and (4.5), i.e., by replacing x with y and y with z, we obtain y' and z' for $R_x(\theta)$:

$$y' = ycos\theta - zsin\theta \tag{4.33}$$

$$z' = ysin\theta + zcos\theta \tag{4.34}$$

Equations (4.32), (4.33), and (4.34) are combined to define $R_x(\theta)$:

$$R_x(\theta) = \begin{pmatrix} 1 & 0 & 0 \\ 0 & cos\theta & -sin\theta \\ 0 & sin\theta & cos\theta \end{pmatrix} \tag{4.35}$$

Shifting from Fig. 4.7-(b) to -(c), we can define the rotation about the y-axis in the same manner:

$$R_y(\theta) = \begin{pmatrix} cos\theta & 0 & sin\theta \\ 0 & 1 & 0 \\ -sin\theta & 0 & cos\theta \end{pmatrix} \tag{4.36}$$

Fig. 4.8 compares counter-clockwise (CCW) and clockwise (CW) rotations about the y-axis. If the rotation is CCW with respect to the axis pointing toward you, the rotation angle is positive. If the rotation is CW, its matrix is defined with the negated rotation angle.

4.3.3 Translation and Homogeneous Coordinates

In order to define the 3D translation that handles homogeneous coordinates, the translation vector, (d_x, d_y, d_z), is inserted into the fourth column of the

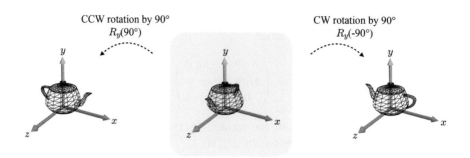

CCW rotation by 90°
$R_y(90°)$

CW rotation by 90°
$R_y(-90°)$

Fig. 4.8: The teapot shown in the middle is rotated CCW about the y-axis to define the one on the left. The rotation matrix is obtained by inserting 90° into Equation (4.36). If rotated CW, we have the result on the right. The rotation matrix is obtained by inserting −90° into Equation (4.36).

4×4 identity matrix:

$$\begin{pmatrix} 1 & 0 & 0 & d_x \\ 0 & 1 & 0 & d_y \\ 0 & 0 & 1 & d_z \\ 0 & 0 & 0 & 1 \end{pmatrix} \tag{4.37}$$

It can be multiplied with the homogeneous coordinates of the 3D point:

$$\begin{pmatrix} 1 & 0 & 0 & d_x \\ 0 & 1 & 0 & d_y \\ 0 & 0 & 1 & d_z \\ 0 & 0 & 0 & 1 \end{pmatrix} \begin{pmatrix} x \\ y \\ z \\ 1 \end{pmatrix} = \begin{pmatrix} x + d_x \\ y + d_y \\ z + d_z \\ 1 \end{pmatrix} \tag{4.38}$$

The 3×3 matrices developed for 3D scaling and rotation are extended to 4×4 matrices. For example, the scaling matrix is defined as

$$\begin{pmatrix} s_x & 0 & 0 & 0 \\ 0 & s_y & 0 & 0 \\ 0 & 0 & s_z & 0 \\ 0 & 0 & 0 & 1 \end{pmatrix} \tag{4.39}$$

4.4   Application: World Transform

The coordinate system used for creating an object is named the *object space*, which is also called the body space or model space. In contrast, the coordinate system for the entire 3D virtual environment is often called the *world space*.

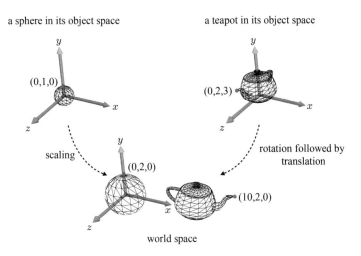

a sphere in its object space   a teapot in its object space

world space

Fig. 4.9: The sphere and teapot are defined in their own object spaces and are assembled into a global space, the world space.

Many objects defined in their own object spaces need to be assembled into the world space. For this, a series of transforms may be applied to each object. This is called the *world transform*[1].

Consider the world shown in Fig. 4.9. It is composed of a sphere and a teapot. They were created in their own object spaces. Initially, the object spaces are assumed to be identical to the world space. The world transform needed for the sphere is a uniform scaling of scaling factor 2, and the world matrix is defined as

$$\begin{pmatrix} 2 & 0 & 0 & 0 \\ 0 & 2 & 0 & 0 \\ 0 & 0 & 2 & 0 \\ 0 & 0 & 0 & 1 \end{pmatrix} \tag{4.40}$$

Consider the north pole of the sphere located at $(0,1,0)$ of the object space. The world matrix transforms it into $(0,2,0)$ in the world space:

$$\begin{pmatrix} 2 & 0 & 0 & 0 \\ 0 & 2 & 0 & 0 \\ 0 & 0 & 2 & 0 \\ 0 & 0 & 0 & 1 \end{pmatrix} \begin{pmatrix} 0 \\ 1 \\ 0 \\ 1 \end{pmatrix} = \begin{pmatrix} 0 \\ 2 \\ 0 \\ 1 \end{pmatrix} \tag{4.41}$$

---

[1] OpenGL ES calls this the *modeling transform*, but the world transform is a better term.

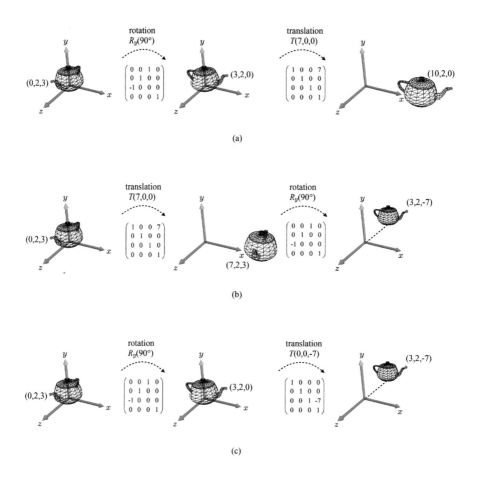

Fig. 4.10: Transform concatenation: (a) The teapot is rotated and then translated. (b) The teapot is translated and then rotated. (c) The affine matrix in (b) is conceptually decomposed into a linear transform (rotation) and a translation.

The world transform of the teapot is the rotation about the y-axis by $90°$, $R_y(90°)$, followed by the translation along the x-axis by seven units, $T(7,0,0)$. See Fig. 4.10-(a). The rotation matrix is obtained from Equation (4.36):

$$R_y(90°) = \begin{pmatrix} 0 & 0 & 1 & 0 \\ 0 & 1 & 0 & 0 \\ -1 & 0 & 0 & 0 \\ 0 & 0 & 0 & 1 \end{pmatrix} \qquad (4.42)$$

The tip of the teapot's mouth at $(0, 2, 3)$ is rotated to $(3, 2, 0)$ by $R_y(90°)$:

$$\begin{pmatrix} 0 & 0 & 1 & 0 \\ 0 & 1 & 0 & 0 \\ -1 & 0 & 0 & 0 \\ 0 & 0 & 0 & 1 \end{pmatrix} \begin{pmatrix} 0 \\ 2 \\ 3 \\ 1 \end{pmatrix} = \begin{pmatrix} 3 \\ 2 \\ 0 \\ 1 \end{pmatrix} \tag{4.43}$$

Now we consider the translation:

$$T(7, 0, 0) = \begin{pmatrix} 1 & 0 & 0 & 7 \\ 0 & 1 & 0 & 0 \\ 0 & 0 & 1 & 0 \\ 0 & 0 & 0 & 1 \end{pmatrix} \tag{4.44}$$

The mouth tip at $(3, 2, 0)$ is translated to $(10, 2, 0)$ by $T(7, 0, 0)$:

$$\begin{pmatrix} 1 & 0 & 0 & 7 \\ 0 & 1 & 0 & 0 \\ 0 & 0 & 1 & 0 \\ 0 & 0 & 0 & 1 \end{pmatrix} \begin{pmatrix} 3 \\ 2 \\ 0 \\ 1 \end{pmatrix} = \begin{pmatrix} 10 \\ 2 \\ 0 \\ 1 \end{pmatrix} \tag{4.45}$$

$R_y(90°)$ and $T(7, 0, 0)$ can be combined into a single matrix:

$$\begin{aligned} T(7, 0, 0) R_y(90°) &= \begin{pmatrix} 1 & 0 & 0 & 7 \\ 0 & 1 & 0 & 0 \\ 0 & 0 & 1 & 0 \\ 0 & 0 & 0 & 1 \end{pmatrix} \begin{pmatrix} 0 & 0 & 1 & 0 \\ 0 & 1 & 0 & 0 \\ -1 & 0 & 0 & 0 \\ 0 & 0 & 0 & 1 \end{pmatrix} \\ &= \begin{pmatrix} 0 & 0 & 1 & 7 \\ 0 & 1 & 0 & 0 \\ -1 & 0 & 0 & 0 \\ 0 & 0 & 0 & 1 \end{pmatrix} \end{aligned} \tag{4.46}$$

This is the world matrix for the teapot. The teapot's mouth tip that is originally located at $(0, 2, 3)$ in the object space is transformed to $(10, 2, 0)$ in the world space by the world matrix:

$$\begin{pmatrix} 0 & 0 & 1 & 7 \\ 0 & 1 & 0 & 0 \\ -1 & 0 & 0 & 0 \\ 0 & 0 & 0 & 1 \end{pmatrix} \begin{pmatrix} 0 \\ 2 \\ 3 \\ 1 \end{pmatrix} = \begin{pmatrix} 10 \\ 2 \\ 0 \\ 1 \end{pmatrix} \tag{4.47}$$

The result is the same as in Equation (4.45).

The discussions we had on 2D affine transforms apply to 3D affine transforms. First of all, matrix multiplication is not commutative. In Fig. 4.10-(b), the order of $R_y(90°)$ and $T(7, 0, 0)$ is changed, and the result is different from Fig. 4.10-(a).

When 3D scaling, rotation, and translation matrices are concatenated to make a 4×4 matrix, the fourth row is always (0 0 0 1), as can be found in

Equation (4.46). The remaining 3×4 elements are denoted by $[L|t]$. L is a 3×3 matrix for the 'combined' linear transform, which does *not* include any terms from the input translations, and t is the 'combined' translation, which may contain the input linear-transform terms. Transforming an object by $[L|t]$ is 'conceptually' decomposed into two steps: L is applied first and then the linearly transformed object is translated by t. For example, the combined matrix in Fig. 4.10-(b) is decomposed into two matrices:

$$R_y(90°)T(7,0,0) = \begin{pmatrix} 0 & 0 & 1 & 0 \\ 0 & 1 & 0 & 0 \\ -1 & 0 & 0 & 0 \\ 0 & 0 & 0 & 1 \end{pmatrix} \begin{pmatrix} 1 & 0 & 0 & 7 \\ 0 & 1 & 0 & 0 \\ 0 & 0 & 1 & 0 \\ 0 & 0 & 0 & 1 \end{pmatrix}$$

$$= \begin{pmatrix} 0 & 0 & 1 & 0 \\ 0 & 1 & 0 & 0 \\ -1 & 0 & 0 & -7 \\ 0 & 0 & 0 & 1 \end{pmatrix} \qquad (4.48)$$

$$= \begin{pmatrix} 1 & 0 & 0 & 0 \\ 0 & 1 & 0 & 0 \\ 0 & 0 & 1 & -7 \\ 0 & 0 & 0 & 1 \end{pmatrix} \begin{pmatrix} 0 & 0 & 1 & 0 \\ 0 & 1 & 0 & 0 \\ -1 & 0 & 0 & 0 \\ 0 & 0 & 0 & 1 \end{pmatrix}$$

The conceptual steps of first applying L (colored in red) and then t (in blue) are illustrated in Fig. 4.10-(c).

4.5   Rotation and Object-space Basis

Once an object is created, it is fixed within its object space. An object can be thought of as being stuck to its object space. In Fig. 4.11-(a), $\{e_1, e_2, e_3\}$ represents the standard basis of the world space and $\{u, v, n\}$ represents the orthonormal basis of the object space. Initially, they are identical. A rotation applied to an object changes its orientation, which can be described by the 'rotated' basis of the object space.

Let R denote the rotation. Then, e_1 and u are related as follows:

$$Re_1 = R\begin{pmatrix} 1 \\ 0 \\ 0 \end{pmatrix} = \begin{pmatrix} u_x \\ u_y \\ u_z \end{pmatrix} \qquad (4.49)$$

Similarly, R transforms e_2 and e_3 into v and n, respectively:

$$Re_2 = R\begin{pmatrix} 0 \\ 1 \\ 0 \end{pmatrix} = \begin{pmatrix} v_x \\ v_y \\ v_z \end{pmatrix} \qquad (4.50)$$

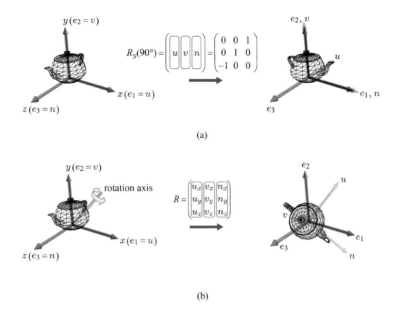

(a)

(b)

Fig. 4.11: The orientation of an object is described by the basis of the rotated object space. (a) Rotation about a principal axis. (b) Rotation about an arbitrary axis.

$$Re_3 = R \begin{pmatrix} 0 \\ 0 \\ 1 \end{pmatrix} = \begin{pmatrix} n_x \\ n_y \\ n_z \end{pmatrix} \tag{4.51}$$

Equations (4.49), (4.50), and (4.51) can be combined into one:

$$R \begin{pmatrix} 1\ 0\ 0 \\ 0\ 1\ 0 \\ 0\ 0\ 1 \end{pmatrix} = \begin{pmatrix} u_x\ v_x\ n_x \\ u_y\ v_y\ n_y \\ u_z\ v_z\ n_z \end{pmatrix} \tag{4.52}$$

In Equation (4.52), the matrix multiplied with R is the identity matrix and therefore the left-hand side is reduced to R:

$$R = \begin{pmatrix} u_x\ v_x\ n_x \\ u_y\ v_y\ n_y \\ u_z\ v_z\ n_z \end{pmatrix} \tag{4.53}$$

It is found that the *columns* of R are u, v, and n. Fig. 4.11-(a) shows the example of $R_y(90°)$, where $u = (0, 0, -1)$, $v = (0, 1, 0)$, and $n = (1, 0, 0)$.

Given the 'rotated' object-space basis, $\{u, v, n\}$, the rotation matrix is immediately determined, and vice versa. This holds in general. Fig. 4.11-(b) shows a rotation about an arbitrary axis, which is not a principal axis. Suppose that its matrix R is obtained somehow. (Section 11.3.4 will present how to compute R.) Then, the rotated object-space basis, $\{u, v, n\}$, is immediately determined by taking the columns of R. Inversely, if $\{u, v, n\}$ is known a priori, R can also be immediately determined.

4.6   Inverse Transforms

In computer graphics, *inverse transforms* are encountered quite frequently. Given a translation T with translation vector (d_x, d_y, d_z), its inverse is simply a translation by $(-d_x, -d_y, -d_z)$, leading to the following matrix:

$$\begin{pmatrix} 1 & 0 & 0 & -d_x \\ 0 & 1 & 0 & -d_y \\ 0 & 0 & 1 & -d_z \\ 0 & 0 & 0 & 1 \end{pmatrix} \tag{4.54}$$

This is the *inverse matrix* of T and is denoted T^{-1}. It is straightforward to show that $T^{-1}T = I$:

$$T^{-1}T = \begin{pmatrix} 1 & 0 & 0 & -d_x \\ 0 & 1 & 0 & -d_y \\ 0 & 0 & 1 & -d_z \\ 0 & 0 & 0 & 1 \end{pmatrix} \begin{pmatrix} 1 & 0 & 0 & d_x \\ 0 & 1 & 0 & d_y \\ 0 & 0 & 1 & d_z \\ 0 & 0 & 0 & 1 \end{pmatrix} = \begin{pmatrix} 1 & 0 & 0 & 0 \\ 0 & 1 & 0 & 0 \\ 0 & 0 & 1 & 0 \\ 0 & 0 & 0 & 1 \end{pmatrix} = I \tag{4.55}$$

Given a scaling with scaling factors (s_x, s_y, s_z), its inverse is defined as

$$\begin{pmatrix} 1/s_x & 0 & 0 & 0 \\ 0 & 1/s_y & 0 & 0 \\ 0 & 0 & 1/s_z & 0 \\ 0 & 0 & 0 & 1 \end{pmatrix} \tag{4.56}$$

Let us now consider inverse rotation. As the object-space basis $\{u, v, n\}$ is an orthonormal basis, $u \cdot u = v \cdot v = n \cdot n = 1$. On the other hand, $u \cdot v = v \cdot u = 0$, $u \cdot n = n \cdot u = 0$, and $v \cdot n = n \cdot v = 0$. Using these, a rotation

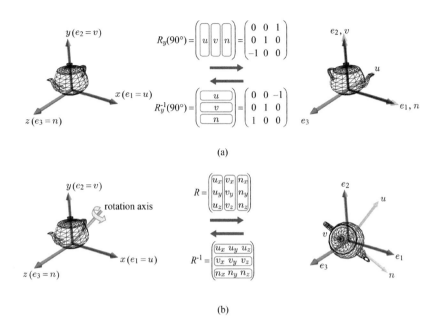

Fig. 4.12: The transpose of a rotation matrix is its inverse, i.e., $R^T = R^{-1}$. (a) $R_y(90°)$ and its inverse. (b) Rotation about an arbitrary axis and its inverse.

matrix and its *transpose* are combined as follows:

$$R^T R = \begin{pmatrix} u_x & u_y & u_z \\ v_x & v_y & v_z \\ n_x & n_y & n_z \end{pmatrix} \begin{pmatrix} u_x & v_x & n_x \\ u_y & v_y & n_y \\ u_z & v_z & n_z \end{pmatrix}$$
$$= \begin{pmatrix} u \cdot u & u \cdot v & u \cdot n \\ v \cdot u & v \cdot v & v \cdot n \\ n \cdot u & n \cdot v & n \cdot n \end{pmatrix}$$
$$= \begin{pmatrix} 1 & 0 & 0 \\ 0 & 1 & 0 \\ 0 & 0 & 1 \end{pmatrix}$$
$$= I$$

(4.57)

This asserts that $R^T = R^{-1}$, i.e., the inverse of a rotation matrix is simply its transpose. Recall that u, v, and n form the *columns* of R. As $R^{-1} = R^T$, u, v, and n form the *rows* of R^{-1}, as illustrated in Fig. 4.12.

Exercises

1. Note the difference between a column vector and a row vector. For matrix-vector multiplication, let us use row vectors.

    (a) Write the translation matrix that translates (x, y) by (dx, dy).

    (b) Write the rotation matrix that rotates (x, y) by θ.

    (c) Write the scaling matrix with scaling factors s_x and s_y.

2. The object-space basis of an object is denoted by $\{u, v, n\}$. Initially, it is the same as the world-space basis. Suppose that $u = (0, 0, -1)$ and $n = (1/\sqrt{2}, 1/\sqrt{2}, 0)$ after a rotation. Compute the matrix for the inverse of the rotation.

3. The following matrix represents a combination of a rotation, R, followed by a translation, T. Write the matrices for R and T.

$$\begin{pmatrix} -1 & 0 & 0 & 3 \\ 0 & 1 & 0 & 4 \\ 0 & 0 & -1 & -1 \\ 0 & 0 & 0 & 1 \end{pmatrix}$$

4. Describe the general procedure for rotating about an arbitrary axis by θ. The procedure should include (1) the step for transforming the arbitrary axis into a principal axis and (2) the cross-product operation.

5. The teapot is to be rotated about $(3, 0, 4)$ by $90°$. The rotation about such an arbitrary axis can be defined as a combination of three matrices: (1) the rotation of the arbitrary axis onto the x-axis, (2) the rotation about the x-axis by $90°$, and (3) the inverse of (1). Compute the three matrices. [Hint: You may use $R_y(\theta)$ for (1).]

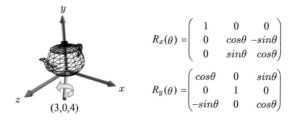

$$R_x(\theta) = \begin{pmatrix} 1 & 0 & 0 \\ 0 & cos\theta & -sin\theta \\ 0 & sin\theta & cos\theta \end{pmatrix}$$

$$R_y(\theta) = \begin{pmatrix} cos\theta & 0 & sin\theta \\ 0 & 1 & 0 \\ -sin\theta & 0 & cos\theta \end{pmatrix}$$

6. The teapot is to be rotated about $(3, 4, 0)$ by $90°$. The rotation about such an arbitrary axis can be defined as a combination of three matrices: (1) the rotation of the arbitrary axis onto the x-axis, (2) the rotation about the x-axis by $90°$, and (3) the inverse of (1). Compute the three matrices. [Hint: You may use $R_z(\theta)$ for (1).]

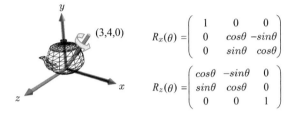

$$R_x(\theta) = \begin{pmatrix} 1 & 0 & 0 \\ 0 & \cos\theta & -\sin\theta \\ 0 & \sin\theta & \cos\theta \end{pmatrix}$$

$$R_z(\theta) = \begin{pmatrix} \cos\theta & -\sin\theta & 0 \\ \sin\theta & \cos\theta & 0 \\ 0 & 0 & 1 \end{pmatrix}$$

Chapter 5

Vertex Processing

The polygon meshes in a 3D scene are passed to the GPU for rendering. The GPU transforms the polygons to their 2D form to appear on the screen and computes the colors of the pixels comprising the 2D polygons. The pixels are written into a memory space called the *color buffer*. The image in the color buffer is displayed on the screen.

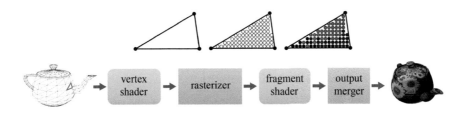

Fig. 5.1: The main stages of the rendering pipeline.

In the GPU, rendering is done in a pipeline architecture, where the output of one stage is taken as the input for the next stage. Fig. 5.1 illustrates the step-by-step process of filling the interior of a polygon in a 3D model. A *shader* in the rendering pipeline is a synonym of a program. We have to provide the pipeline with two programs, i.e., the vertex and fragment shaders. In contrast, the rasterizer and output merger are hard-wired stages that perform fixed functions.

The vertex shader performs various operations on every input vertex stored in the vertex array. The output is passed to the rasterizer. It assembles triangles from the vertices and converts each triangle into what are called the *fragments*. A fragment is defined for a pixel location covered by the triangle on the screen and refers to a set of data used to determine a color. The fragment shader operates on each fragment and determines its color through various operations such as texturing and lighting. In the output merger stage, each fragment competes or combines with a pixel stored in the color buffer to update the pixel's color.

Fig. 5.2: Transforms and spaces for the vertex shader: Sections 5.1, 5.2, and 5.4 present the three transforms in order.

This and the next chapters present the first stage of the rendering pipeline, the vertex shader. Among the operations performed by the vertex shader, the most essential is applying a series of transforms to the vertex, as shown in Fig. 5.2. The first is the world transform presented in Section 4.4. Section 5.1 revisits it and discusses an issue which was not covered. Then, the next sections present the subsequent transforms shown in Fig. 5.2.

5.1 World Transform Revisited

The role of the world transform is to assemble all objects defined in their own object spaces into a single environment named the world space. In Section 4.4, the world transform was applied to "vertex position" in the vertex array. Another indispensable element of the vertex array is "vertex normal." Can it be transformed by the same world transform?

As discussed in Section 4.4, the world matrix composed of affine transforms is denoted by $[L|t]$, where L is the 'combined' linear transform and t is the 'combined' translation. We ignore t and consider only L for transforming normals because vectors are not affected by translations.

In Fig. 5.3-(a), the line segment represents the cross section of a triangle that is perpendicular to the xy-plane of the 3D coordinate system. Its normal is denoted as n. Suppose that L is a non-uniform scaling where $s_x = 0.5$ and $s_y = 1$. Fig. 5.3-(a) shows that Ln is no longer orthogonal to the triangle scaled by L.

In order for the normal to remain orthogonal to the triangle transformed by L, it should be transformed by $(L^{-1})^T$. [Note: Normal transform] proves this. $(L^{-1})^T$ is named the *inverse transpose* of L and is denoted simply by L^{-T}. Fig. 5.3-(b) depicts the result of applying L^{-T} to the triangle's normal.

If L does not contain non-uniform scaling, i.e., if L is a rotation, a uniform scaling, or a combination of both, Ln remains orthogonal to the triangle transformed by L. For the sake of consistency, however, we transform n by

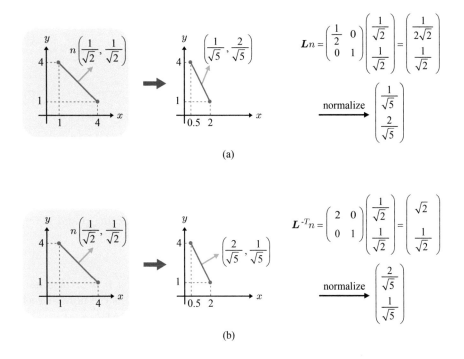

Fig. 5.3: Normal transform (modified from [3]): (a) Two vertices and a triangle normal are transformed by the same matrix, L. As L is a scaling, the transformed normal is normalized. (b) Whereas the vertices are transformed by L, the normal is transformed by L^{-T}.

L^{-T} regardless of whether L contains non-uniform scaling or not. Note that $L^{-T}n$ will be normalized such that the world-transformed normal remains a unit vector.

Fig. 5.3 shows "triangle normals" for easy discussions. Stored in the vertex array are "vertex normals." They are also transformed by L^{-T}.

[Note: Normal transform]
Consider the triangle $\langle p, q, r \rangle$ in Fig. 5.4. Its normal n is orthogonal to the vector connecting p and q. The dot product of orthogonal vectors is zero, and we have the following:

$$n^T(q - p) = 0 \qquad (5.1)$$

where n, q, and p represent column vectors. A linear transform L transforms p and q to p' and q', respectively, i.e., $Lp = p'$ and $Lq = q'$. Using the *inverse* transform, $\boldsymbol{L}^{-1}$, we can rewrite Equation (5.1) as follows:

$$n^T(\boldsymbol{L}^{-1}q' - \boldsymbol{L}^{-1}p') = 0 \tag{5.2}$$

Rearranging Equation (5.2) leads to the following:

$$n^T\boldsymbol{L}^{-1}(q' - p') = 0 \tag{5.3}$$

Let us take the *transpose* of Equation (5.3):

$$(q' - p')^T(\boldsymbol{L}^{-1})^T n = 0 \tag{5.4}$$

Equation (5.4) asserts that $(\boldsymbol{L}^{-1})^T n$ is a vector orthogonal to $(q' - p')$ which is the edge vector of the triangle transformed by $\boldsymbol{L}$.

The same discussion can be made for the vector connecting p and r:

$$(r' - p')^T(\boldsymbol{L}^{-1})^T n = 0 \tag{5.5}$$

As shown in Equations (5.4) and (5.5), the vector $(\boldsymbol{L}^{-1})^T n$ is orthogonal to both $(q' - p')$ and $(r' - p')$, and therefore it can be taken as the normal vector n' of the transformed triangle. This concludes that $(\boldsymbol{L}^{-1})^T$ is the correct transform to be applied to n.

$(\boldsymbol{L}^{-1})^T$ is multiplied with $\boldsymbol{L}^T$ to return the identity matrix:

$$(\boldsymbol{L}^{-1})^T\boldsymbol{L}^T = (\boldsymbol{L}\boldsymbol{L}^{-1})^T = I^T = I \tag{5.6}$$

This shows that $(\boldsymbol{L}^{-1})^T$ is the inverse of $\boldsymbol{L}^T$, i.e., $(\boldsymbol{L}^{-1})^T = (\boldsymbol{L}^T)^{-1}$. Both $(\boldsymbol{L}^{-1})^T$ and $(\boldsymbol{L}^T)^{-1}$ are denoted simply by $\boldsymbol{L}^{-T}$.

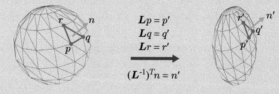

Fig. 5.4: Before $\boldsymbol{L}$ is applied, n is orthogonal to the triangle $\langle p, q, r \rangle$. Whereas $\langle p, q, r \rangle$ is transformed by $\boldsymbol{L}$, n is transformed by $(\boldsymbol{L}^{-1})^T$. Then, the transformed normal n' remains orthogonal to the transformed triangle $\langle p', q', r' \rangle$.

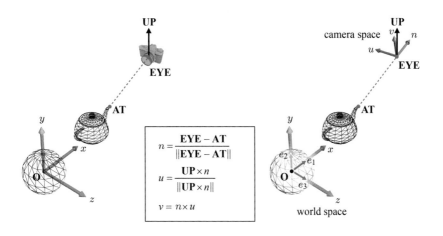

Fig. 5.5: **EYE**, **AT**, and **UP** define the camera space $\{u, v, n, \mathbf{EYE}\}$. With respect to the camera space, the camera is located at the origin and points in the $-n$ direction.

5.2 View Transform

Suppose that the world transform has been completed and all objects are now defined in the world space. In order to capture the scene, we then have to specify the pose of a *virtual camera* in the world space. The camera is often called the *eye* or *viewer*.

5.2.1 Camera Space

The camera pose is specified in terms of three parameters, **EYE**, **AT**, and **UP**, as shown on the left of Fig. 5.5.

- **EYE** is the camera position in the world space.
- **AT** is a reference point in the scene at which the camera is pointing. (In the example, **AT** is located at the tip of the teapot's mouth.)
- **UP** is a vector that roughly describes where the top of the camera is pointing. (In most cases, **UP** is set to the vertical axis of the world space, i.e., the y-axis.)

These parameters are used to build the *camera space*, which is also called the eye space or view space. Its origin is **EYE**. The box in the middle of Fig. 5.5 shows the sequential process of building the basis, $\{u, v, n\}$, of the camera space. First, the vector connecting **AT** and **EYE** is normalized to compose a unit vector n. The cross product of **UP** and n is normalized to define another unit vector u. Finally, the cross product of n and u determines a unit vector v. Observe that $\{u, v, n\}$ is an orthonormal basis. The camera space is denoted as $\{u, v, n, \mathbf{EYE}\}$.

5.2.2   View Matrix for Space Change

We have two distinct spaces: the camera space $\{u, v, n, \mathbf{EYE}\}$ and the world space $\{e_1, e_2, e_3, \mathbf{O}\}$. Suppose that the tip of the teapot's mouth has the coordinates $(10, 2, 0)$ in the world space and it is designated as **AT**, as depicted in the first box of Fig. 5.6. On the other hand, **EYE**'s coordinates are $(18, 8, 0)$. With respect to the camera space, the mouth tip is on the $-n$ axis, and therefore its u- and v-coordinates are zero. The distance between the tip and **EYE** is 10. Then, the "camera-space coordinates" of the tip are $(0, 0, -10)$ whereas its "world-space coordinates" are $(10, 2, 0)$.

It becomes much easier to develop the rendering algorithms if all of the world-space objects are redefined in the camera space in the same manner as the tip of the teapot's mouth, i.e., from $(10, 2, 0)$ to $(0, 0, -10)$. This is generally called a *space change* and can be intuitively described by the process of *superimposing* the camera space $\{u, v, n, \mathbf{EYE}\}$ onto the world space $\{e_1, e_2, e_3, \mathbf{O}\}$. Along the way, we keep the relative pose of each object with respect to the camera space. It will be helpful if you imagine an invisible rod connecting the object and the camera space. In Fig. 5.6, **EYE** is first translated to **O**, and then $\{u, v, n\}$ is rotated to $\{e_1, e_2, e_3\}$. Accordingly, the scene objects are translated and then rotated. As the world and camera spaces are made identical, the world-space positions of the transformed objects can be taken as the camera-space ones. In our example, the mouth tip is translated and then rotated to have the coordinates $(0, 0, -10)$, which represent its camera-space position.

The space change from the world space to the camera space is named the *view transform* or *camera transform*. Its translation (denoted by T) is defined by the translation vector $\mathbf{O} - \mathbf{EYE}$, i.e., $(-\mathbf{EYE}_x, -\mathbf{EYE}_y, -\mathbf{EYE}_z)$:

$$T = \begin{pmatrix} 1 & 0 & 0 & -\mathbf{EYE}_x \\ 0 & 1 & 0 & -\mathbf{EYE}_y \\ 0 & 0 & 1 & -\mathbf{EYE}_z \\ 0 & 0 & 0 & 1 \end{pmatrix} \tag{5.7}$$

In our example, the tip of the teapot's mouth is translated by T from $(10, 2, 0)$ into $(-8, -6, 0)$:

$$T\begin{pmatrix} 10 \\ 2 \\ 0 \\ 1 \end{pmatrix} = \begin{pmatrix} 1 & 0 & 0 & -18 \\ 0 & 1 & 0 & -8 \\ 0 & 0 & 1 & 0 \\ 0 & 0 & 0 & 1 \end{pmatrix} \begin{pmatrix} 10 \\ 2 \\ 0 \\ 1 \end{pmatrix} = \begin{pmatrix} -8 \\ -6 \\ 0 \\ 1 \end{pmatrix} \tag{5.8}$$

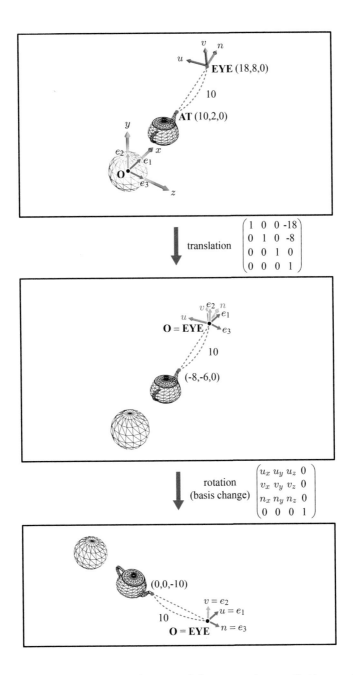

Fig. 5.6: The world-space coordinates of the teapot's mouth tip are $(10, 2, 0)$ and are transformed to $(0, 0, -10)$ in the camera space.

Due to translation, the world space and the camera space now share the same origin, as illustrated in the second box of Fig. 5.6. We then need a rotation that transforms $\{u, v, n\}$ onto $\{e_1, e_2, e_3\}$. As presented in Fig. 4.12-(b), u, v, and n fill the rows of the rotation matrix:

$$R = \begin{pmatrix} u_x & u_y & u_z & 0 \\ v_x & v_y & v_z & 0 \\ n_x & n_y & n_z & 0 \\ 0 & 0 & 0 & 1 \end{pmatrix} \tag{5.9}$$

The scene objects are rotated by R, as shown in the last box of Fig. 5.6. The rotation component of a space change (R in our example) is called a *basis change* in the sense that it changes the coordinates defined in a basis into those in another one, e.g., from $(-8, -6, 0)$ defined in $\{e_1, e_2, e_3\}$ to $(0, 0, -10)$ in $\{u, v, n\}$. In fact, every basis change is represented in a rotation matrix.

The view transform matrix denoted by M_{view} is a combination of T and R:

$$\begin{aligned} M_{view} &= RT \\ &= \begin{pmatrix} u_x & u_y & u_z & 0 \\ v_x & v_y & v_z & 0 \\ n_x & n_y & n_z & 0 \\ 0 & 0 & 0 & 1 \end{pmatrix} \begin{pmatrix} 1 & 0 & 0 & -\mathbf{EYE}_x \\ 0 & 1 & 0 & -\mathbf{EYE}_y \\ 0 & 0 & 1 & -\mathbf{EYE}_z \\ 0 & 0 & 0 & 1 \end{pmatrix} \\ &= \begin{pmatrix} u_x & u_y & u_z & -u \cdot \mathbf{EYE} \\ v_x & v_y & v_z & -v \cdot \mathbf{EYE} \\ n_x & n_y & n_z & -n \cdot \mathbf{EYE} \\ 0 & 0 & 0 & 1 \end{pmatrix} \end{aligned} \tag{5.10}$$

M_{view} is applied to all objects in the world space to transform them into the camera space.

The space/basis change plays quite an important role in many algorithms of computer graphics, computer vision, augmented reality, and robotics. It also frequently appears later in this book.

5.3   Right-hand System versus Left-hand System

A 3D Cartesian coordinate system is either *right-handed* or *left-handed*, as shown in Fig. 5.7. In the right-hand system (RHS), the thumb of the right hand points toward the positive end of the z-axis when the other four fingers curl from the x-axis to the y-axis. In the left-hand system (LHS), the same rule is applied with the left hand. OpenGL uses the RHS, but Direct3D uses the LHS. The coordinate system used in this OpenGL ES book is the RHS by default. However, you will encounter an LHS in the next section.

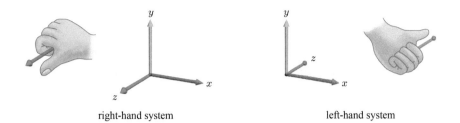

Fig. 5.7: Right-hand system versus left-hand system.

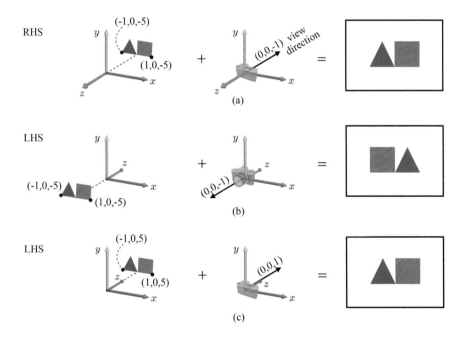

Fig. 5.8: Conversion between the RHS and LHS.

Fig. 5.8-(a) shows an object composed of a triangle and a square. It is located in the $-z$ side of the RHS. Assume that the camera's position (**EYE**) is at the origin and its view direction (connecting **EYE** and **AT**) is $(0, 0, -1)$. Then, the camera captures the image shown on the right of Fig. 5.8-(a).

Fig. 5.8-(b) shows the object and camera parameters ported into the LHS. Observe that the coordinates of the vertices and view direction are not changed. Then, we will obtain a horizontally flipped image shown on the right of Fig. 5.8-(b).

A simple solution to this inconsistency is to negate the z-coordinates of the object and camera parameters. Fig. 5.8-(c) shows that z-negation enables us to capture a consistent image. Intuitively, z-negation is equivalent to *inverting* the z-axis, as can be observed when we move from Fig. 5.8-(a) to -(c).

5.4 Projection Transform

EYE, **AT**, and **UP** defined in the world space are considered as the external parameters of the camera. Now it is time to define the camera's internal parameters. It is analogous to choosing a camera lens and controlling zoom.

The view transform has converted all vertices of the world-space objects into the camera space, $\{u, v, n, \mathbf{EYE}\}$. The internal parameters are defined in the camera space. We do not need the world space any longer, and therefore we will use $\{x, y, z\}$ to denote the camera-space axes simply because $\{x, y, z\}$ is more familiar to us.

5.4.1 View Frustum

In general, a camera cannot capture all objects in the scene because its *field of view* is limited. The visible region in a scene is called the *view volume*. It is specified in terms of four parameters: *fovy*, *aspect*, *n*, and *f*. See Fig. 5.9. First of all, *fovy* specifies the field of view with respect to the y-axis, and *aspect* denotes the aspect ratio of the view volume, i.e., the width divided by the height of the view volume. The volume defined by *fovy* and *aspect* can be considered as an infinite pyramid. Its apex is located at the origin and its axis is the $-z$ axis. In Fig. 5.9, the cylinder is invisible because it is out of the field of view.

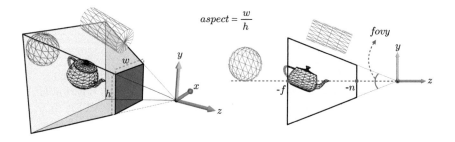

Fig. 5.9: The pyramid-like volume is named the view frustum. The polygons outside of the view frustum (illustrated in red) are considered invisible.

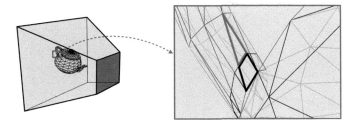

Fig. 5.10: If a polygon intersects the view frustum's boundary, the part of the polygon outside of the view frustum is discarded.

The other parameters of the view volume, n and f, denote the distances from the origin to the *near plane* and *far plane*, respectively. The infinite pyramid defined by *fovy* and *aspect* is truncated by the planes, $z = -n$ and $z = -f$. The truncated pyramidal view volume is called the *view frustum*.

Observe that, in Fig. 5.9, not only the cylinder but also the sphere is invisible because it is outside of the view frustum. The near and far planes run counter to a real-world camera or human vision system but have been introduced for the sake of computational efficiency. The out-of-frustum objects do not contribute to the final image and are usually discarded before entering the GPU pipeline[1].

In Fig. 5.9, only the teapot is taken as a visible object. Note however that its handle intersects the far plane of the view frustum. If a polygon intersects the boundary of the view frustum, it is *clipped* with respect to the boundary, and only the portion inside of the view frustum is processed for display. See Fig. 5.10. The clipped polygons with black edges are further processed whereas those with red edges are discarded. Clipping is done by the rasterizer[2], which is the second stage of the rendering pipeline presented in Fig. 5.1.

5.4.2 Projection Matrix and Clip Space

Fig. 5.10 shows the concept of clipping with the pyramidal view frustum. In reality, however, clipping is not done with it. Consider a transform that

---

[1] This process is named the *view-frustum culling*. In computer graphics, culling refers to the process of eliminating parts of a scene that are not visible to the camera.

[2] If the view-frustum culling is not done by the CPU, the cylinder and sphere in Fig. 5.9 enter the GPU rendering pipeline. All of their triangles lie outside of the view frustum and thus are discarded by the clipping algorithm. This shows a lack of efficiency because invisible objects unnecessarily consume GPU resources.

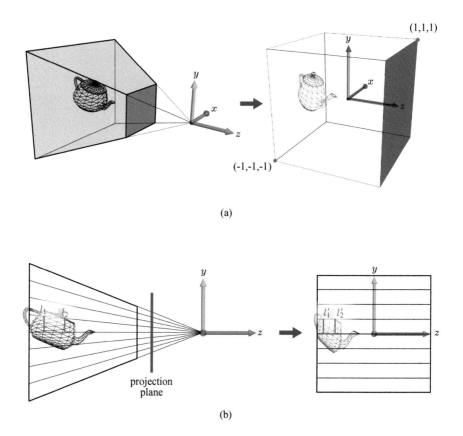

(a)

(b)

Fig. 5.11: Projection transform: (a) The view frustum is deformed into a cube. The deformation is in fact applied to the objects in the scene. The teapot is deformed in a way that the part closer to the camera is blown-up and that farther from it is shrunken. (b) Cross-section views show how the perspective projection effect (often called *foreshortening*) is achieved through the projection transform.

deforms the view frustum into the axis-aligned 2×2×2-sized cube centered at the origin, as shown in Fig. 5.11-(a). It is called the *projection transform*. The camera-space objects are projection-transformed and then clipped against the cube. In order to put emphasis on this, the projection-transformed objects are said to be defined in the *clip space*, which can be considered as the renamed camera space.

The cross section of the view frustum is shown on the left of Fig. 5.11-(b). The view frustum can be taken as a convergent pencil of *projection lines*. The lines converge on the origin, where the camera is located. Imagine a *projection plane* that is parallel to the xy-plane and is located between the view frustum and the origin. The projection lines would form the image of the scene on the projection plane.

All 3D points on a projection line would be mapped onto a single point on the projection plane. Consider the line segments, l_1 and l_2, in Fig. 5.11-(b). They appear to be of equal length in the projection plane even though l_1 is longer than l_2 in the 3D space. It is the effect of *perspective projection*, where objects farther away look smaller.

Now look at the right of Fig. 5.11-(b). The projection transform ensures that all projection lines become parallel to the z-axis, i.e., we now have a universal projection line. Observe that the projection transform *deforms* the 3D objects in the scene. The polygons near the origin (camera) are relatively blown-up whereas those at the rear of the view frustum are relatively shrunken. Consequently, the projection-transformed line segments l_1' and l_2' are made to be of equal length. The projection transform does not actually 'project' the 3D objects into the 2D projection plane, but brings the effect of perspective projection within the 3D space.

Later, the 2×2×2-sized cube will be scaled such that the lightly-shaded face (pointed by the z-axis) in Fig. 5.11-(a) fits to the screen. The objects are scaled accordingly and then *orthographically* projected to the screen along the z-axis. Consequently, l_1' and l_2' will appear to be of equal length on the screen. Chapter 7 will present the scaling and orthographic projection.

Shown below is the projection matrix defined by the view frustum parameters, *fovy*, *aspect*, n, and f:

$$M = \begin{pmatrix} \frac{cot\frac{fovy}{2}}{aspect} & 0 & 0 & 0 \\ 0 & cot\frac{fovy}{2} & 0 & 0 \\ 0 & 0 & \frac{f+n}{f-n} & \frac{2nf}{f-n} \\ 0 & 0 & -1 & 0 \end{pmatrix} \tag{5.11}$$

Section 5.4.3 will present how to derive the projection matrix. An important feature of the projection matrix is that, unlike affine matrices, the last row is not (0 0 0 1). Its implication will be discussed in Section 7.2.

Observe that the clip space in Fig. 5.11 is right-handed. The projection transform is the last operation in the vertex shader, and the teapot's vertices

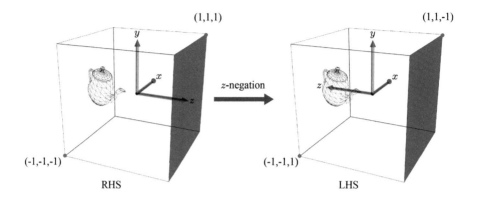

Fig. 5.12: The z-coordinates are negated to switch from the right-handed space to the left-handed space. Z-negation is conceptually equivalent to z-axis inversion.

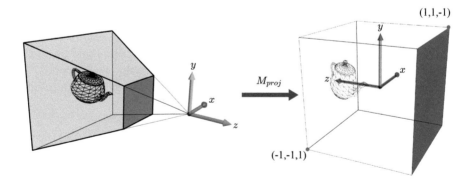

Fig. 5.13: The last transform in the vertex shader, M_{proj}, converts the right-handed camera-space object into the left-handed clip space. This illustrates the combination of Fig. 5.11-(a) and Fig. 5.12.

will then enter the 'hard-wired' rasterizer, as shown in Fig. 5.1. In the raster-izer, the clip space is left-handed by default. In order for the vertex shader to be compatible with the rasterizer, we need to change the right-handed clip space into the left-handed one. It requires z-negation. Fig. 5.12 shows the result of z-negation.

When a vertex v is transformed into v' by M presented in Equation (5.11), the z-coordinate of v' is determined by the third row of M. Therefore, negat-ing the z-coordinate of v' is achieved by negating the third row of M:

$$M_{proj} = \begin{pmatrix} \frac{cot\frac{fovy}{2}}{aspect} & 0 & 0 & 0 \\ 0 & cot\frac{fovy}{2} & 0 & 0 \\ 0 & 0 & -\frac{f+n}{f-n} & -\frac{2nf}{f-n} \\ 0 & 0 & -1 & 0 \end{pmatrix} \tag{5.12}$$

Fig. 5.13 shows that M_{proj} transforms the object defined in the right-handed camera space to that of the left-handed clip space.

5.4.3 Derivation of Projection Matrix*

The projection matrix converts the view frustum into the $2\times2\times2$-sized cube. When a camera-space point located at (x, y, z) is transformed into (x', y', z'), each coordinate should be in the range of $[-1, 1]$. Using this constraint, the transformed coordinates, (x', y', z'), can be defined.

Fig. 5.14-(a) shows the cross section of the pyramidal view volume. The coordinates of a point v are represented in 2D: (y, z). Suppose a projection plane orthogonal to the z-axis. Conceptually, v will be projected to v' on the plane. The coordinates of v' are represented in (y', z'). If the projection plane is at the z-coordinate of $-cot\frac{fovy}{2}$, y' is confined to the range of $[-1, 1]$. This satisfies our constraint, and we can compute y' using the principle of similar triangles:

$$y' = -cot\frac{fovy}{2} \cdot \frac{y}{z} \tag{5.13}$$

If $fovx$ were given as the 'horizontal' field of view, we could find that

$$x' = -cot\frac{fovx}{2} \cdot \frac{x}{z} \tag{5.14}$$

through the same method used for computing y'. On the other hand, Fig. 5.14-(b) shows that

$$aspect = \frac{cot\frac{fovy}{2}}{cot\frac{fovx}{2}} \tag{5.15}$$

It is rewritten as follows:

$$cot\frac{fovx}{2} = \frac{cot\frac{fovy}{2}}{aspect} \tag{5.16}$$

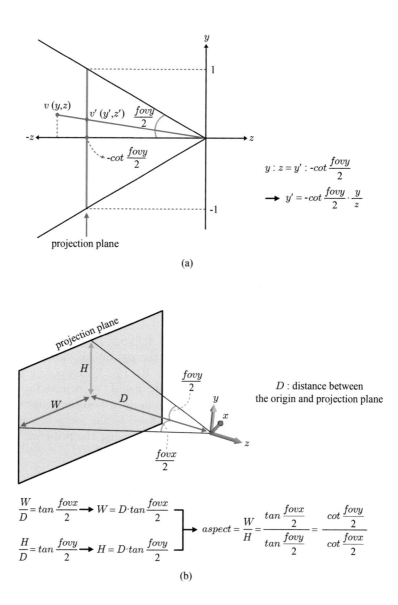

(a)

(b)

Fig. 5.14: Computing the projection matrix: (a) The normalized coordinate y' is computed. (b) The aspect ratio can be defined in terms of *fovx* and *fovy*.

By inserting Equation (5.16) into Equation (5.14), we can define x' in terms of $fovy$ and $aspect$:

$$x' = -\cot\frac{fovx}{2}\cdot\frac{x}{z} = -\frac{\cot\frac{fovy}{2}}{aspect}\cdot\frac{x}{z} \tag{5.17}$$

For simplicity, let us abbreviate $\cot\frac{fovy}{2}$ to D and $aspect$ to A. Then, using Equations (5.13) and (5.17), the projection-transformed point v' is represented in homogeneous coordinates as follows:

$$v' = (x', y', z', 1) = (-\frac{D}{A}\cdot\frac{x}{z}, -D\frac{y}{z}, z', 1) \tag{5.18}$$

where z' remains unknown. Let us multiply all coordinates of Equation (5.18) by $-z$:

$$(-\frac{D}{A}\cdot\frac{x}{z}, -D\frac{y}{z}, z', 1) \rightarrow (\frac{D}{A}x, Dy, -zz', -z) \tag{5.19}$$

The two homogeneous coordinates represent the same Cartesian coordinates. Let us abbreviate $-zz'$ to z''. In Equation (5.19), $\frac{D}{A}x$, Dy, and $-z$ are linear combinations of x, y, and z, and therefore we can define the following matrix multiplication form:

$$\begin{pmatrix} \frac{D}{A}x \\ Dy \\ z'' \\ -z \end{pmatrix} = \begin{pmatrix} \frac{D}{A} & 0 & 0 & 0 \\ 0 & D & 0 & 0 \\ m_1 & m_2 & m_3 & m_4 \\ 0 & 0 & -1 & 0 \end{pmatrix} \begin{pmatrix} x \\ y \\ z \\ 1 \end{pmatrix} \tag{5.20}$$

The 4×4 matrix is the projection matrix. We will complete the matrix by filling its third row.

Note that z' (the z-coordinate of the projection-transformed point v') is independent of the x- and y-coordinates of v. It can be intuitively understood if you consider a quad that is orthogonal to the z-axis of the camera space. When the quad is projection-transformed, it remains orthogonal to the z-axis of the clip space, i.e., every point on the transformed quad has the same z' regardless of its original position, (x, y), within the quad. As $z'' = -zz'$, z'' is also independent of x and y. Therefore, the third row of the projection matrix in Equation (5.20) is simplified to $(0\ 0\ m_3\ m_4)$, and the coordinates of v' are defined as follows:

$$\begin{pmatrix} \frac{D}{A} & 0 & 0 & 0 \\ 0 & D & 0 & 0 \\ 0 & 0 & m_3 & m_4 \\ 0 & 0 & -1 & 0 \end{pmatrix} \begin{pmatrix} x \\ y \\ z \\ 1 \end{pmatrix} = \begin{pmatrix} \frac{D}{A}x \\ Dy \\ m_3z + m_4 \\ -z \end{pmatrix} \rightarrow \begin{pmatrix} -\frac{D}{A}\cdot\frac{x}{z} \\ -D\frac{y}{z} \\ -m_3 - \frac{m_4}{z} \\ 1 \end{pmatrix} = \begin{pmatrix} x' \\ y' \\ z' \\ 1 \end{pmatrix} \tag{5.21}$$

We found that

$$z' = -m_3 - \frac{m_4}{z} \tag{5.22}$$

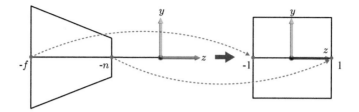

Fig. 5.15: The projection transform converts the z-range $[-f, -n]$ to $[-1, 1]$.

As shown in Fig. 5.15, the z-coordinates $-f$ and $-n$ are mapped to -1 and 1, respectively, by the projection transform. Putting them into Equation (5.22), we obtain the following:

$$-1 = -m_3 + \frac{m_4}{f}$$
$$1 = -m_3 + \frac{m_4}{n}$$

$$(5.23)$$

Solving Equation (5.23) for m_3 and m_4 gives

$$m_3 = \frac{f+n}{f-n}$$
$$m_4 = \frac{2nf}{f-n}$$

$$(5.24)$$

Now the third row of the 4×4 matrix presented in Equation (5.20) is determined. Restoring D and A back to $cot\frac{fovy}{2}$ and $aspect$, respectively, we obtain the matrix:

$$M = \begin{pmatrix} \frac{cot\frac{fovy}{2}}{aspect} & 0 & 0 & 0 \\ 0 & cot\frac{fovy}{2} & 0 & 0 \\ 0 & 0 & \frac{f+n}{f-n} & \frac{2nf}{f-n} \\ 0 & 0 & -1 & 0 \end{pmatrix}$$

$$(5.25)$$

The projection matrix is defined by negating the third row of M:

$$M_{proj} = \begin{pmatrix} \frac{cot\frac{fovy}{2}}{aspect} & 0 & 0 & 0 \\ 0 & cot\frac{fovy}{2} & 0 & 0 \\ 0 & 0 & -\frac{f+n}{f-n} & -\frac{2nf}{f-n} \\ 0 & 0 & -1 & 0 \end{pmatrix}$$

$$(5.26)$$

Exercises

1. Given two non-standard orthonormal bases in 2D space, $\{a, b\}$ and $\{c, d\}$, compute the 2×2 matrix that converts a vector defined in terms of $\{a, b\}$ into that of $\{c, d\}$.

2. Given two non-standard orthonormal bases in 3D space, $\{a, b, c\}$ and $\{d, e, f\}$, compute the 3×3 matrix that converts a vector defined in terms of $\{a, b, c\}$ into that of $\{d, e, f\}$.

3. Consider scaling along two orthonormal vectors, a and b, neither of which is identical to the standard basis vector, e_1 or e_2. The scaling factors along a and b are denoted by s_a and s_b, respectively. The scaling matrix is a combination of three 2×2 matrices. Write the three matrices.

4. Consider scaling along three orthonormal vectors, a, b, and c, any of which is not identical to the standard basis vector, e_1, e_2, or e_3. The scaling factors along a, b, and c are denoted by s_a, s_b, and s_c, respectively. It is also observed that $a \times b = c$ where $\times$ denotes the cross product. The scaling matrix is a combination of three 3×3 matrices. Write the three matrices.

5. The standard coordinate system is defined as $\{e_1, e_2, e_3, \mathbf{O}\}$, where $e_1 = (1, 0, 0)$, $e_2 = (0, 1, 0)$, $e_3 = (0, 0, 1)$, and $\mathbf{O} = (0, 0, 0)$. Consider another coordinate system named S. Its origin is at $(5, 0, 0)$ and basis is $\{(0, 1, 0), (-1, 0, 0), (0, 0, 1)\}$. Given a point defined in the standard coordinate system, compute the matrix that converts the point into S.

6. We are given the following view parameters: $\mathbf{EYE} = (0, 0, -\sqrt{3})$, $\mathbf{AT} = (0, 0, 0)$, and $\mathbf{UP} = (0, 1, 0)$.

   (a) Write the basis and origin of the camera space.

   (b) The view transform consists of a translation and a rotation. Write their matrices.

7. We are given the following view parameters: $\mathbf{EYE} = (0, 0, 3)$, $\mathbf{AT} = (0, 0, -1)$, and $\mathbf{UP} = (-1, 0, 0)$.

   (a) Write the basis and origin of the camera space.

   (b) The view transform consists of a translation and a rotation. Write their matrices.

8. We are given the following view parameters: $\mathbf{EYE} = (0, 0, 3)$, $\mathbf{AT} = (0, 0, -1)$, and $\mathbf{UP} = (-1, 0, 0)$. Compute the matrix that transforms the camera-space coordinates into the world space. Notice that this is not the view matrix but its inverse.

9. In the world space, two different sets of view parameters are given, {**EYE**, **AT**, **UP1**} and {**EYE**, **AT**, **UP2**}, where **EYE** = $(18, 8, 0)$, **AT** = $(10, 2, 0)$, **UP1** = $(0, 8, 0)$, and **UP2** = $(-13, 2, 0)$. Discuss whether the resulting camera spaces are identical to each other or not.

10. We have two camera spaces, S_1 and S_2, and want to transform a point defined in S_1 into that in S_2. A solution is to transform from S_1 to the world space and then transform from the world space to S_2.

    (a) S_1 is defined using the following parameters: **EYE** = $(0, 0, 3)$, **AT** = $(0, 0, -1)$, and **UP** = $(-1, 0, 0)$. Compute the matrix that transforms a point in S_1 to that in the world space.

    (b) S_2 is defined using the following parameters: **EYE** = $(0, 0, -3)$, **AT** = $(0, 0, 0)$, and **UP** = $(0, 1, 0)$. Compute the matrix that transforms a point in the world space to that in S_2.

11. Suppose that the world space is left-handed. The view parameters are defined as follows: **EYE** = $(0, 0, 3)$, **AT** = $(0, 0, -1)$, and **UP** = $(-1, 0, 0)$.

    (a) Assuming that the camera space is also left-handed, compute its basis, $\{u, v, n\}$.

    (b) Compute the view matrix that converts the world-space objects into the camera space.

12. Shown below is a cross section of the view frustum. It is orthogonal to the z-axis. We are given $\{fovy, fovx, n, f\}$, where $fovx$ stands for field of view along x-axis. D denotes the distance from the camera to the center of the cross section. Define *aspect* as a function of $fovx$ and $fovy$.

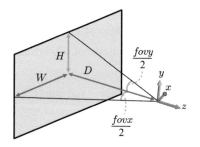

13. Section 5.4.3 derives the projection matrix based on the fact that the z-range of the cuboidal view volume is $[-1, 1]$. Assume that the z-range of the view volume is changed to $[-1, 0]$ whereas the x- and y-ranges remain $[-1, 1]$. Derive the new projection matrix.

14. In (a), a sphere travels about a fixed camera in a circle. Suppose that the rotating sphere is rendered through the GPU pipeline and the camera periodically captures five images while the sphere is inside of the view frustum. If the captured images were overlapped, we would expect the result in (b). The distance between the camera and sphere is unchanged and therefore the sphere's size would remain the same wherever it is located on the circle. However, the overlapped images produced by the GPU rendering pipeline appear as in (c). As soon as the sphere enters the view frustum (the leftmost sphere), it looks the largest. If the sphere is on the $-n$ axis of the camera space (the sphere in the middle), it looks the smallest. Right before the sphere leaves the view frustum (the rightmost sphere), it looks the largest. Explain why.

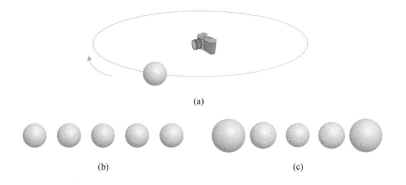

(a)

(b)   (c)

Chapter 6

OpenGL ES and Shader

The vertex array input to the rendering pipeline contains the per-vertex data such as positions and normals. The vertex shader runs once for each vertex. GPU has a massively parallel architecture with a lot of independently working fine-grained cores. The architecture is well suited for processing a large number of vertices simultaneously.

6.1 OpenGL ES and Shading Language

OpenGL ES is a subset of OpenGL. OpenGL ES 2.0 is derived from OpenGL 2.0. It requires two programs to be provided: the vertex and fragment shaders. OpenGL ES 3.0 is derived from OpenGL 3.3 and adds many enhanced features to OpenGL ES 2.0. It is backward compatible with OpenGL ES 2.0, i.e., applications built upon OpenGL ES 2.0 work with OpenGL ES 3.0. This book focuses on OpenGL ES 3.0.

OpenGL ES 3.1 supports the *compute shader* for general-purpose GPU computing and OpenGL ES 3.2 includes the *geometry shader* and *tessellation shader*. The compute and geometry shaders are not covered in this book, but Chapter 18 will present the tessellation shader.

The shaders are written in a GPU-specialized language, named OpenGL ES Shading Language. Henceforth, we call OpenGL ES simply 'GL' and OpenGL ES Shading Language 'GLSL.' (We do not use abbreviation for OpenGL.) This book presents the minimal syntax of GL and GLSL, which would be enough to understand the given sample programs. Readers are referred to a manual such as [4] for serious programming in GL and GLSL.

6.2 Vertex Shader

GLSL is a C-like language, and therefore programmers with experiences in C would not have difficulty in understanding the data types, operations,

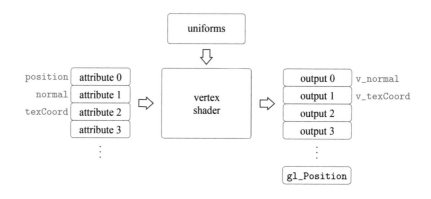

Fig. 6.1: Input and output of the vertex shader.

and control flow in GLSL. However, GLSL works on the GPU, the goal and architecture of which are different from those of the CPU. The differences shape GLSL in a distinct way. Vectors and matrices are good examples. In addition to the basic types such as `float`, GLSL supports vectors with up to four elements. For example, `vec4` is a floating-point 4D vector and `ivec3` is an integer 3D vector. GLSL also supports matrices with up to 4×4 elements. For example, `mat3` and `mat4` represent 3×3 and 4×4 square matrices, respectively, whereas `mat3x4` represents a 3×4 matrix. The matrix elements are all `float` values.

Two major inputs to the vertex shader are named the *attributes* and *uniforms*. See Fig. 6.1. The per-vertex data stored in the vertex array, such as position and normal, make up the attributes. Each vertex of a polygon mesh is processed by a distinct copy of the vertex shader, and the vertex attributes are unique to each execution of the vertex shader. In contrast, the uniforms remain constant for multiple executions of a shader. A good example is the world transform. The same world matrix is applied to all vertices of an object.

Sample code 6-1 shows a vertex shader. The first line declares that it is written in GLSL 3.0. Three 4×4 matrices for world, view, and projection transforms are preceded by the keyword `uniform`. The vertex shader takes three attributes, `position`, `normal`, and `texCoord`, which are preceded by the keyword `in`. (Here, `texCoord` is used to access a 2D texture. Chapter 8 will present how it works.) When we have m attributes, their locations are indexed by $0, 1, 2, \ldots, m - 1$. An attribute variable is bound to a location using a `layout` qualifier. In the sample code, `position` is bound to location 0, `normal` to 1, and `texCoord` to 2.

Sample code 6-1 Vertex shader

```
 1: #version 300 es
 2:
 3: uniform mat4 worldMat, viewMat, projMat;
 4:
 5: layout(location = 0) in vec3 position;
 6: layout(location = 1) in vec3 normal;
 7: layout(location = 2) in vec2 texCoord;
 8:
 9: out vec3 v_normal;
10: out vec2 v_texCoord;
11:
12: void main() {
13:     gl_Position = projMat * viewMat * worldMat * vec4(position, 1.0);
14:     v_normal = normalize(transpose(inverse(mat3(worldMat))) * normal);
15:     v_texCoord = texCoord;
16: }
```

Two output variables, v_normal and v_texCoord, are defined using the keyword out. They will be returned by the main function. The first statement of the main function transforms the object-space vertex into the clip space. Computing the clip-space vertex position is the required task for every vertex shader. The result is stored in the built-in variable gl_Position. All transforms are 4×4 matrices but position is a 3D vector. Therefore, position is converted into a 4D vector by invoking vec4 as a *constructor*.

In the second statement of the main function, mat3(worldMat) represents the upper-left 3×3 sub-matrix of the world matrix. As discussed in Section 5.1, it is L extracted from $[L|t]$. Its inverse transpose (L^{-T}) is applied to normal. The result is normalized and assigned to the output variable, v_normal. GLSL provides many library functions. Among them are normalize, transpose, and inverse. On the other hand, the vertex shader simply copies the input attribute, texCoord, to the output variable, v_texCoord. The output variables (gl_Position, v_normal, and v_texCoord) are sent to the rasterizer.

6.3 OpenGL ES for Shaders

The previous section presented a vertex shader. The fragment shader is more complicated in general but is written in a similar fashion. (Fragment shaders will be presented starting from Chapter 8.) While the vertex and fragment shaders are in charge of low-level details in rendering, the GL program manages the shaders and provides them with various data needed for rendering. The GL commands begin with the prefix gl, and GL data types begin with GL.

Sample code 6-2 GL program for shader object

```
1: GLuint shader = glCreateShader(GL_VERTEX_SHADER);
2: glShaderSource(shader, 1, &source, NULL);
3: glCompileShader(shader);
```

Sample code 6-2 is a fraction of a GL program for the vertex shader:

- A *shader object* is a container for storing the shader's source code and is created using glCreateShader. It takes either GL_VERTEX_SHADER or GL_FRAGMENT_SHADER and returns the shader object's ID (shader).
- Suppose that the shader's source code is loaded into the GL program and is pointed to by source, which is of type char*. The source code is then stored in the shader object (shader) by glShaderSource. (This book presents only the key arguments of GL commands, thus passing over the second and fourth arguments of glShaderSource, for which readers are referred to GL programming manuals.)
- The shader object is compiled using glCompileShader.

Sample code 6-3 GL program for program object

```
1: GLuint program = glCreateProgram();
2: glAttachShader(program, shader);
3: glLinkProgram(program);
4: glUseProgram(program);
```

The vertex and fragment shader objects should be 'attached' to a *program object*, which is then 'linked' to the final executable. See Sample code 6-3:

- The program object is created by glCreateProgram.
- The vertex shader object (shader) is attached to the program object by glAttachShader. The fragment shader object should also be attached to the program object in the same manner.
- The program object is linked by glLinkProgram.
- So as to use the program object for rendering, glUseProgram is invoked.

6.4   Attributes and Uniforms

An important task of the GL program is to make the attributes and uniforms available for the vertex shader. The GL program not only hands them over to the vertex shader but also informs the vertex shader of their structures.

6.4.1 Attributes and Buffer Objects

Sample code 6-4 GL program for vertex and index arrays

```
1: struct Vertex {
2:     glm::vec3 pos; // position
3:     glm::vec3 nor; // normal
4:     glm::vec2 tex; // texture coordinates
5: };
6: typedef GLushort Index;
7:
8: struct ObjData {
9:     std::vector<Vertex> vertices;
10:    std::vector<Index> indices;
11: };
12:
13: ObjData objData;
```

In Sample code 6-4, the per-vertex data (position, normal, and texture coordinates) are specified in `Vertex`. OpenGL Mathematics (`glm`) is a library that provides classes and functions with the same naming conventions and functionalities as GLSL. Suppose that the polygon mesh data stored in a file (such as a .obj file) are loaded into the vertex and index arrays of the GL program and they are pointed to by `vertices` and `indices`, respectively. The arrays are stored in `objData`.

The vertex and index arrays residing in the CPU memory will be transferred into the *buffer objects* in the GPU memory. For the indexed representation of a mesh, GL supports two types of buffer objects: (1) *Array buffer object* which is for the vertex array and is specified by `GL_ARRAY_BUFFER`. (2) *Element array buffer object* which is for the index array and is specified by `GL_ELEMENT_ARRAY_BUFFER`. Fig. 6.2 shows their relation.

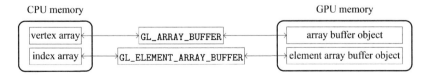

Fig. 6.2: Vertex and index arrays in the CPU memory versus buffer objects in the GPU memory.

Sample code 6-5 GL program for array buffer object

```
1: GLuint abo;
2: glGenBuffers(1, &abo);
3: glBindBuffer(GL_ARRAY_BUFFER, abo);
4: glBufferData(GL_ARRAY_BUFFER,
            (GLsizei) objData.vertices.size() * sizeof(Vertex),
            objData.vertices.data(), GL_STATIC_DRAW);
```

Sample code 6-6 GL program for element array buffer object

```
1: GLuint eabo;
2: glGenBuffers(1, &eabo);
3: glBindBuffer(GL_ELEMENT_ARRAY_BUFFER, eabo);
4: glBufferData(GL_ELEMENT_ARRAY_BUFFER,
            (GLsizei) objData.indices.size() * sizeof(Index),
            objData.indices.data(), GL_STATIC_DRAW);
```

Sample code 6-7 GL program for vertex attributes

```
1: glEnableVertexAttribArray(0); // position = attribute 0
2: glVertexAttribPointer(0, 3, GL_FLOAT, GL_FALSE,
        sizeof(Vertex), (const GLvoid*) offsetof(Vertex, pos));
3:
4: glEnableVertexAttribArray(1); // normal = attribute 1
5: glVertexAttribPointer(1, 3, GL_FLOAT, GL_FALSE,
        sizeof(Vertex), (const GLvoid*) offsetof(Vertex, nor));
6:
7: glEnableVertexAttribArray(2); // texture coordinates = attribute 2
8: glVertexAttribPointer(2, 2, GL_FLOAT, GL_FALSE,
        sizeof(Vertex), (const GLvoid*) offsetof(Vertex, tex));
```

Sample code 6-5 presents how to create and bind a buffer object for the vertex array:

- The buffer object is created by invoking glGenBuffers(GLsizei n, GLuint* buffers), which returns n buffer objects in buffers.
- The buffer object is bound to the vertex array by invoking glBindBuffer with GL_ARRAY_BUFFER.
- In order to fill the buffer object with objData.vertices defined in Sample code 6-4, glBufferData is invoked. The second argument specifies the size of the vertex array, and the third argument is the pointer to the array.

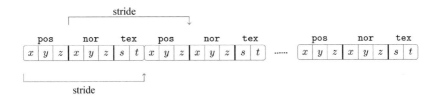

Fig. 6.3: Vertex attributes in the buffer object: The size of `Vertex` in Sample code 6-4 is 32 bytes and so is the stride.

The index array is processed in a similar fashion. In Sample code 6-6, `glBindBuffer` and `glBufferData` are called with `GL_ELEMENT_ARRAY_BUFFER`. The vertex and index arrays are now in the GPU memory. Fig. 6.3 shows how the vertex attributes are put together in the buffer object. The first occurrence of `pos` is located at the very beginning of the buffer object and the next is 32-bytes away from the first. The byte distance between the consecutive attributes of the same type is called the *stride*. By repeating the same stride, all position attributes can be retrieved. The same applies to `nor` and `tex`. The vertex shader should be informed of that structure.

Recall that, in the vertex shader presented in Sample code 6-1, the vertex position is bound to location 0. Sample code 6-7 first *enables* the attribute using `glEnableVertexAttribArray` in the first line and then details it using `glVertexAttribPointer` in the second line, where the first argument implies the position attribute, the second and third arguments specify that it is composed of three float elements, the fifth argument is the stride, and the last argument is the offset (in bytes) to the first occurrence of the position attribute in the buffer object. See the shaded box presented below for `glVertexAttribPointer`.

void	glVertexAttribPointer(GLuint index,
	GLint size,
	GLenum type,
	GLboolean normalized,
	GLsizei stride,
	const GLvoid* pointer);
index	index of the vertex attribute
size	number of components in the attribute
type	data type such as `GL_INT` and `GL_FLOAT`
normalized	If `GL_TRUE`, integer data are mapped to [-1,1] or [0,1].
stride	byte distance between the same attributes
pointer	offset (in bytes) to the first occurrence of the attribute

In the vertex shader presented in Sample code 6-1, the vertex normal and texture coordinates are bound to locations 1 and 2, respectively. They are enabled and detailed in the same manner as the vertex position. See lines 4 through 8 in Sample code 6-7. We use the same stride but the offset is distinct for each attribute.

6.4.2   Uniforms

Sample code 6-8 GL program for the world matrix

```
1: glm::mat4 worldMatrix; // repeatedly updated for a dynamic object
2:
3: GLint loc = glGetUniformLocation(program, "worldMat");
4: glUniformMatrix4fv(loc, 1, GL_FALSE, glm::value_ptr(worldMatrix));
```

The vertex shader in Sample code 6-1 takes three uniforms, `worldMat`, `viewMat`, and `projMat`. These are provided by the GL program. Sample code 6-8 shows the case of `worldMat`. Suppose that the GL program computes the world matrix and names it `worldMatrix`. In order to assign `worldMatrix` to the vertex shader's uniform, `worldMat`, the GL program has to find its *location* in the program object, which was determined during the link phase. For this, `glGetUniformLocation` is invoked with **program** (the program object ID) and `worldMat`.

A list of functions, which we collectively name `glUniform*`, is available for loading uniforms with specific data. In order to load a 4×4 matrix, we use `glUniformMatrix4fv`. In Sample code 6-8, its first argument is the location index returned by `glGetUniformLocation`. If a scene object moves, the GL program should update `worldMatrix` and reassigns it to `worldMat` using `glUniformMatrix4fv`.

void	glUniformMatrix4fv(GLint location,
	GLsizei count,
	GLboolean transpose,
	const GLfloat* value);
location	uniform location
count	the number of matrices to be modified
transpose	must be GL_FALSE
value	pointer to an array of 16 GLfloat values

6.5 Drawcalls

Suppose that we have passed the attributes and uniforms to the vertex shader using the GL commands presented so far. Then, we can draw a polygon mesh by making a *drawcall*. Consider the polygon mesh shown in Fig. 3.9. It has 48 triangles and its index array has 144 (48 times 3) elements. We invoke glDrawElements(GL_TRIANGLES, 144, GL_UNSIGNED_SHORT, 0). If the polygon mesh were represented in the *non-indexed* fashion, we would invoke glDrawArrays(GL_TRIANGLES, 0, 144).

void	glDrawElements(GLenum mode,
	GLsizei count,
	GLenum type,
	const GLvoid* indices);
mode	GL_TRIANGLES for a polygon mesh
count	number of indices to draw
type	index type
indices	byte offset into the buffer bound to
	GL_ELEMENT_ARRAY_BUFFER

void	glDrawArrays(GLenum mode,
	GLint first,
	GLsizei count);
mode	GL_TRIANGLES for a polygon mesh
first	start index in the vertex array
count	the number of vertices to draw

Exercises

1. Given an OpenGL ES program and its vertex shader shown below, fill in the boxes. Assume that `worldMat` includes a non-uniform scaling. The second argument of `glVertexAttribPointer` specifies the number of components in the attribute and the fifth argument specifies the stride.

```
 1: #version 300 es
 2:
 3: uniform mat4 worldMat, viewMat, projMat;
 4:
 5: layout(location = 2) in vec3 position;
 6: layout(location = 3) in vec3 normal;
 7: layout(location = 7) in vec2 texCoord;
 8:
 9: out vec3 v_normal;
10: out vec2 v_texCoord;
11:
12: void main() {
13:       gl_Position = [                              ];
14:       v_normal = [                                 ];
15:       v_texCoord = texCoord;
16: }
```

```
 1: struct Vertex
 2: {
 3:     glm::vec3 pos; // position
 4:     glm::vec3 nor; // normal
 5:     glm::vec2 tex; // texture coordinates
 6: };
 7: typedef GLushort Index;
 8:
 9: glEnableVertexAttribArray(□); // position
10: glVertexAttribPointer(□, □, GL_FLOAT, GL_FALSE,
                  [          ], (const GLvoid*) offsetof(Vertex, pos));
11:
12: glEnableVertexAttribArray(□); // normal
13: glVertexAttribPointer(□, □, GL_FLOAT, GL_FALSE,
                  [          ], (const GLvoid*) offsetof(Vertex, nor));
14:
15: glEnableVertexAttribArray(□); // texture coordinates
16: glVertexAttribPointer(□, □, GL_FLOAT, GL_FALSE,
                  [          ], (const GLvoid*) offsetof(Vertex, tex));
```

2. The triangle mesh shown below is composed of eight triangles.

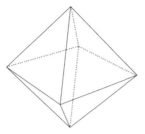

(a) If we have the indexed representation of the mesh, we will invoke
glDrawElements(mode, count, type, indices). What will mode
be? What will count be?

(b) If we have the non-indexed representation of the mesh, we will
invoke glDrawArrays(mode, first, count). What will mode be?
What will count be?

Chapter 7

Rasterizer

In the GPU rendering pipeline, the geometric entity to be drawn is referred to as a *primitive*. It may be a point or a line as well as a triangle. They are all defined in terms of vertices. The vertices processed by the vertex shader are assembled into primitives. Each primitive is further processed to determine its 2D form appearing on the screen and is then rasterized into *fragments*. A fragment is defined at each pixel location covered by the primitive. The per-vertex data such as the vertex normals are interpolated across the primitive and assigned to each fragment.

This process of *primitive assembly and rasterization* is done by a hard-wired stage of the rendering pipeline, which we simply call the rasterizer. Focusing on triangle primitives, this chapter presents the rasterizer's substages for clipping, perspective division, back-face culling, viewport transform, and scan conversion.

7.1 Clipping

Clipping refers to the process of cutting the polygons with the cubic view volume defined in the clip space. To create a better sense of understanding, however, this section presents the idea of clipping triangles "with the view frustum in the camera space." Consider the spatial relationships between the triangles and the view frustum in Fig. 7.1: (1) Triangle t_1 is completely outside of the view frustum and is discarded. (2) Triangle t_2 is completely inside and is passed *as is* to the next step. (3) Triangle t_3 intersects the view frustum and is thus clipped. Only the part of the triangle located inside of the view frustum proceeds to the next step in the rendering pipeline. As a result of clipping, vertices are added to and deleted from the triangle.

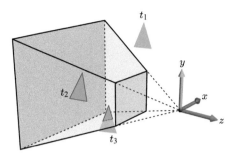

Fig. 7.1: Clipping triangles with the view frustum.

7.2   Perspective Division

Suppose that the projection matrix M_{proj} presented in Equation (5.12) is applied to a camera-space vertex with coordinates $(x, y, z, 1)$:

$$
\begin{pmatrix}
m_{11} & 0 & 0 & 0 \\
0 & m_{22} & 0 & 0 \\
0 & 0 & m_{33} & m_{34} \\
0 & 0 & -1 & 0
\end{pmatrix}
\begin{pmatrix}
x \\ y \\ z \\ 1
\end{pmatrix}
=
\begin{pmatrix}
m_{11}x \\ m_{22}y \\ m_{33}z + m_{34} \\ -z
\end{pmatrix}
\rightarrow
\begin{pmatrix}
-m_{11}\frac{x}{z} \\ -m_{22}\frac{y}{z} \\ -m_{33} - m_{34}\frac{1}{z} \\ 1
\end{pmatrix}
$$

$$(7.1)$$

where m_{11} stands for $\frac{cot\frac{fovy}{2}}{aspect}$ and similarly the other symbols represent the non-zero elements of M_{proj}. Unlike affine matrices, the last row of M_{proj} is not $(0\,0\,0\,1)$ but $(0\,0\,-1\,0)$. Consequently, the w-coordinate of the projection-transformed vertex is $-z$, which is not necessarily 1. Converting the homogeneous coordinates to the Cartesian coordinates requires division by $-z$, as denoted by $\rightarrow$ in Equation (7.1).

Fig. 7.2 shows an example of the projection transform. Compare the results of applying M_{proj} to the end points of two line segments, l_1 and l_2. Note that $-z$ is a positive value representing the *distance* from the xy-plane of the camera space. It is two for P_1 and Q_1 but is one for P_2 and Q_2. Division by $-z$ makes distant objects smaller. In Fig. 7.2, l_1 and l_2 are of the same length in the camera space, but l_1' becomes shorter than l_2' due to the division. This is the effect of perspective projection or foreshortening, and the division by $-z$ is called the *perspective division*.

Due to the perspective division, a vertex is defined in the so-called *normalized device coordinates* (NDC). The coordinates are named normalized because the x-, y-, and z-components are all in the range of $[-1,1]$.

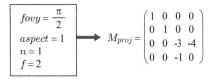

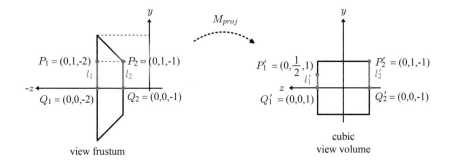

Fig. 7.2: The projection transform returns the vertices in the homogeneous clip space. Dividing each vertex by its w-coordinate converts the homogeneous coordinates into the Cartesian coordinates. This causes the effect of perspective projection and therefore is called the perspective division.

7.3 Back-face Culling

In computer graphics, culling refers to the process of eliminating parts of a scene that are invisible to the camera. The polygons facing away from the viewpoint of the camera are called the *back faces*. They are culled. The polygons facing the camera are called the *front faces*. They are preserved.

7.3.1 Concept

In the camera space, a triangle is taken as a back face if the camera (**EYE**) is on the opposite side of the triangle's normal. In Fig. 7.3-(a), t_1 is a back face whereas t_2 is a front face. Such a distinction can be made by taking the dot product of the triangle normal n and the vector c connecting the triangle and the camera. Recall that $n \cdot c = \|n\|\|c\|cos\theta$ where θ is the angle between n and c. If n and c form an acute angle, $n \cdot c$ is positive and the triangle is a front face. If n and c form an obtuse angle, $n \cdot c$ is negative and the triangle is a back face. For t_3 in Fig. 7.3-(a), $n \cdot c = 0$, which implies that n and c are perpendicular and thus t_3 is an edge-on face.

7.3.2 Implementation

Note that c_i in Fig. 7.3-(a) is equivalent to a *projection line* presented in Section 5.4.2. The projection transform makes all projection lines parallel to the z-axis. Fig. 7.3-(b) shows the universal projection line in a cross section. Given the projection-transformed sphere in Fig. 7.3-(c), let us conceptually project the triangles along the universal projection line onto the xy-plane, i.e., consider only the x- and y-coordinates of each vertex.

Fig. 7.3-(d) illustrates t_1's projection onto the xy-plane. Note that its vertices appear to be ordered clockwise (CW) even though they are counterclockwise (CCW) in the 3D space. It is not surprising because the CCW order in the 3D space is observed when we see t_1 from outside of the sphere, but t_1 in Fig. 7.3-(d) looks as if it were captured from inside of the sphere. It is said that t_1 in Fig. 7.3-(d) has the CW *winding order* of vertices. On the other hand, t_2 in Fig. 7.3-(e) has the CCW winding order. These two examples show that a projected triangle with the CW winding order is a back face and that with the CCW winding order is a front face.

Given a projected triangle $\langle v_1, v_2, v_3 \rangle$, where v_i has the coordinates (x_i, y_i), it is straightforward to determine whether the triangle has the CW or CCW winding order. Connect v_1 and v_2 to define a vector $(x_2 - x_1, y_2 - y_1)$, and connect v_1 and v_3 to define another vector $(x_3 - x_1, y_3 - y_1)$. Then, compute the following determinant:

$$\begin{vmatrix} (x_2 - x_1) & (y_2 - y_1) \\ (x_3 - x_1) & (y_3 - y_1) \end{vmatrix} = (x_2 - x_1)(y_3 - y_1) - (y_2 - y_1)(x_3 - x_1) \qquad (7.2)$$

If the determinant is negative, as in Fig. 7.3-(d), the winding order is CW and the triangle is a back face. If positive, as in Fig. 7.3-(e), the winding order is CCW and the triangle is a front face. If zero, it is an edge-on face.

The back faces are not always culled. Consider rendering a hollow translucent sphere. For the back faces to show through the front faces, no face should be culled. On the other hand, consider culling only the front faces of a sphere. Then the cross-section view of the sphere will be obtained.

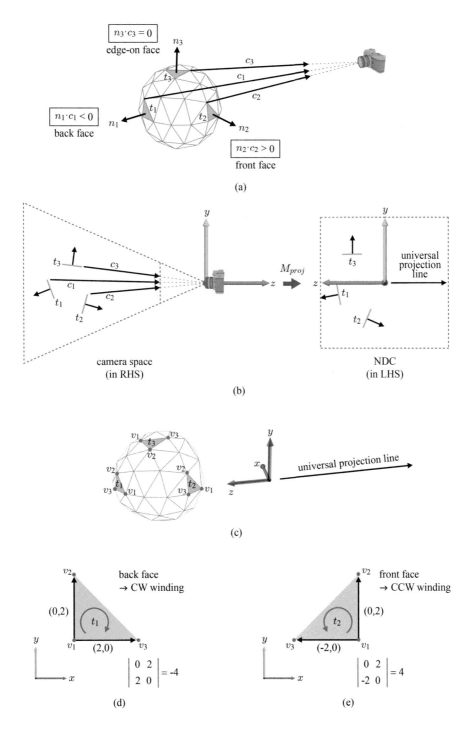

Fig. 7.3: Back-face culling: concept and implementation.

The back-face culling algorithm is implemented in hardware, as is the case for every substage of the rasterizer. Unlike clipping and perspective division, however, it allows us to control the way it works. In the rendering pipeline, various GL capabilities are enabled by `glEnable` and disabled by `glDisable`. In order to enable face culling, `glEnable(GL_CULL_FACE)` is invoked. Then, `glCullFace` specifies whether front or back faces are culled. Its default argument is `GL_BACK`, i.e., back faces are culled by default. Finally, `glFrontFace` specifies the winding order of front faces. The default argument of `glFrontFace` is `GL_CCW`. It is compatible with Fig. 7.3-(e).

```
void glCullFace(GLenum mode);
mode GL_FRONT, GL_BACK, or GL_FRONT_AND_BACK
```

```
void glFrontFace(GLenum mode);
mode GL_CW or GL_CCW
```

The back faces of an opaque object are culled because they are invisible and cannot contribute to the final image. However, a front face may not be visible if it is occluded from the camera position by other front faces. Such an invisible face is handled by the well-known per-fragment visibility algorithm, *z-buffering*, at the output merger stage of the rendering pipeline. It will be presented in Section 10.1.

7.4 Viewport Transform

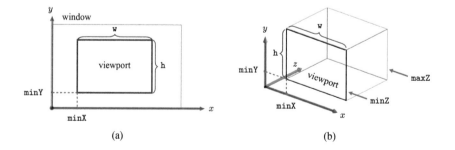

(a)   (b)

Fig. 7.4: Screen space and viewport: (a) In the screen space, a viewport is defined by its lower-left corner point and its dimensions, i.e., width and height. (b) 3D viewport = 2D viewport + depth range.

A window is associated with its own coordinate system, which is called the *window space* or *screen space*. Its origin is located at the lower-left corner of the window. See Fig. 7.4-(a). A *viewport* is a rectangle into which the scene is projected. It does not necessarily take up the entire window but can be a sub-area of the window. The viewport is defined by `glViewport`. Its first two arguments, `minX` and `minY`, represent the screen-space coordinates of the lower-left corner of the viewport whereas the last two arguments, `w` (for width) and `h` (for height), specify the viewport's size. The aspect ratio of the viewport is `w/h`. In general, the view-frustum parameter *aspect* (presented in Section 5.4.1) is made to be identical to this.

void	glViewport(GLint minX,
	GLint minY,
	GLsizei w,
	GLsizei h);
minX, minY	lower-left corner point
w, h	width and height

The screen space is 3D. As shown in Fig. 7.4-(b), its z-axis goes into the window. (It will be clarified in Chapter 10 why we need the 3D screen space.) The viewport is also 3D. It is defined by augmenting the 2D viewport with a depth range, which is provided through `glDepthRangef(minZ, maxZ)`. The default depth range is $[0, 1]$.

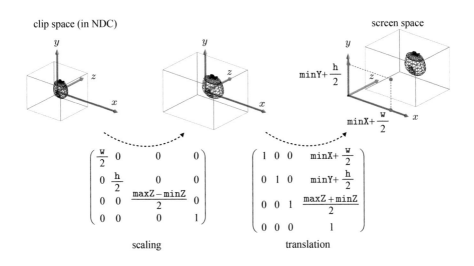

Fig. 7.5: The viewport transform is a combination of a scaling and a translation. Note that both the clip space and the screen space are left-handed.

Consider the transform that converts the 2×2×2-sized cubic view volume (in NDC) into the 3D viewport. As shown in Fig. 7.5, it is defined as a scaling followed by a translation. The two matrices are combined into a single matrix:

$$\begin{pmatrix} \frac{w}{2} & 0 & 0 & minX + \frac{w}{2} \\ 0 & \frac{h}{2} & 0 & minY + \frac{h}{2} \\ 0 & 0 & \frac{maxZ - minZ}{2} & \frac{maxZ + minZ}{2} \\ 0 & 0 & 0 & 1 \end{pmatrix} \tag{7.3}$$

We call this *viewport transform*. It transforms all of the objects defined in NDC into the 3D viewport.

In many applications, the viewport takes up the entire window, and therefore both minX and minY are zero. Furthermore, if minZ and maxZ take the default values, i.e., 0.0 and 1.0, respectively, the above matrix is simplified as follows:

$$\begin{pmatrix} \frac{w}{2} & 0 & 0 & \frac{w}{2} \\ 0 & \frac{h}{2} & 0 & \frac{h}{2} \\ 0 & 0 & \frac{1}{2} & \frac{1}{2} \\ 0 & 0 & 0 & 1 \end{pmatrix} \tag{7.4}$$

7.5　Scan Conversion

The viewport transform has converted every primitive into the screen-space viewport. The last substage in the rasterizer breaks up each primitive into a set of fragments. Specifically, it identifies the pixels covered by the primitive and interpolates the vertex attributes for each pixel location. This process is called the *scan conversion*.

Consider the screen-space triangle shown in Fig. 7.6-(a). For the scan conversion, we use only the (x, y) coordinates of the triangle's vertices, i.e., the scan conversion is made in the 2D screen space shown in Fig. 7.6-(b). As shown on the right of Fig. 7.6-(c), the triangle encompasses 18 pixels. For each pixel's location, the vertex attributes will be interpolated.

The scan conversion is considered as the key feature of real-time graphics and needs to be clearly understood for writing the subsequent stage, the fragment shader. Graphics hardware vendors have employed various optimized algorithms for scan conversion. This section presents the skeleton of an implementation. Even though the vertex attributes rarely include color, we will assume that vertex colors exist, just for the sake of presentation, and show how the red (R) components are interpolated.

First of all, the vertex attributes are linearly interpolated "along the edges" of a triangle. Fig. 7.6-(c) shows how R_1 and R_3 are interpolated along the left edge. For interpolation, a set of *slopes* is computed per edge. One slope

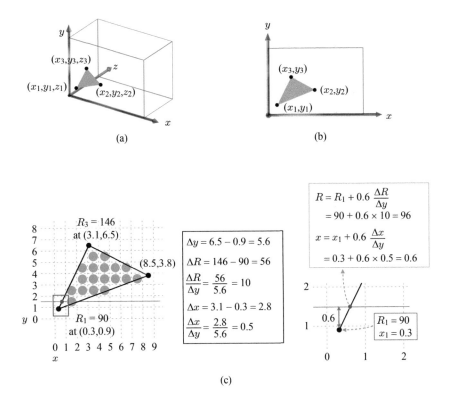

Fig. 7.6: Scan conversion through bilinear interpolation: (a) A triangle in the 3D viewport. (b) Ignoring the z-coordinate of every vertex, the triangle is defined in the 2D screen space. (c) For the left edge, the attribute slopes are computed, and the attributes are initialized at the first scan line with y-coordinate 1.5.

is $\Delta R/\Delta y$, which describes the ratio of a change in R to the vertical distance. Another slope is $\Delta x/\Delta y$. The box in the middle of Fig. 7.6-(c) shows $\Delta R/\Delta y$ and $\Delta x/\Delta y$ for the left edge.

In the screen, a horizontal line of pixels is named a *scan line*. Observe that the first scan line intersecting the left edge has the y-coordinate 1.5. The box on the right of Fig. 7.6-(c) shows how the R value and x-coordinate are initialized at the intersection. After the initialization step, the R values and x-coordinates of the next scan lines are obtained by repeatedly adding the slopes, $\Delta R/\Delta y$ and $\Delta x/\Delta y$, respectively. Fig. 7.6-(d) shows the interpolated results along the left edge.

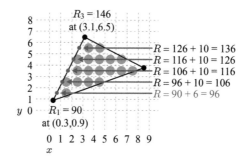

(d)

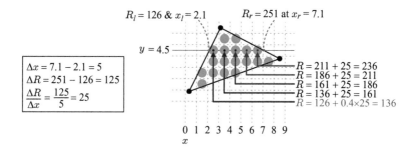

(e)

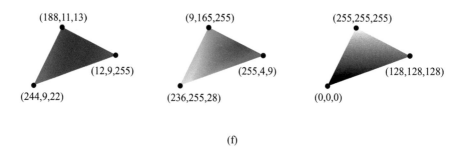

(f)

Fig. 7.6: Scan conversion through bilinear interpolation (*continued*): (d) Interpolation of the attributes along the edge. (e) Interpolation of the attributes along the scan line. (f) Examples of color-interpolated triangles.

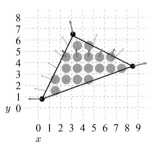

Fig. 7.7: The normals interpolated along the two upper edges and those along the scan line at y-coordinate 4.5 are visualized. The x-, y-, and z-components of the normals are interpolated independently.

The process is repeated for the other two edges of the triangle. Then, for each scan line, we obtain the left- and right-bound red values (R_l and R_r) and x-coordinates (x_l and x_r). Next, we interpolate the boundary attributes "along the scan lines." It is quite similar to interpolation along the edges. Fig. 7.6-(e) shows the scan line at y-coordinate 4.5. $\Delta R/\Delta x$ is computed, where $\Delta R = R_r - R_l$ and $\Delta x = x_r - x_l$. For the first pixel located at $(2.5, 4.5)$, the R value is initialized. The R values of the next pixels are obtained by repeatedly adding $\Delta R/\Delta x$ from left to right.

Observe that *linear interpolation* was performed in two phases: along the edges first and then along the scan lines. It is called the *bilinear interpolation*. If the G and B color components are interpolated using the same method, the per-fragment colors are obtained. Fig. 7.6-(f) shows examples of color-interpolated triangles.

Sample code 6-1 in Section 6.2 outputs v_normal and v_texCoord. These will be processed by the scan conversion algorithm. Fig. 7.7 visualizes how the per-vertex normals are interpolated to define the per-fragment ones. The next stage in the GPU pipeline is the fragment shader. It processes one fragment at a time using the per-fragment normal and texture coordinates.

[Note: Top-left rule]

When a pixel is on the edge shared by two triangles, we have to decide to which triangle it belongs. Otherwise, it would be processed twice by the scan conversion algorithm.

Intuitively speaking, a triangle may have right, left, top or bottom edges. For example, t_1 in Fig. 7.8 has two left edges and one right edge. In contrast, t_2 has a bottom edge, and t_3 has a top edge. GL adopts the *top-left rule*, which declares that a pixel belongs to a triangle if it lies on the top or left edge of the triangle. In Fig. 7.8, p_1 belongs to t_1, not t_2, because it lies on the left edge of t_1. The top-left rule also judges that p_2 belongs to t_3, not t_2, because it lies on the top edge of t_3.

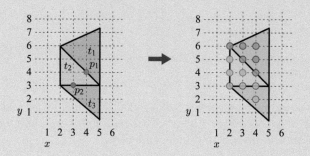

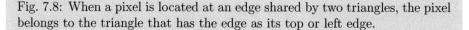

Fig. 7.8: When a pixel is located at an edge shared by two triangles, the pixel belongs to the triangle that has the edge as its top or left edge.

[Note: Perspective correction]

The projection transform maps lines to lines, i.e., collinear points remain collinear after the transform. However, it does not preserve the distance ratio of collinear points. (In contrast, affine transforms do.) Consider the view frustum and the projection matrix M_{proj} in Fig. 7.9. The collinear points, v_1, v_2, and v_3, are projection-transformed to v_1', v_2', and v_3', respectively. Observe that the projected points are also collinear. However, the distance ratio is changed, i.e., $\|v_1 - v_2\| : \|v_2 - v_3\| = 1 : 1$ in the camera space, but $\|v_1' - v_2'\| : \|v_2' - v_3'\| = 3 : 4$ in the clip space. The clip-space ratio will be maintained in the screen space because the viewport transform is affine.

Suppose that v_1 and v_3 are the end vertices of a line segment and its color linearly changes from white (v_1) to black (v_3). Let us denote white by 1 and black by 0. Because, v_2 is the midpoint of the line segment, v_2's color is 0.5. When the colors of v_1' and v_3' are interpolated in the screen space, v_2' is assigned a gray color $\frac{4}{7}$. It is not 0.5 and is incorrect. We have the incorrect result because the bilinear interpolation process presented in this section uses the 'distorted' screen-space distance ratio instead of the 'undistorted' camera-space ratio, i.e., the ratio before the projection transform.

Using such a 'distorted' distance ratio often produces an annoying artifact especially for texturing. In order to avoid this, the GPU adds a procedure to the bilinear interpolation, which is called the *perspective correction*. Many classic computer graphics textbooks present the correction method.

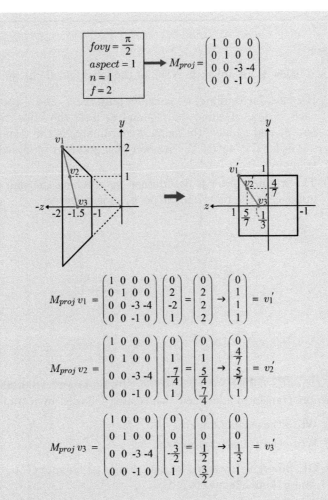

Fig. 7.9: The projection transform distorts the distance ratio of the camera space, and therefore bilinear interpolation using the distorted distance ratio produces incorrect results.

Exercises

1. Shown below is an object in NDC of the left-handed clip space.

   (a) For back-face culling, we consider only the x- and y-coordinates of each vertex. Assume that v_1 and v_2 have the same x-coordinate and v_1 and v_3 have the same y-coordinate. Is the triangle's winding order CW or CCW? Answer this question by drawing the 2D triangle.

   (b) The winding order is determined by checking the sign of a determinant. Is the determinant positive or negative?

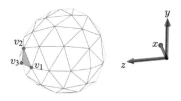

2. A viewport's corners are located at $(10, 20, 1)$ and $(100, 200, 2)$. The viewport transform is defined as a scaling followed by a translation.

   (a) Write the scaling matrix.

   (b) Write the translation matrix.

3. Our GL program invokes two functions: `glViewport(10, 20, 200, 100)` and `glDepthRangef(0, 1)`.

   (a) Write the scaling matrix for the viewport transform.

   (b) Write the translation matrix for the viewport transform.

4. Shown below is a 3D viewport. Compute the viewport transform matrix.

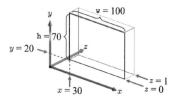

5. Shown below is a screen-space triangle. Each vertex is associated with $\{(R, G, B), z\}$. Compute R and z for the fragment at $(5.5, 3.5)$. Instead of taking the mechanical steps based on *slopes*, use the *linear interpolation* for the intersection of the left edge of the triangle with the scan line at y-coordinate 3.5. Along the scan line, also use the linear interpolation.

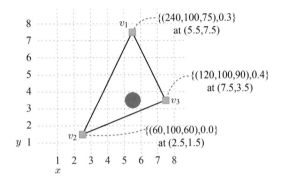

6. Shown below is a screen-space triangle. The vertex attributes are the RGB color, 2D texture coordinates, and z. Interpolate the attributes for the fragment at $(4.5, 3.5)$. Instead of taking the mechanical steps based on *slopes*, use the *linear interpolation* for the intersection of the right edge of the triangle with the scan line at y-coordinate 3.5. Along the scan line, also use the linear interpolation.

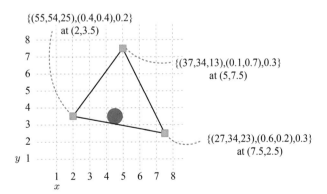

7. Shown below is the projection matrix. Suppose that $n = 1$, $f = 2$, $fovy = \frac{\pi}{2}$, and the view frustum's width equals its height. Apply the projection transform to the camera-space points, $(0, 2, -2)$ and $(0, 0, -1)$. Then, apply the projection transform to $(0, 1, -1.5)$, which is the midpoint between $(0, 2, -2)$ and $(0, 0, -1)$. Is the result still the midpoint in NDC? Discuss why or why not.

$$\begin{pmatrix} \frac{\cot \frac{fovy}{2}}{aspect} & 0 & 0 & 0 \\ 0 & \cot \frac{fovy}{2} & 0 & 0 \\ 0 & 0 & -\frac{f+n}{f-n} & -\frac{2nf}{f-n} \\ 0 & 0 & -1 & 0 \end{pmatrix}$$

8. Shown below is an example of the projection matrix.

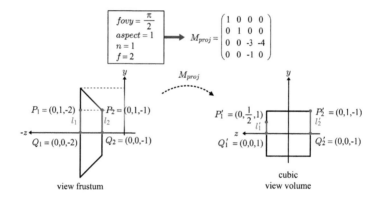

(a) Suppose that a camera-space point at $(0, 1, -1.5)$ is projection-transformed. Compute the transformed point.

(b) With the result of (a), you may be able to guess the following figure. Discuss why this *non-linearity* happens.

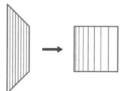

Chapter 8

Image Texturing

The per-fragment attributes produced by the rasterizer usually include a normal vector and texture coordinates. Using the attributes, the fragment shader determines the color of each fragment. The fragment shader has the strongest impact on the quality of the final image and has employed a variety of algorithms. The algorithms largely focus on *lighting* and *texturing*. This chapter presents the basics of texturing and the next chapter presents lighting.

8.1 Texture Coordinates

(a)   (b)

Fig. 8.1: Image texturing: (a) An image texture is an array of color texels. (b) The image is pasted on a curved surface.

For now, consider a texture as an image. Non-image textures will be presented later in this book. A texture is typically represented as a 2D array of *texels* (texture elements). In image textures, a texel is nothing but a pixel (picture element) but is called so in order to distinguish it from the screen-space pixel. See Fig. 8.1-(a). A texel's location can be described by the coordinates of its center. For example, the lower-left corner texel in Fig. 8.1-(a) is located at $(0.5, 0.5)$, and its neighbor on the right is at $(1.5, 0.5)$.

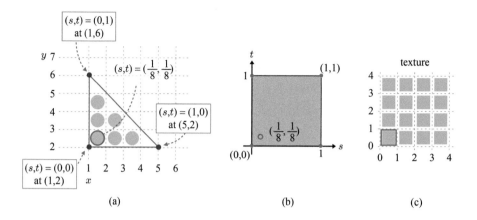

(a)   (b)   (c)

Fig. 8.2: Scan conversion and texture lookup: (a) The scan conversion algorithm computes per-fragment texture coordinates. (b) Normalized parameter space. (c) The texture coordinates are projected into the texture space.

Image texturing is often described as pasting an image on an object's surface. The texture in Fig. 8.1-(a) is pasted on the cylindrical surface in Fig. 8.1-(b). For texturing, we assign the *texture coordinates* to each vertex of the polygon mesh "at the modeling step." This will be presented in Section 8.2.

The texture coordinates are represented in (s,t) and it is customary to normalize both s and t to the range of $[0,1]$. Fig. 8.2-(a) shows a screen-space triangle. The texture coordinates assigned to the vertices are $(0,0)$, $(1,0)$ and $(0,1)$. The rasterizer interpolates them for the fragments. For example, the texture coordinates of the lower-left corner fragment are $(1/8, 1/8)$. Fig. 8.2-(b) illustrates the coordinates in the normalized space.

The normalized texture coordinates (s,t) are *projected* into the texture space. GL adopts a simple projection scheme:

$$s' = s \times r_x$$
$$t' = t \times r_y \tag{8.1}$$

where $r_x \times r_y$ denotes the texture's resolution. Consider a toy texture composed of 4×4 texels shown in Fig. 8.2-(c). As $r_x = r_y = 4$, the texture coordinates $(1/8, 1/8)$ are projected to $(0.5, 0.5)$. Then, the lower-left corner texel at $(0.5, 0.5)$ is fetched and is used to determine the fragment color.

The normalized texture coordinates do not depend on a specific texture resolution and can be freely plugged into various textures. In the example of Fig. 8.3, the texture coordinates $(0.5, 0.5)$ represent the texture's center and are projected to the center texel located at $(2.5, 2.5)$ in texture 1, but to $(3.5, 3.5)$ in texture 2. Fig. 8.4 shows that two images with different resolutions can be pasted on a cylindrical surface without altering the texture coordinates.

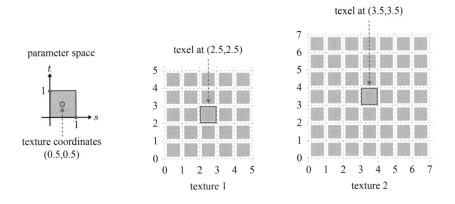

Fig. 8.3: Normalized texture coordinates.

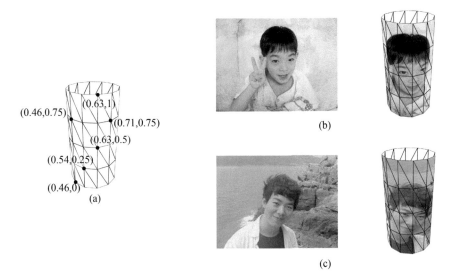

Fig. 8.4: Texture coordinates and image texturing: (a) Each vertex is associated with its own texture coordinates. To avoid clutter, only a few vertices are illustrated with their texture coordinates. (b) The surface is textured with an image. The polygon mesh is overlaid just for visualization purposes. (c) Using the same texture coordinates, the surface is textured with another image of a different resolution.

Unlike the contrived examples in Fig. 8.2 and Fig. 8.3, (s', t') computed in Equation (8.1) may not fall onto the center of a texel. Therefore, the texels *around* (s', t') need to be collected and combined. This issue will be discussed in Section 8.5.

The texture's dimension is not limited to 2D. Consider medical imaging data acquired by a CT (computed tomography) scan or an MRI (magnetic resonance imaging). When 2D slice images are regularly stacked, e.g., one slice per millimeter, the stack can be taken as a 3D texture. It is often called a volume texture and is widely used for medical image visualization. GL supports such 3D textures. Nonetheless, most of the textures in computer graphics are 2D, and this chapter focuses on 2D image texturing.

8.2   Surface Parameterization

The process of assigning texture coordinates, i.e., s and t parameters, to the vertices of a polygon mesh is called *surface parameterization* or simply *parameterization*. Parameterization requires *unfolding* a 3D surface onto a 2D planar domain. See Fig. 8.5-(a). Parameterizing a cylindrical surface is conceptually equivalent to cutting the surface along a vertical seam and then flattening it. Given such an unfolded 2D mesh, (s, t) coordinates can be assigned to each vertex by mapping the rectangular area to the unit square domain of s and t. The texture coordinates are recorded in the vertex array of the polygon mesh such that they are input to the vertex shader.

Unless a surface is *developable* like a cylinder or a cone, parameterization is not straightforward and incurs *distortion*, e.g., the relative triangle areas of the 3D polygon mesh are not preserved in the 2D domain. This problem has been well studied in computer graphics, and many parameterization techniques have been proposed aiming at minimizing the distortion. Graphics packages such as 3ds Max also provide parameterization tools, which are often based on a combination of automatic and manual procedures.

A complex polygon mesh is usually subdivided into a number of *patches* such that the patches are unfolded individually. Fig. 8.5-(b) shows the unfolded patch for a character's face. Once unfolded, it is straightforward to assign the texture coordinates to the vertices of the patch.

The artist draws an image on the unfolded patch using an image editing tool such as Adobe Photoshop. Fig. 8.6-(a) shows the image texture to be pasted on the character's face. An image texture for a patch is often called a *chart*. Multiple charts are usually packed and arranged in a larger texture, which is called an *atlas*. Fig. 8.6-(b) shows the atlas for the whole body of the baseball player.

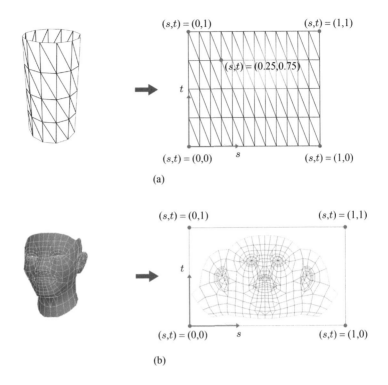

(a)

(b)

Fig. 8.5: Surface parameterization: (a) It is easy to parameterize developable surfaces. To avoid clutter, only a few vertices are illustrated with their texture coordinates. (b) Most 3D surfaces are distorted during parameterization, but well-designed parameterization algorithms keep the distortion to a minimum.

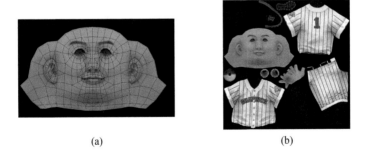

(a)   (b)

Fig. 8.6: Chart and atlas: (a) The chart for the face patch. The unfolded patch is overlaid on the chart just for visualization purposes. (b) An atlas is a collection of charts.

8.3   Texture Definition in GL

Sample code 8-1 GL program for texture object

```
1: struct Texel {
2:     GLubyte r; // red
3:     GLubyte g; // green
4:     GLubyte b; // blue
5:     GLubyte a; // alpha
6: };
7:
8: struct TexData {
9:     std::vector<Texel> texels;
10:    GLsizei width;
11:    GLsizei height;
12: };
13:
14: TexData texData;
15:
16: GLuint texture;
17: glGenTextures(1, &texture);
18: glBindTexture(GL_TEXTURE_2D, texture);
19: glTexImage2D(GL_TEXTURE_2D, 0, GL_RGBA, texData.width, texData.height,
          0, GL_RGBA, GL_UNSIGNED_BYTE, texData.texels.data());
```

Assume that an image texture file is loaded into the GL program to fill `texData` in Sample code 8-1, where `texels` points to the actual texels, and `width×height` represents the texture resolution. Recall that, as presented in Sample code 6-5, the buffer object for the vertex array was created by invoking `glGenBuffers`, `glBindBuffer`, and `glBufferData` one after the other. Textures are handled in a similar manner:

- In order to create *texture objects*, `glGenTextures(GLsizei n, GLuint* textures)` is invoked, which returns `n` texture objects in `textures`.
- In order to bind a texture object to a particular type, `glBindTexture` is invoked. Its first argument is `GL_TEXTURE_2D` for a 2D texture and the second argument is the texture object ID returned by `glGenTextures`.
- The texture object is filled with the image texture using `glTexImage2D`.

In Sample code 8-1, `glTexImage2D` is invoked without `texture`. Understand that `glTexImage2D` does not have any argument for the texture object's ID. Once a texture object is bound, subsequent operations such as `glTexImage2D` work on the bound texture object.

void	glTexImage2D(GLenum target,
	GLint level,
	GLint internalFormat,
	GLsizei width,
	GLsizei height,
	GLint border,
	GLenum format,
	GLenum type,
	const GLvoid* data);
target	GL_TEXTURE_2D for 2D image texture
level	mipmap level (later on this)
internalFormat	number of color components such as GL_RGBA
width	width of the texture image
height	height of the texture image
border	OpenGL's legacy argument that must be 0
format	pixel format such as GL_RGBA
type	pixel data type such as GL_UNSIGNED_BYTE
data	pointer to the image data in memory

8.4   Texture Wrapping

GL allows the texture coordinates to be defined outside the normalized range of $[0, 1]$. Those texture coordinates are processed by the *texture wrapping mode*. Consider the image texture in Fig. 8.7-(a) and the quad in Fig. 8.7-(b). The texture coordinates of three vertices of the quad are outside of the range $[0, 1]$. Many fragments of the quad will be assigned the out-of-range texture coordinates. The simplest solution is to project those texture coordinates to the edge of the texture. If the s-coordinate of a fragment is 1.1, for example, it is clamped to 1.0. Fig. 8.7-(c) shows the textured result.

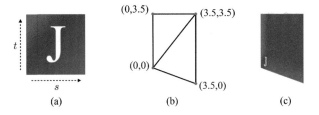

Fig. 8.7: Texture wrapping modes: (a) Image texture. (b) A quad with out-of-range texture coordinates. (c) Clamp-to-edge mode.

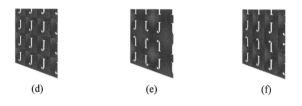

(d)   (e)   (f)

Fig. 8.7: Texture wrapping modes (*continued*): (d) Repeat mode. (e) Mirrored-repeat mode. (f) The *s*-axis follows the repeat mode whereas the *t*-axis follows the mirrored-repeat mode.

Another, more popular, solution is to use the fractional part of each texture coordinate. If *s* is 1.1, it is set to 0.1. This is called the *repeat* mode. The texture is tiled at every integer junction, as shown in Fig. 8.7-(d). However, the boundaries between the repeated textures are visible and can be annoying. If the *mirrored-repeat* mode is used instead, the texture is mirrored at every integer junction. If *s* is 1.1, 0.9 is taken. If *s* is 1.2, 0.8 is taken. We then have a smooth transition at the boundaries, as shown in Fig. 8.7-(e). The wrapping modes along the *s*- and *t*-axes can be specified independently. Fig. 8.7-(f) shows the result of setting the repeat and mirrored-repeat modes to the *s*- and *t*-axes, respectively.

`void   glTexParameteri(GLenum target,`	
`                       GLenum pname,`	
`                       GLint param);`	
`target`	target is `GL_TEXTURE_2D` for a 2D image texture
`pname`	either `GL_TEXTURE_WRAP_S` or `GL_TEXTURE_WRAP_T` in the context of texture wrapping
`param`	either `GL_CLAMP_TO_EDGE` (Fig. 8.7-(c)), `GL_REPEAT` (Fig. 8.7-(d)), or `GL_MIRRORED_REPEAT` (Fig. 8.7-(e))

In GL, the texture wrapping modes are specified using `glTexParameteri`. For example, Fig. 8.7-(f) is obtained by invoking `glTexParameteri` twice, as shown below.

Sample code 8-2 GL program for texture wrapping

```
1: glTexParameteri(GL_TEXTURE_2D, GL_TEXTURE_WRAP_S, GL_REPEAT);
2: glTexParameteri(GL_TEXTURE_2D, GL_TEXTURE_WRAP_T, GL_MIRRORED_REPEAT);
```

8.5   Texture Filtering

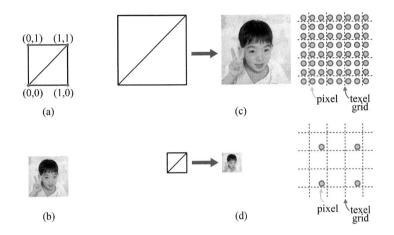

Fig. 8.8: Texture magnification and minification: (a) A quad to be textured. (b) An image texture. (c) Magnification. (d) Minification.

The texture coordinates (s, t) of a fragment are projected into (s', t') in the texture space, as presented in Equation (8.1). Then the texels *around* (s', t') are collected and combined to determine the color of the fragment. This process is called *texture filtering*.

Consider the quad shown in Fig. 8.8-(a). It is going to be textured with the image of Fig. 8.8-(b). Depending on the view, view-frustum, and viewport parameters, the size of the quad may vary in the screen. Shown on the left of Fig. 8.8-(c) is the screen-space quad. When textured, it appears larger than the texture of Fig. 8.8-(b). Conceptually, the texture is *magnified* so as to fit to the larger quad. Shown on the right of Fig. 8.8-(c) is a part of the texture space depicted as a grid of dotted lines, where a texel is located at a grid cell. The green dots represent the screen-space pixels projected onto the texture space. We have more pixels than texels[1].

In contrast, the screen-space quad in Fig. 8.8-(d) appears smaller than the image texture, and the texture is *minified* so as to fit to the smaller quad. As shown on the right, there are more texels than pixels. Sparsely projected onto the texture space, the pixels take large jumps in the space.

---

[1]More precisely, we have more 'fragments' than texels. However, this and the next sections will simply call fragments 'pixels' for a clearer contrast with 'texels.'

(a)

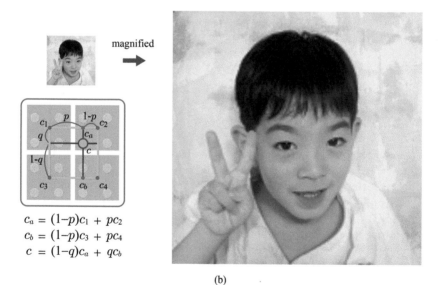

$$c_a = (1-p)c_1 + pc_2$$
$$c_b = (1-p)c_3 + pc_4$$
$$c = (1-q)c_a + qc_b$$

(b)

Fig. 8.9: Texture filtering for magnification: (a) Sixteen pixels are projected onto the area of 2×2 texels, and each pixel takes the color of the nearest texel. (b) The colors (denoted by c_i) of four texels surrounding the projected pixel are bilinearly interpolated.

8.5.1 Magnification

A filtering method for magnification is *nearest point sampling*. For a projected pixel, the nearest texel is selected. Fig. 8.9-(a) illustrates the method. Observe that a block of projected pixels is mapped to a single texel. Consequently, the nearest point sampling method usually produces a blocky image. See the boundary between the boy's hair and the background.

A better filtering method is *bilinear interpolation*, where the four texels surrounding a projected pixel are bilinearly interpolated. See Fig. 8.9-(b). With bilinear interpolation, the adjacent pixels are likely to have different texture colors, and the textured result does not suffer from the blocky-image problem. In most cases, the textured result obtained by bilinear interpolation has better quality.

8.5.2 Minification

Consider the checkerboard image texture shown in Fig. 8.10. Recall that, in the minification case, the pixels are sparsely projected onto the texture space. In Fig. 8.10-(a), they are depicted as green dots. Each pixel is surrounded by the dark-gray texels and is then assigned the dark-gray color, regardless of whether nearest point sampling or bilinear interpolation is adopted for texture filtering. If every projected pixel of the screen-space primitive is surrounded by dark-gray texels, the textured primitive will appear dark gray. The checkerboard image is not properly reconstructed. In contrast, the primitive appears just light gray if every projected pixel happens to be surrounded by light-gray texels, as shown in Fig. 8.10-(b).

This problem is an instance of *aliasing*. It refers to a sampling error that occurs when a high-frequency signal (in our example, the checkerboard image texture) is sampled at a lower resolution (in our example, the sparsely projected pixels). Aliasing is an ever-present problem in computer graphics. We need an *anti-aliasing* technique to reduce the aliasing artifact, and the next section presents a solution in the context of texturing.

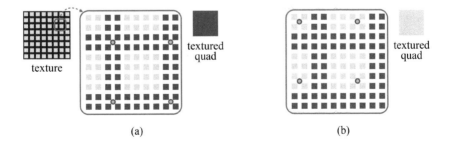

Fig. 8.10: Aliasing problem in minification.

8.6　Mipmapping

The aliasing problem observed in minification is caused by the fact that we have more texels than pixels. The pixels take large jumps in the texture space, leaving many texels not involved in texture filtering. Then, a simple solution is to reduce the number of texels such that the texel count becomes as close as possible to the pixel count.

8.6.1　Mipmap Construction

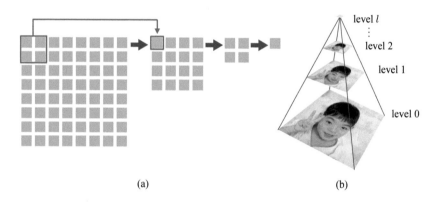

(a)　　　　　　　　　　　　　　　(b)

Fig. 8.11: Mipmap construction: (a) The 2×2 texels are repeatedly combined into a single texel. (b) If the input texture has a resolution of $2^l \times 2^l$, a pyramid of $(l+1)$ textures is generated.

Consider an 8×8-resolution texture shown in Fig. 8.11-(a). We can *down-sample* it to a quarter of its size, i.e., 4×4-resolution texture. The colors of 2×2 neighboring texels are averaged to determine the color of a texel in the down-sampled texture. Such down-sampling is repeated until a single-texel texture is obtained, which contains the average color of the original texture.

Given an original texture with a $2^l \times 2^l$ resolution, l down-sampled textures can be generated. The original and down-sampled textures are conceptually stacked to construct a *texture pyramid* of $(l+1)$ levels, as shown in Fig. 8.11-(b). The original texture is located at level 0. The pyramid is called a *mipmap*. (The prefix 'mip' is an acronym of the Latin phrase *multum in parvo*, meaning "many things in a small space.") Given a mipmap composed of $(l+1)$ levels, we will look for the level whose texel count is close to the pixel count.

8.6.2 Mipmap Filtering

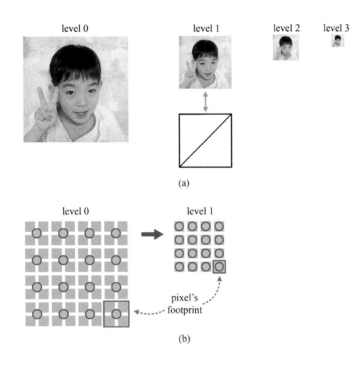

Fig. 8.12: Mipmap filtering example 1: (a) The screen-space quad and the level-1 texture have the same size. (b) A pixel's footprint covers four texels in the level-0 texture but covers a single texel in the level-1 texture.

Consider a minification case shown in Fig. 8.12-(a), where the original texture at level 0 is four times larger than the screen-space quad. For presenting mipmap filtering, some contrived examples would help. Illustrated on the left of Fig. 8.12-(b) is a part of the level-0 texture, where 4×4 pixels are projected onto the area of 8×8 texels.

So far, we have regarded a pixel as a point, i.e., a pixel located at a point in the screen space is projected onto another point in the texture space. In reality, however, a pixel covers an area on the screen. For simplicity, take the area as square such that the entire screen is considered to be tiled by an array of square pixels. Then, a pixel's projection onto the texture space is not a point but an area centered at (s', t') computed in Equation (8.1). The projected area is called the *footprint* of the pixel. In Fig. 8.12-(b), the red box at the lower-right corner of the level-0 texture represents a pixel's footprint. It covers 2×2 texels. We have too many texels for a pixel.

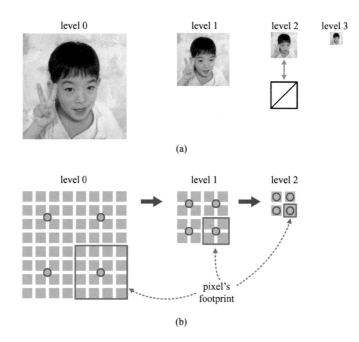

(a)

(b)

Fig. 8.13: Mipmap filtering example 2: (a) The screen-space quad and the level-2 texture have the same size. (b) A pixel's footprint covers exactly a single texel in the level-2 texture.

We move up the texture pyramid by one level. Then, as shown in Fig. 8.12-(b), the pixel's footprint covers a single texel. The texel count is equal to the pixel count. This is the best place for filtering. In this contrived example, the pixel's center coincides with the texel's center at level 1, and both nearest point sampling and bilinear interpolation return the same result.

Fig. 8.13-(a) shows another example, where the level-0 (original) texture is 16 times larger than the screen-space quad. Fig. 8.13-(b) shows that the pixel footprint covers 4×4, 2×2, and a single texel(s) in levels 0, 1, and 2, respectively. Therefore, the level-2 texture is filtered.

In a mipmap, *every* texel at level 0 contributes to all of the upper levels. Consequently, no texel of the "original texture" may be excluded in mipmap filtering, and the aliasing artifact is largely resolved.

When a pixel's footprint covers $m \times m$ texels in the level-0 texture, $\log_2 m$ determines the level to visit in the mipmap structure. By convention it is called the *level of detail* and is denoted by λ. In Fig. 8.12, $m = 2$ and $\lambda = \log_2 m = \log_2 2 = 1$. In Fig. 8.13, $m = 4$ and $\lambda = \log_2 m = \log_2 4 = 2$.

In general, m is not the power of 2 and λ is a floating-point value. Fig. 8.14-(a) shows an example. The pixel footprint covers 3×3 texels at the level-0

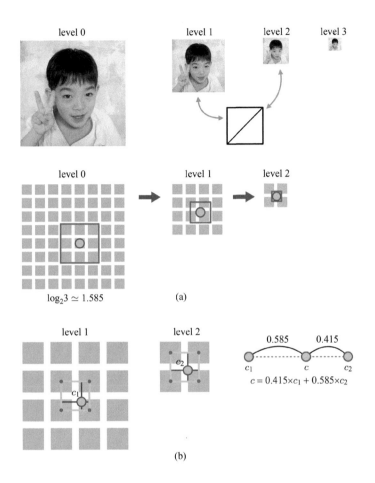

Fig. 8.14: Mipmap filtering example 3: (a) The screen-space quad is smaller than the level-1 texture but is larger than the level-2 texture. The two levels are the candidates to filter. (b) Trilinear interpolation.

texture, and $\lambda = \log_2 3 \simeq 1.585$. Given a floating-point λ, an option is to take the level that is *nearest* to λ. It is computed as $\lfloor \lambda + 0.5 \rfloor$. In the example of Fig. 8.14-(a), level 2 will be selected. In the selected level, we have two choices: nearest point sampling and bilinear interpolation.

In contrast, we can choose two levels ($\lfloor \lambda \rfloor$ and $\lceil \lambda \rceil$) and then linearly interpolate the filtered results from the levels. In Fig. 8.14-(a), levels 1 and 2 can be filtered either by nearest point sampling or by bilinear interpolation. In Fig. 8.14-(b), levels 1 and 2 are bilinearly interpolated. The results are then linearly interpolated using the fractional part of λ, 0.585. This process is called the *trilinear interpolation*.

8.7   Texture Filtering in GL

Given a screen-space pixel, GL itself computes its footprint to determine whether the texture is magnified or minified. In either case, the filtering method has yet to be specified by invoking `glTexParameteri` presented in Section 8.4. In the context of texture filtering, its second argument, `pname`, is either `GL_TEXTURE_MAG_FILTER` (for magnification) or `GL_TEXTURE_MIN_FILTER` (for minification). When `pname` is `GL_TEXTURE_MAG_FILTER`, the last argument of `glTexParameteri` (`param`) is either `GL_NEAREST` (for nearest point sampling) or `GL_LINEAR` (for bilinear interpolation).

When `pname` is `GL_TEXTURE_MIN_FILTER`, we have six options for `param`. The first two do not use the mipmap but filter the original texture either by nearest point sampling or by bilinear interpolation:

- `GL_NEAREST` (for nearest point sampling)
- `GL_LINEAR` (for bilinear interpolation)

Obviously, they are not preferred. The remaining four options are to use the mipmap[2]. Every option shares the structure, `GL_B_MIPMAP_A`, where `A` specifies which level(s) to choose in the mipmap and `B` specifies how to filter the chosen level(s):

- `GL_NEAREST_MIPMAP_NEAREST` takes the nearest level in the mipmap, e.g., level 2 in Fig. 8.14-(a), and filters the level by nearest point sampling.
- `GL_LINEAR_MIPMAP_NEAREST` filters the nearest level by bilinear interpolation.
- `GL_NEAREST_MIPMAP_LINEAR` takes two levels in the mipmap, e.g., levels 1 and 2 in Fig. 8.14-(a), and filters each by nearest point sampling.
- `GL_LINEAR_MIPMAP_LINEAR` corresponds to trilinear interpolation presented in Fig. 8.14-(b).

8.8   Mipmappig Examples in GL*

Fig. 8.15-(a) shows a mipmap of blue-stripe textures. Let us replace level 0 by a red-stripe texture to make an artificial mipmap shown in Fig. 8.15-(b). This would help us understand mipmapping. Fig. 8.15-(c) shows a long thin quad with texture coordinates. Suppose that it is angled obliquely away from the viewer such that its top is quite far from the viewpoint whereas its bottom

---

[2]The mipmap is constructed by invoking `glGenerateMipmap(GL_TEXTURE_2D)`. This does not have the argument for the texture object's ID but simply works on the current texture object bound by `glBindTexture` presented in Sample code 8-1.

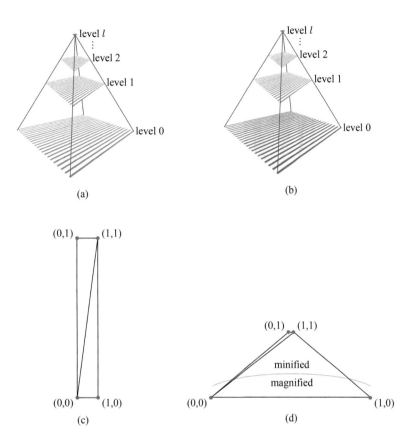

Fig. 8.15: Mipmap and quad: (a) The mipmap of a blue-stripe texture. (b) The level-0 texture in (a) is replaced by a red-stripe texture. (c) A long thin quad. (d) An extremely oriented quad.

is very close to the viewpoint. Then, the screen-space quad would look like Fig. 8.15-(d). It will be textured using the mipmap in Fig. 8.15-(b). For each pixel covered by the quad, GL determines whether the texture is magnified or minified. Then, the quad is partitioned into two parts. The texture is magnified in the lower part whereas it is minified in the upper part.

Fig. 8.16 shows the quads textured with different filtering methods. (The screen-space quad is cut at both right and left ends for visualization purposes.) In Fig. 8.16-(a), param is set to GL_NEAREST for both magnification and minification. Because magnification does not use the mipmap, the magnified part is always textured with the level-0 texture. On the other hand, GL_NEAREST specified for minification also makes the minified part textured only with the level-0 texture. Consequently, the entire quad is textured with red stripes.

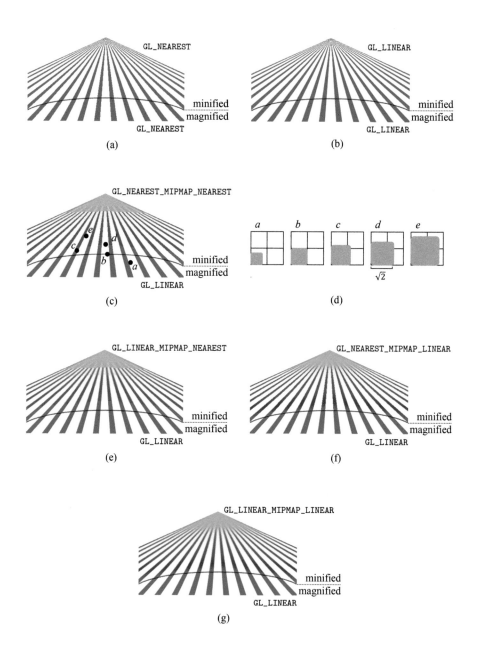

Fig. 8.16: Mipmapping examples.

Fig. 8.16-(b) shows the textured result when `param` is changed to `GL_LINEAR` for both magnification and minification. The entire quad is still textured with red stripes, but the stripes appear smooth because the texture is filtered by bilinear interpolation.

While fixing the magnification filter to `GL_LINEAR`, let us change the minification filter one by one. When we use `GL_NEAREST_MIPMAP_NEAREST`, we have the result shown in Fig. 8.16-(c). The quad is now textured with the mipmap in Fig. 8.15-(b), and therefore not only level 0 but also its upper levels are involved in texturing the minified part.

Consider the five pixels depicted as black dots in Fig. 8.16-(c). Fig. 8.16-(d) visualizes their footprint sizes against the texel grid. Pixel a is in the magnified area and its footprint is smaller than a texel. In contrast, pixel b is located on the boundary between the magnified and minified parts and its footprint has the same size as a texel. Now consider pixel d located on the boundary between the red-stripe texture at level 0 and the blue-stripe texture at level 1. Its footprint area is 2 and the side length is $\sqrt{2}$, making $\lambda = \log_2 \sqrt{2} = 0.5$, i.e., λ is the midpoint between levels 0 and 1. If a pixel, such as c, has a slightly smaller footprint, level 0 will be selected. If a pixel, such as e, has a slightly larger footprint, level 1 will be selected.

Fig. 8.16-(e) shows the textured result when we take `GL_LINEAR_MIPMAP_NEAREST` for the minification filter. The stripes in the minified part are made smoother.

Let us take `GL_NEAREST_MIPMAP_LINEAR` for the minification filter. Then, each pixel at the minified part is no longer dominated by a single mipmap level. Instead, two levels are filtered (through nearest point sampling) and the filtered results are linearly interpolated. It is clearly demonstrated by the blended red and blue stripes in Fig. 8.16-(f). Finally, Fig. 8.16-(g) shows that `GL_LINEAR_MIPMAP_LINEAR` smoothes the stripes in the minified part.

8.9 Fragment Shader for Texturing

Shown in Sample code 8-3 is a fragment shader for texturing. It runs once for each fragment so that each fragment is textured independently of the others. A fragment shader may take *uniforms*, and the texture is provided as a uniform. At line 5, a uniform, `colorMap`, is declared with type `sampler2D`, which represents a 2D texture. In GL, a texture is called a sampler.

The texture coordinates should be input to the fragment shader. Such input data must be output by the vertex shader. Our fragment shader works together with the vertex shader presented in Sample code 6-1. It copied the attribute `texCoord` into `v_texCoord`. The per-vertex texture coordinates were passed to the rasterizer and interpolated for each fragment. Now, the

Sample code 8-3 Fragment shader for texturing

```
1: #version 300 es
2:
3: precision mediump float;
4:
5: uniform sampler2D colorMap;
6:
7: in vec2 v_texCoord;
8:
9: layout(location = 0) out vec4 fragColor;
10:
11: void main() {
12:     fragColor = texture(colorMap, v_texCoord);
13: }
```

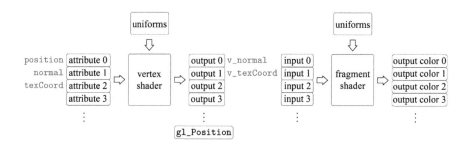

Fig. 8.17: Vertex and fragment shaders.

per-fragment texture coordinates are input to the fragment shader with the same name, v_texCoord, at line 7 of Sample code 8-3. Fig. 8.17 shows the relation between the vertex and fragment shaders. The fragment shader does not have to take all data provided by the vertex shader and rasterizer. In fact, our fragment shader does not take as input v_normal, which was output by the vertex shader in Sample code 6-1. (The next chapter will present a different fragment shader that uses v_normal for lighting.)

The fragment shader in GL 3.0 may output multiple colors whereas only a single color can be output in GL 2.0. For the sake of simplicity, however, this book considers outputting only a single color. It is fragColor at line 9 of Sample code 8-3. It is a 4D vector that stores RGBA[3].

The main function invokes the built-in function, texture, which accesses colorMap using v_texCoord to return fragColor. As presented in Section 8.7, the filtering method is set up by glTexParameteri, and colorMap is

---

[3]'A' stands for 'alpha' and describes the *opacity* of the RGB color. If it is in the normalized range $[0, 1]$, 0 denotes "fully transparent," 1 denotes "fully opaque," and the other values specify the degrees of opacity.

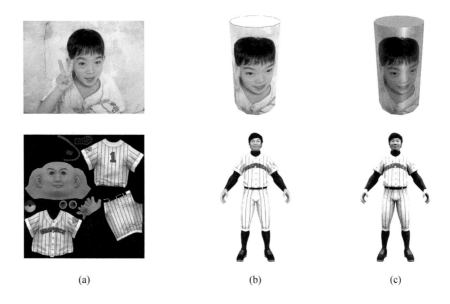

(a)   (b)   (c)

Fig. 8.18: Textured results: (a) Textures. (b) Texturing only. (c) Texturing + lighting.

filtered accordingly. The output of the fragment shader is passed to the next stage of the rendering pipeline, the output merger.

In the vertex and fragment shaders, a variable can be declared to have either low, medium, or high precision. Those precisions denoted by the keywords, `lowp`, `mediump`, and `highp`, are implementation-dependent. For example, two bytes can be assigned to a float variable of `mediump` whereas four bytes to `highp`. The precision is specified using the keyword `precision`. Line 3 in Sample code 8-3 declares that all float variables in the fragment shader have the medium precision by default.

Fig. 8.18-(a) shows two image textures and Fig. 8.18-(b) shows the textured objects, where texturing is completed by the simple fragment shader in Sample code 8-3. Observe that the textured objects are not really 'shaded,' i.e., there is no difference in shading across the objects' surfaces, making the objects look less realistic. We need *lighting* to produce the shaded objects shown in Fig. 8.18-(c). It will be presented in the next chapter.

Exercises

1. Consider the scan line at y-coordinate 3.5.

   (a) Compute the texture coordinates at the intersection points between the scan line and two edges.

   (b) Compute the texture coordinates of two fragments at the scan line.

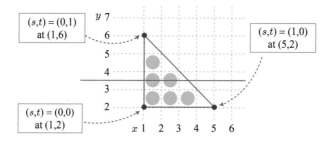

2. Suppose that the texture coordinate s is outside of the range $[0, 1]$. Assuming that the texture wrapping mode is *repeat*, write an equation that converts s into the range $[0, 1]$. Use the floor or ceiling function.

3. Suppose that a pixel is projected into (s', t') in the texture space. Using the floor or ceiling function, write the equations to compute the texel *index* for nearest point sampling. The index of a texel is the coordinates of its lower-left corner. For example, the index of the texel located at $(1.5, 3.5)$ is $(1, 3)$.

4. Shown below is a fragment projected into the texture space. It is surrounded by four texels. The color of each texel is denoted by c_i. Compute the fragment color, c, using bilinear interpolation.

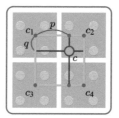

5. A pixel is projected onto an 8×8-resolution image texture. On the left of the figure, the red dot represents the projected point, and the yellow rectangle is the footprint.

   (a) The texture is a gray-scale image. The numbers in the level-0 and level-1 textures represent the texel intensities. Construct the level-2 and level-3 textures.

   (b) Suppose that trilinear interpolation is used for texture filtering and λ is set to the length of the *longest* side of the footprint. Which levels are selected? Compute the filtered result at each level.

   (c) Suppose that trilinear interpolation is used for texture filtering and λ is set to the length of the *shortest* side of the footprint. Which levels are selected? Compute the filtered result at each level.

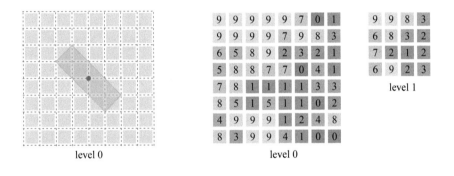

level 0   level 0   level 1

6. Suppose that, for the OpenGL ES function glTexParameteri(GLenum target, GLenum pname, GLint param), target is GL_TEXTURE_2D and pname is GL_TEXTURE_MIN_FILTER.

   (a) If we choose GL_LINEAR for param, what problem might we have?

   (b) Suppose that we choose GL_LINEAR_MIPMAP_NEAREST for param, which implies that we choose the nearest level in the mipmap. How many "linear interpolations" are performed in total? (Note that this question is not asking the count of bilinear interpolations.)

   (c) Suppose that we choose GL_NEAREST_MIPMAP_LINEAR for param. How many "linear interpolations" are performed in total?

   (d) Suppose that we choose GL_LINEAR_MIPMAP_LINEAR for param. How many "linear interpolations" are performed in total?

7. Some applications such as medical imaging require 3D texturing. Given a 3D image with a $2^l \times 2^l \times 2^l$ resolution, describe how to construct the

mipmap. How many levels are in the mipmap? What is the size of the top-level image in the mipmap?

8. Shown below are a mipmap, a textured quad, and five cases of pixel projection, where the gray box represents a pixel's footprint and the 2×2 grid represents 4 texels. Make five alphabet-number pairs.

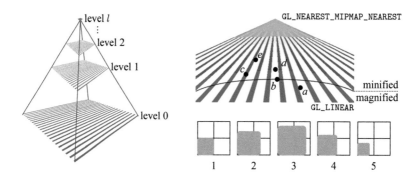

9. Consider a checkerboard image composed of two gray-scale values, 0 (black) and 0.8 (light gray) in the range of $[0, 1]$. The footprint of a projected pixel is square. Its center is exactly in the middle of 4 texels, and the side length is $2\sqrt{2}$.

   (a) Suppose that each level in the mipmap is filtered by nearest point sampling and the filtered results are linearly interpolated. What is the final textured color? (If there are multiple texels whose distances to the pixel are the same, we choose the upper or upper-right one for nearest point sampling.)

   (b) Now suppose that each level is filtered by bilinear interpolation. What is the final textured color?

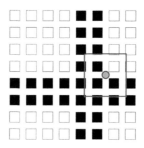

Chapter 9

Lighting

Lighting or *illumination* refers to the technique that handles the interaction between lights and objects. This chapter presents a widely-used lighting model named the *Phong model* and shows how the shaders are programmed for it. Later, Chapter 16 will discuss the problems of the Phong model and introduce significantly different lighting models, *ray tracing* and *radiosity*.

9.1 Phong Lighting Model

For lighting computation, it is necessary to specify the light sources. A simple light source is the *point light*. Located at a point in space, it emits light uniformly in all directions. The light is attenuated over distance. As the distance from the light source increases, the intensity of the light decreases.

Suppose that a strong light source is considerably far from the scene. A good example is the sun. It is safely assumed that all objects in the scene receive the sunlight along a universal direction. The light source is called *directional*. It is assumed that, unlike the point light, the directional light is not attenuated over distance. The only factors to be considered are the light's direction and color. This chapter presents lighting with a directional light.

For rendering a surface illuminated by a light source, we need to measure the *irradiance* (incoming light) at the surface and the outgoing *radiance* reaching the camera. The relationship between them is described by BRDF (bidirectional reflectance distribution function) [5]. The Phong model simplifies the BRDF for real-time purposes. The perceived color of a surface point is defined by four terms named *diffuse, specular, ambient,* and *emissive*. See Fig. 9.1. The diffuse and specular terms deal with the light ray coming directly from the light source to the surface point whereas the ambient term accounts for *indirect lighting*. The emissive term applies to the object emitting light itself. The following subsections present the four terms in order.

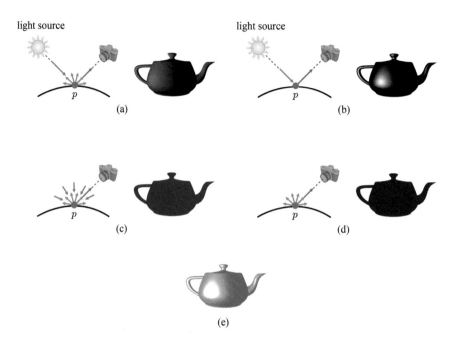

Fig. 9.1: The light incident on a surface point p is illustrated in blue, and the reflected light is in orange. Outgoing radiance reaching the camera is illustrated in red. (a) Diffuse reflection. (b) Specular reflection. (c) Ambient reflection. (d) Emissive light. (e) The RGB colors computed in (a) through (d) are accumulated to determine the final color.

9.1.1　Diffuse Reflection

The diffuse term is based on *Lambert's law*, which states that reflections from ideally diffuse surfaces (called the Lambertian surfaces) are scattered with equal intensity in *all* directions, as illustrated in Fig. 9.1-(a). Therefore, the amount of perceived reflection is independent of the view direction and is just proportional to the amount of incoming light.

We assume a directional light. Consequently the *light vector* denoted as l is constant for the entire scene[1]. In Fig. 9.2-(a), l is defined to be opposite to the direction the light actually travels. It is for computational efficiency. At a surface point p, the angle θ between l and the surface normal n is named the *incident angle*. As θ becomes smaller, p receives more light. Assuming that n and l are unit vectors, their dot product is used to measure the amount of

---

[1] In contrast, a point light source is located at a specific position in the 3D scene, and the light vector is not constant but varies across the scene.

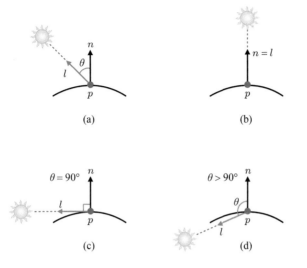

Fig. 9.2: Diffuse reflection: (a) The amount of light incident on p is defined by $n \cdot l$. (b) When $n = l$, the light incident on p reaches the maximum amount. (c) When $\theta = 90°$, it is zero. (d) When $\theta > 90°$, it is also zero.

incident light:

$$n \cdot l = \|n\|\|l\|cos\theta = cos\theta \qquad (9.1)$$

When $\theta = 0$, i.e., when $n = l$, $n \cdot l$ equals one, implying that p receives the maximum amount of light (Fig. 9.2-(b)). When $\theta = 90°$, $n \cdot l$ equals zero, and p receives no light (Fig. 9.2-(c)). Note that, when $\theta > 90°$, p does not receive any light (Fig. 9.2-(d)). The amount of incident light should be zero, but $n \cdot l$ becomes negative. To resolve this problem, $n \cdot l$ is extended to

$$max(n \cdot l, 0) \qquad (9.2)$$

Note that $max(n \cdot l, 0)$ describes the 'amount' of incident light. The perceived 'color' of the surface point p is defined as

$$s_d \otimes m_d \qquad (9.3)$$

where s_d is the RGB color of the light source, m_d is the *diffuse reflectance* of the object material, and $\otimes$ represents the component-wise multiplication. (In our notations, s denotes the light source, and m denotes the material.) Suppose that s_d is $(1, 1, 0)$, i.e., the light source's color is yellow. If m_d is $(1, 1, 1)$, for example, the diffuse color term $s_d \otimes m_d$ is $(1, 1, 0)$, i.e., the yellow light is reflected as is. If m_d is $(0, 1, 1)$, however, the diffuse color term becomes

$(0, 1, 0)$, i.e., the red component of the light source is absorbed by the material, and only the green component is reflected.

The diffuse reflection term of the Phong model is defined by combining the amount of incident light and the perceived color of the surface:

$$max(n \cdot l, 0)s_d \otimes m_d \qquad (9.4)$$

Fig. 9.1-(a) shows the teapot rendered with only the diffuse term.

9.1.2 Specular Reflection

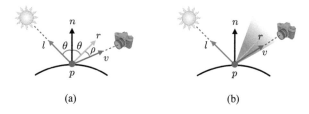

(a)   (b)

Fig. 9.3: Specular reflection: (a) Reflected light vector and view vector are denoted by r and v, respectively. (b) If v falls into the conceptual cone of the reflected vectors centered around r, a highlight is visible to the camera.

The specular term is used to make a surface look shiny via *highlights*, and it requires a *view vector* and a *reflection vector* in addition to the light vector. The normalized view vector, denoted as v in Fig. 9.3-(a), connects the surface point p and the camera position. For computational efficiency, v is defined to be opposite to the view direction.

The light vector, l, is reflected at p to define the reflection vector, denoted as r. It is easy to compute r. In Fig. 9.4, the incident angle θ is equal to the reflection angle. The two right triangles in the figure share the side represented by the vector $ncos\theta$. Consider the base s of the triangle at the left-hand side. It connects l and $ncos\theta$, and is defined as follows:

$$s = ncos\theta - l \qquad (9.5)$$

The base of the triangle at the right-hand side is also s and is defined as follows:

$$s = r - ncos\theta \qquad (9.6)$$

Equations (9.5) and (9.6) should be identical, and therefore we can derive r:

$$r = 2ncos\theta - l \qquad (9.7)$$

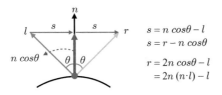

$$s = n\,\cos\theta - l$$
$$s = r - n\,\cos\theta$$

$$r = 2n\,\cos\theta - l$$
$$ = 2n\,(n{\cdot}l) - l$$

Fig. 9.4: Computing reflection vector.

As $n \cdot l = \cos\theta$, r is rephrased as follows:

$$r = 2n(n \cdot l) - l \qquad\qquad (9.8)$$

Because l is assumed to be a unit vector, r is also a unit vector.

Return to Fig. 9.3-(a) and consider the angle ρ between r and v. For a perfectly shiny surface, the highlight at p is visible to the camera only when $\rho = 0$. This is because the incoming light is reflected only along r. For a surface that is not perfectly shiny, however, the highlight reaches the maximum when $\rho = 0$ but decreases as ρ increases. Fig. 9.3-(b) illustrates the cone of the reflected light rays, the axis of which is r. If v is inside the cone, the highlight is visible to the camera. The decrease of highlights is often approximated by

$$(r \cdot v)^{sh} \qquad\qquad (9.9)$$

where sh represents the *shiniess* of the surface. If $r = v$, $(r \cdot v)^{sh} = 1$ and the maximum highlight is visible to the camera. Otherwise, the highlight becomes less visible. A larger sh results in a smaller, sharper highlight whereas a smaller sh results in a larger highlight.

The specular term is defined as

$$(max(r \cdot v, 0))^{sh} s_s \otimes m_s \qquad\qquad (9.10)$$

where s_s is the RGB color of the specular light, and m_s is the *specular reflectance* of the object material. The *max* function is needed for the same reason as in the diffuse reflection term. In general, s_s is equal to s_d, the RGB color of the diffuse light. Unlike m_d (diffuse reflectance), m_s is usually a gray-scale value rather than an RGB color. It enables the highlight on the surface to be the color of the light source. Imagine a white light shining on a red-colored metallic object. Most of the object surfaces would appear red, but the highlight would be white. Fig. 9.1-(b) shows the teapot rendered with only the specular term.

9.1.3 Ambient Reflection

Ambient light describes the light reflected from the various objects in the scene, i.e., it accounts for indirect lighting. The ambient light has bounced around in the scene and arrives at a surface point from *all* directions, rather than from a specific direction. As a consequence, reflections from the surface point are also scattered with equal intensity in all directions. These facts imply that the amount of ambient light incident on a surface point is independent of the surface orientation, and that the amount of perceived reflection is independent of the view direction. Therefore, the ambient reflection term is simply defined as

$$s_a \otimes m_a \qquad (9.11)$$

where s_a is the RGB color of the ambient light, and m_a is the *ambient reflectance* of the object material. Fig. 9.1-(c) shows the teapot rendered with only the ambient term. The rendered result simply looks like a 2D object because there is no difference in shading across the teapot's surface.

The ambient term approximates the inter-reflection of real-world lighting and enables us to see into shadowy corners of the scene that are not directly lit by light sources. For example, in Fig. 9.1-(a) and -(b), the lower-right part of the teapot is completely dark because it is not directly lit. In contrast, the same part of the teapot in Fig. 9.1-(c) is not completely dark but slightly illuminated. However, the ambient term of the Phong model is too simple to capture the subtleties of real-world indirect lighting. Section 16.4 will present a technique to make the ambient reflection more realistic.

9.1.4 Emissive Light

The emissive term describes the amount of light emitted by a surface itself. It is simply an RGB color value and is denoted by m_e. Fig. 9.1-(d) shows the teapot rendered with only the emissive term. The object has little emissive color. The rendered result looks 2D as in the case of the ambient reflection. Note that, in the Phong illumination model, an emissive object is not a light source per se, and it does not illuminate the other objects in the scene. This is an obvious limitation of the Phong model.

The Phong model sums the four terms to determine the color of a surface point:

$$max(n \cdot l, 0)s_d \otimes m_d + (max(r \cdot v, 0))^{sh} s_s \otimes m_s + s_a \otimes m_a + m_e \qquad (9.12)$$

Fig. 9.1-(e) shows the result of adding the four terms. If an object does not emit light, the emissive term m_e is simply deleted. If an object is close to a Lambertian surface, the RGB components of m_s are small. In contrast, m_s is made large in order to describe a shiny metallic object.

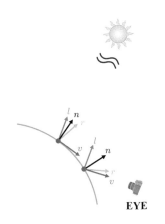

Fig. 9.5: Vectors involved in lighting.

9.2 Shaders for Phong Lighting

This section presents how the vertex and fragment shaders cooperate to implement the Phong model. Fig. 9.5 illustrates two points on an object's surface, each of which is assumed to make up a distinct fragment. The fragment shader computes lighting using the four vectors involved in Equation (9.12): light vector l, normal n, reflection vector r, and view vector v. Since we assume a directional light, l is constant for all surface points. It is provided for the fragment shader as a uniform. In contrast, n, r, and v vary across the object's surface. A distinct pair of n and v is given to each execution of the fragment shader, which then computes r using Equation (9.8) and finally implements Equation (9.12).

Because l is a world-space vector, n should also be defined in the world space. For this, the vertex shader world-transforms the object-space normal of each vertex and passes the world-space normal to the rasterizer. The rasterizer interpolates the vertex normals to provide n for each fragment. Consider the two vertices, p_1 and p_2, of the sphere mesh in Fig. 9.6-(a). The cross-section illustration in Fig. 9.6-(b) shows their world-space normals, n_1 and n_2. On the edge connecting p_1 and p_2, consider two points, a and b, each of which is assumed to make up a distinct fragment. The rasterizer assigns normals, n_a and n_b, to them by interpolating n_1 and n_2.

For the fragments, a and b, we also need world-space view vectors denoted by v_a and v_b, respectively. For this, the vertex shader transforms the object-space position of each vertex to the world space and connects it to the camera position, **EYE**, defined in the world space. In Fig. 9.6-(c), v_1 and v_2 represent

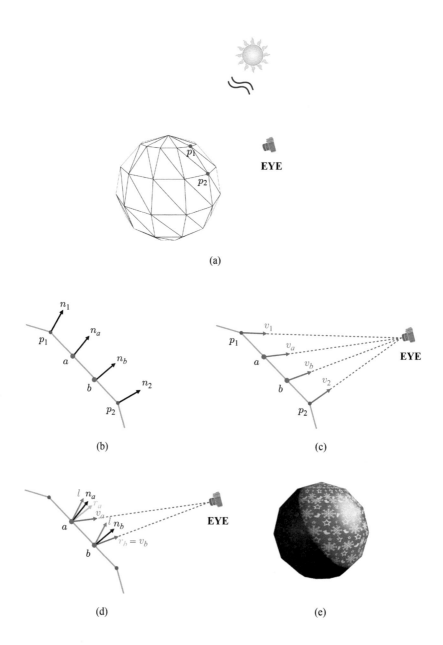

Fig. 9.6: Per-fragment lighting: (a) Two vertices in a low-resolution polygon mesh of a sphere. (b) Interpolated normals. (c) Interpolated view vectors. (d) Four vectors at each fragment. (e) Lit and textured mesh.

Sample code 9-1 Vertex shader for Phong lighting

```
 1: #version 300 es
 2:
 3: uniform mat4 worldMat, viewMat, projMat;
 4: uniform vec3 eyePos;
 5:
 6: layout(location = 0) in vec3 position;
 7: layout(location = 1) in vec3 normal;
 8: layout(location = 2) in vec2 texCoord;
 9:
10: out vec3 v_normal, v_view;
11: out vec2 v_texCoord;
12:
13: void main() {
14:     v_normal = normalize(transpose(inverse(mat3(worldMat))) * normal);
15:     vec3 worldPos = (worldMat * vec4(position, 1.0)).xyz;
16:     v_view = normalize(eyePos - worldPos);
17:     v_texCoord = texCoord;
18:     gl_Position = projMat * viewMat * vec4(worldPos, 1.0);
19: }
```

the per-vertex world-space view vectors. They are passed to the rasterizer and interpolated to produce v_a and v_b.

Given n and v provided by the rasterizer and l provided as a uniform by the GL program, the fragment shader first computes the reflection vector, i.e., $r = 2n(n \cdot l) - l$, and finally implements Equation (9.12). Note that l, n, r, and v are all defined in the world space. Do not get confused! The fragment shader processes such *world-space* vectors for determining the color of the *screen-space* fragment.

Fig. 9.6-(d) compares lighting at two fragments, a and b. They share l, the directional light vector. For a, the reflection vector (r_a) makes a considerable angle with the view vector (v_a) and therefore the camera perceives little specular reflection. In contrast, the reflection vector at b (r_b) happens to be identical to the view vector (v_b) and therefore the camera perceives the maximum amount of specular reflection. Fig. 9.6-(e) shows the sphere lit by the Phong model.

Shown in Sample code 9-1 is the vertex shader. It extends our first vertex shader presented in Sample code 6-1. A uniform, eyePos, is added at line 4, which represents **EYE**, and an output variable, v_view, is added at line 10. The first statement of the main function computes the world-space vertex normal and assigns it to the output variable, v_normal. The second and third statements compute the world-space view vector and assign it to v_view. As usual, the texture coordinates are copied to v_texCoord (the fourth statement). The rasterizer will interpolate v_normal, v_view, and v_texCoord. The required task of the vertex shader is to compute the clip-space vertex position, and the final statement of the main function assigns it to gl_Position.

Sample code 9-2 Fragment shader for Phong lighting

```
1: #version 300 es
2:
3: precision mediump float;
4:
5: uniform sampler2D colorMap;
6: uniform vec3 matSpec, matAmbi, matEmit; // Ms, Ma, Me
7: uniform float matSh; // shininess
8: uniform vec3 srcDiff, srcSpec, srcAmbi; // Sd, Ss, Sa
9: uniform vec3 lightDir; // directional light
10:
11: in vec3 v_normal, v_view;
12: in vec2 v_texCoord;
13:
14: layout(location = 0) out vec4 fragColor;
15:
16: void main() {
17:     // normalization
18:     vec3 normal = normalize(v_normal);
19:     vec3 view = normalize(v_view);
20:     vec3 light = normalize(lightDir);
21:
22:     // diffuse term
23:     vec3 matDiff = texture(colorMap, v_texCoord).rgb;
24:     vec3 diff = max(dot(normal, light), 0.0) * srcDiff * matDiff;
25:
26:     // specular term
27:     vec3 refl = 2.0 * normal * dot(normal, light) - light;
28:     vec3 spec = pow(max(dot(refl, view), 0.0), matSh) * srcSpec * matSpec;
29:
30:     // ambient term
31:     vec3 ambi = srcAmbi * matAmbi;
32:
33:     fragColor = vec4(diff + spec + ambi + matEmit, 1.0);
34: }
```

Shown in Sample code 9-2 is the fragment shader for Phong lighting. The uniforms declared at lines 6 through 9 are the ingredients of the Phong lighting model. Specifically, `lightDir` at line 9 is the directional light vector defined in the world space. Lines 11 and 12 show three input variables provided by the rasterizer.

The main function computes the diffuse, specular, and ambient terms one by one. Line 24 is the straight implementation of the diffuse term. It invokes two built-in functions: `dot(a,b)` for calculating the dot product of two vectors a and b, and `max(a,b)` for taking the larger between two input arguments a and b. Note that the diffuse reflectance, `matDiff` corresponding to m_d in Equation (9.12), is fetched from the image texture (line 23). It is also straightforward to compute the specular and ambient terms. Line 28 invokes a built-in function, `pow(a,b)` for raising a to the power b.

It is worth paying attention to `normalize(v_normal)` at line 18. Even though `v_normal` output by the vertex shader in Sample code 9-1 is a unit vector, the fragment shader's input, `v_normal`, is not necessarily so because it is generated by interpolating the vertex normals across the triangle[2]. Because every normal used for lighting is assumed to be a unit vector, `v_normal` should be normalized by invoking the built-in function `normalize`. By the same token, another input variable, `v_view`, is also normalized (line 19).

---

[2]Consider interpolating two 2D unit vectors, $(-\frac{1}{\sqrt{2}}, \frac{1}{\sqrt{2}})$ and $(\frac{1}{\sqrt{2}}, \frac{1}{\sqrt{2}})$. When their weights are both 0.5, for example, the interpolated vector is $(0, \frac{1}{\sqrt{2}})$. It is not a unit vector.

Exercises

1. The Phong model shown below assumes a directional light source.

   $$max(n \cdot l, 0)s_d \otimes m_d + (max(r \cdot v, 0))^{sh}s_s \otimes m_s + s_a \otimes m_a + m_e$$

   (a) How would you modify it for handling multiple directional light sources?

   (b) How would you modify it for replacing the directional light source by a point light source? Assume that the light intensity a surface point receives is inversely proportional to the square of distance that the light has traveled.

2. At line 16 of Sample code 9-1, v_view is a unit vector, but line 19 of Sample code 9-2 normalizes it again. Explain why.

3. At line 24 of Sample code 9-2, why do we need max?

4. For specular reflection, it is necessary to compute the refection vector r using the surface normal n and the light vector l. Write the equation for r using the dot product of n and l.

5. Consider the figure shown below. It is for the specular reflection term of the Phong lighting model: $(max(r \cdot v, 0))^{sh}s_s \otimes m_s$. Illustrated in the middle column are the cones representing the ranges where we can see the highlights. Connect the black dots. For example, if you think that a smaller sh leads to a smaller cone, connect the upper-left box to the upper-middle box.

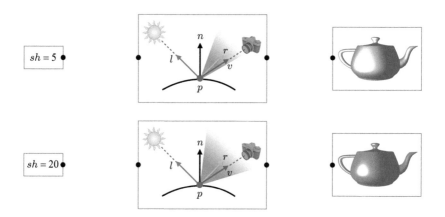

Chapter 10

Output Merger

We are approaching the end of the rendering pipeline. Its last stage is the output merger[1]. As is the rasterizer, the output merger is hard-wired but controllable through GL commands. This chapter focuses on two main functionalities of the output merger: z-buffering and alpha blending.

10.1 Z-buffering

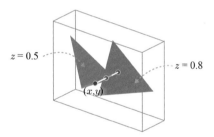

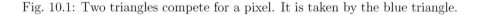

Fig. 10.1: Two triangles compete for a pixel. It is taken by the blue triangle.

Fig. 10.1 shows two triangles in the viewport and a pixel located at (x, y). The pixel will be colored in blue because the blue triangle is in front of the red triangle. In the GPU, such a decision is made by comparing the z-values of the triangles at (x, y).

GL supports three types of buffers: the *color buffer*, *depth buffer*, and *stencil buffer*. The collection of these three is called the *frame buffer*. This

---

[1]GL calls this stage *per-fragment operations*, but then readers might get confused because the fragment shader also operates per fragment. Therefore, we call it the output merger. It is the term used in Direct3D.

chapter does not present the stencil buffer but focuses on the color and depth buffers. Those buffers have the same resolution as the 2D viewport. The color buffer is a memory space storing the pixels to be displayed on the 2D viewport. The depth buffer, also called the *z-buffer*, records the z-values of the pixels currently stored in the color buffer. The z-values are defined in the 3D viewport's depth range.

Sample code 10-1 GL program for color and depth buffers

```
1: glClearDepthf(1.0f); // initialized with depth 1.0
2: glClearColor(1.0f, 1.0f, 1.0f, 1.0f); // initialized with white
3: glClear(GL_DEPTH_BUFFER_BIT | GL_COLOR_BUFFER_BIT); // clear buffers
```

Fig. 10.2-(a) illustrates how the z-buffer and color buffer are updated when we process the red triangle first and then the blue one shown in Fig. 10.1. Suppose that the depth range of the viewport is $[0, 1]$. Then, the z-buffer is initialized with 1.0, which represents the background depth. On the other hand, the color buffer is initialized with the background color, white in our example. In Sample code 10-1, `glClearDepthf` and `glClearColor` preset the initialization values and `glClear` clears the z-buffer and color buffer to the preset values.

When the fragment shader returns an RGBA color of a fragment, its screen-space coordinates (x, y, z) are automatically passed to the output merger. Then, the z-value of the fragment is compared with the current z-buffer value of the pixel at (x, y). If the fragment's value is smaller, the fragment is judged to be in front of the pixel and thus hide it. Then, the fragment's color and z-value update the color buffer and z-buffer at (x, y), respectively. Otherwise, the fragment is judged to lie behind the pixel and thus be invisible. It is discarded.

For simplicity, the triangles in Fig. 10.1 are assumed to be parallel to the xy-plane of the screen space, and the blue and red triangles' equations are $z = 0.5$ and $z = 0.8$, respectively. Shown in the middle of Fig. 10.2-(a) is the result of processing the red triangle. The blue triangle is processed next, and the result is shown on the right of Fig. 10.2-(a). The color-buffer pixels located at $(38, 56)$, $(38, 57)$ and $(39, 56)$ are changed from red to blue. The same locations in the z-buffer are also updated from 0.8 to 0.5. This method of determining visible surfaces is named *z-buffering* or *depth buffering*.

Fig. 10.2-(b) shows the case where the processing order is reversed. Observe that, when rendering is completed, the z-buffer and color buffer contain the same information as those in Fig. 10.2-(a). In principle, z-buffering allows primitives to be processed in an arbitrary order. It is one of the key features making the method so popular. However, primitive ordering is important for handling translucent objects, as will be discussed in the next section.

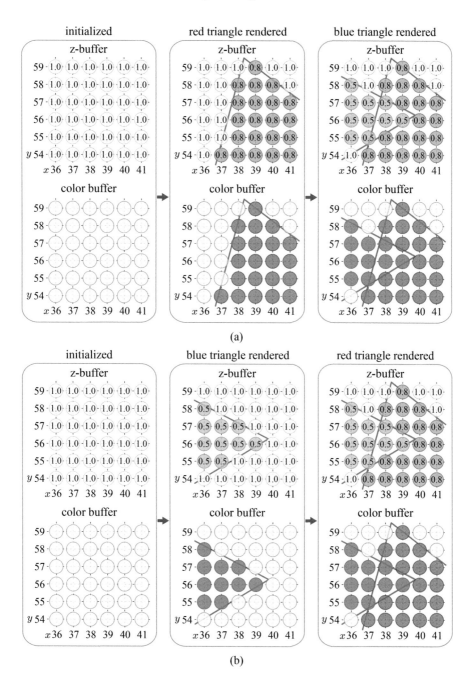

Fig. 10.2: Z-buffering: (a) Rendering order is red to blue triangles. (b) Rendering order is blue to red triangles.

To enable the z-buffering, we first invoke `glEnable(GL_DEPTH_TEST)`. Then, the function used for depth comparison is specified via `glDepthFunc`. The color and depth buffers are updated if the incoming fragment's depth is "less than" the current pixel's. The default argument of `glDepthFunc` is `GL_LESS`.

10.2 Alpha Blending

The previous section presents how the incoming fragment competes with the pixel stored in the color buffer. The fragment either replaces the pixel or is discarded. This section shows that the fragment color may be blended with the pixel color.

To this point, all surfaces are implicitly assumed to be opaque so that, when two surface points compete for a pixel position, one point fully occludes the other. However, some surfaces may be translucent (partially transparent). Suppose that the current fragment has a smaller depth than the pixel in the color buffer and is translucent. Then, the pixel should be visible through the fragment. This is achieved by *blending* the fragment's color with the pixel's.

The blending process uses the alpha value of the fragment, often called the *alpha channel*, and is named *alpha blending*. The alpha channel typically contains as many bits as a color channel. If the red channel is assigned 8 bits, for example, the alpha channel may also be assigned 8 bits, leading to 32-bit RGBA color, where A stands for alpha. With 8 bits, the alpha channel can represent 256 degrees of opacity: 0 denotes "fully transparent" and 255 denotes "fully opaque." For the opacity representation, the normalized range $[0, 1]$ is preferred to the integer range $[0, 255]$. A typical blending equation is described as follows:

$$c = \alpha c_f + (1 - \alpha)c_p \tag{10.1}$$

where c is the blended color, α represents the fragment's opacity, c_f is the fragment color, and c_p is the pixel color. If α is 1, for example, the fragment is fully opaque and hides the pixel. If α is 0.5, c will be the mean of the fragment and pixel colors.

Fig. 10.3-(a) shows that the blue triangle's RGBA color is $(0, 0, 1, 0.5)$ and the red triangle's is $(1, 0, 0, 1)$. Suppose that, after processing the red triangle is completed, the blue fragment at $(38, 56)$ comes in. As shown in Fig. 10.3-(b), the color buffer at the location is updated by Equation (10.1) from red to dim magenta, which is the blended color of blue and red. The pixels at $(38, 57)$ and $(39, 56)$ are updated in the same manner.

What if the rendering order is blue-to-red triangles? At the pixel location $(38, 56)$, for example, the z-value of the incoming red fragment is 0.8. It is larger than the current value of the z-buffer, 0.5, and therefore is discarded. The red fragment does not have a chance to get blended with the blue pixel.

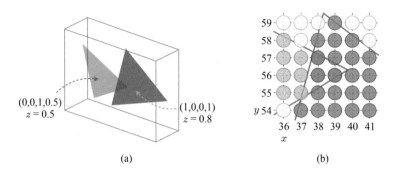

(a)   (b)

Fig. 10.3: Alpha blending: (a) The red triangle is opaque but the blue triangle is translucent. (b) In the color buffer, three pixels have the blended colors.

Even though z-buffering generally allows the primitives to be processed in an arbitrary order, it does not apply to translucent primitives. They must be processed in a *back-to-front* order after all opaque primitives are processed. For this, the translucent objects should be *sorted*. Unfortunately, sorting triangles is not an easy problem. For example, the view direction may change frame by frame, and sorting based on the view direction should be done in real time. The more triangles we have, the more computational overhead we encounter.

Sample code 10-2 GL program for alpha blending

```
1:  glEnable(GL_BLEND);
2:  glBlendFunc(GL_SRC_ALPHA, GL_ONE_MINUS_SRC_ALPHA);
3:  glBlendEquation(GL_FUNC_ADD);
```

Sample code 10-2 shows the GL code for alpha blending. As is the case for z-buffering, alpha blending must be enabled by invoking `glEnable`. Then, the method of blending a pixel with a fragment is specified via `glBlendFunc` and `glBlendEquation`. The first argument of `glBlendFunc` specifies the weight of the fragment, and the second argument specifies that of the pixel. In Sample code 10-2, `GL_SRC_ALPHA` means α of the fragment, which is often called source, and `GL_ONE_MINUS_SRC_ALPHA` means $1 - \alpha$. The weighted colors are combined using the operator defined by `glBlendEquation`, the default argument of which is `GL_FUNC_ADD`. Sample code 10-2 implements Equation (10.1).

Exercises

1. Consider four triangles competing for a pixel location. They have distinct depth values at the pixel location. If the triangles are processed in an arbitrary order, how many times would the z-buffer be updated on average for the pixel location?

2. You have three surface points competing for a pixel location. Their RGBA colors and z-coordinates are given as follows: $\{(1,0,0,0.5),0.25\}$, $\{(0,1,0,0.5),0.5\}$, and $\{(0,0,1,1),0.75\}$. They are processed in the back-to-front order. Compute the final color of the pixel.

3. Consider three triangles in the viewport. They are all perpendicular to the z-axis. The red triangle is behind the green, which is behind the blue. Three fragments with RGBA colors, $(1,0,0,1)$, $(0,1,0,0.5)$ and $(0,0,1,0.5)$, compete for a pixel location and they are processed in the back-to-front order. Compute the final color of the pixel.

4. Consider five fragments competing for a pixel location. Their RGBA colors and z-coordinates are given as follows:
   $f_1 = \{(1,0,0,0.5),0.2\}$
   $f_2 = \{(0,1,1,0.5),0.4\}$
   $f_3 = \{(0,0,1,1),0.6\}$
   $f_4 = \{(1,0,1,0.5),0.8\}$
   $f_5 = \{(0,1,0,1),1.0\}$

   (a) What is the correct order of processing the fragments?

   (b) Compute the final color of the pixel.

5. Fog is often used to enhance the realism of outdoor scenes. The simplest implementation is a *linear* fog, which starts from the near plane and ends at the far plane of the view frustum. The objects located at the near plane are clearly visible whereas objects at the far plane are completely obscured by the fog. Such a linear fog can be described by the following blending equation:
   $$c = fc_f + (1 - f)c_o$$
   where c is the fogged color, f represents the fog factor which increases with the distance from the viewer, c_f is the fog color, and c_o is the fragment color. Define the fog factor f as a function of the near plane's depth (denoted as N) and the far plane's depth (denoted as F).

6. Consider three polygons shown below. They occlude one another in a circle.

(a) Assume that the polygons are translucent and the rendering order is red, green, and then blue. Sketch the rendered result.

(b) What problem do you find? How would you resolve the problem?

Part II
Advanced Topics

Chapter 11

Euler Transforms and Quaternions

A rotation applied to an object changes its orientation. In Section 4.3.2, we defined rotations about the principal axes. This chapter first shows that a combination of such rotations gives an object an arbitrary orientation, and then presents how to rotate an object about an arbitrary axis, which is not necessarily a principal axis.

11.1 Euler Transforms

The *Euler transform* is defined as a succession of rotations about three principal axes. The rotation axes can be taken from the fixed coordinate system, such as the world space, or from the object space that rotates together with the object.

11.1.1 World-space Euler Transforms

Suppose that we successively rotate an object about the x-, y-, and z-axes of the world space, as shown in Fig. 11.1-(a). The rotation angles are called the *Euler angles*. The rotation matrices defined by the Euler angles are combined into a single matrix:

$$R_z(-45°)R_y(60°)R_x(45°) = \begin{pmatrix} \frac{\sqrt{2}}{2} & \frac{\sqrt{2}}{2} & 0 \\ -\frac{\sqrt{2}}{2} & \frac{\sqrt{2}}{2} & 0 \\ 0 & 0 & 1 \end{pmatrix} \begin{pmatrix} \frac{1}{2} & 0 & \frac{\sqrt{3}}{2} \\ 0 & 1 & 0 \\ -\frac{\sqrt{3}}{2} & 0 & \frac{1}{2} \end{pmatrix} \begin{pmatrix} 1 & 0 & 0 \\ 0 & \frac{\sqrt{2}}{2} & -\frac{\sqrt{2}}{2} \\ 0 & \frac{\sqrt{2}}{2} & \frac{\sqrt{2}}{2} \end{pmatrix}$$

$$= \begin{pmatrix} \frac{\sqrt{2}}{4} & \frac{2+\sqrt{3}}{4} & \frac{-2+\sqrt{3}}{4} \\ -\frac{\sqrt{2}}{4} & \frac{2-\sqrt{3}}{4} & \frac{-2-\sqrt{3}}{4} \\ -\frac{\sqrt{3}}{2} & \frac{\sqrt{2}}{4} & \frac{\sqrt{2}}{4} \end{pmatrix}$$

The orientation of the teapot shown on the right of Fig. 11.1-(a) cannot be obtained by a single rotation about a principal axis.

The rotation axes are not necessarily taken in the order of x, y, and z. Fig. 11.1-(b) shows the order of y, x, and z. Observe that the teapots in Fig. 11.1-(a) and -(b) have different orientations.

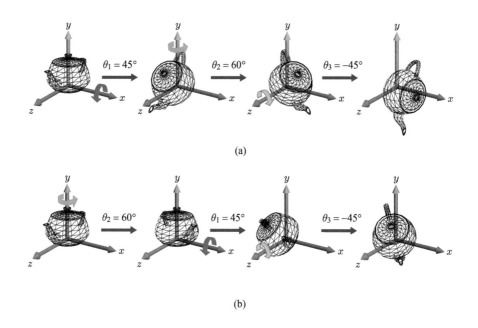

Fig. 11.1: The Euler transforms are made with the fixed global coordinate system, i.e., with the world space. (a) The rotations are in the order of the x-, y-, and z-axes. (b) The rotations are in the order of the y-, x-, and z-axes.

11.1.2 Object-space Euler Transforms[*]

The Euler transform was presented with the world space, but it can be defined with respect to the object space. In Fig. 11.2-(a), the object is successively rotated about its object-space basis vectors, which we denote by u, v, and n.

When the object is first rotated about u, the other basis vectors, v and n which are stuck to the object, are rotated accordingly. Consequently, v is no longer parallel to the y-axis of the world space, making the next rotation about v totally different from the rotation about the y-axis. In Fig. 11.1-(a) and Fig. 11.2-(a), the same sequence of Euler angles is used but the final orientations are different.

Let us compute the matrix for the object-space Euler transform. First of all, consider $R_v(\theta_2)R_u(\theta_1)$, i.e., rotating about u by θ_1 and then rotating about v by θ_2. Because the object space is initially identical to the world space, $R_u(\theta_1)$ equals $R_x(\theta_1)$. We know the matrix for R_x. It was defined in Equation (4.35).

How about $R_v(\theta_2)$? Due to $R_u(\theta_1)$, v is no longer parallel to the y-axis but becomes an arbitrary axis in the world space. We do not know the matrix for

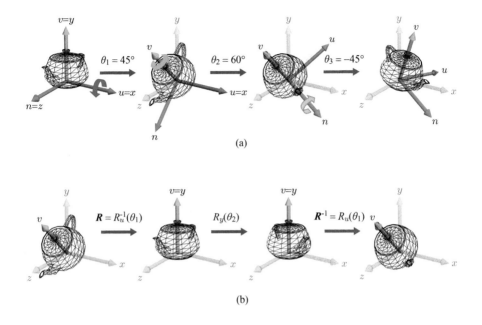

Fig. 11.2: Object-space Euler transforms: (a) The Euler transform is made with the object space. (b) $R_v(\theta_2)$ is defined as a combination of three simple rotations.

such a rotation about an arbitrary axis. Fortunately, $R_v(\theta_2)$ is conceptually defined as a combination of three matrices, as illustrated in Fig. 11.2-(b): (1) The matrix that rotates v onto the y-axis, which we denote by $\boldsymbol{R}$. (2) The matrix for rotation about the y-axis by θ_2, i.e., $R_y(\theta_2)$, which we do know. It was defined in Equation (4.36). (3) The inverse of $\boldsymbol{R}$.

Observe that $\boldsymbol{R}$ undoes $R_u(\theta_1)$, restoring v to the y-axis. $\boldsymbol{R}$ equals $R_u^{-1}(\theta_1)$. Therefore, the object-space Euler transform $R_v(\theta_2)R_u(\theta_1)$ is defined as follows:

$$\begin{aligned} R_v(\theta_2)R_u(\theta_1) &= \boldsymbol{R}^{-1}R_y(\theta_2)\boldsymbol{R}R_u(\theta_1) \\ &= [R_u^{-1}(\theta_1)]^{-1}R_y(\theta_2)R_u^{-1}(\theta_1)R_u(\theta_1) \\ &= R_u(\theta_1)R_y(\theta_2) \\ &= R_x(\theta_1)R_y(\theta_2) \end{aligned} \qquad (11.1)$$

It asserts that the object-space Euler transform (with u first and then v) is implemented as if the Euler angles were applied "in reverse order" to the world-space axes (with y first and then x).

Now consider the object-space Euler transform with all of three axes involved: $R_n(\theta_3)R_v(\theta_2)R_u(\theta_1)$. As in the case of $R_v(\theta_2)$ presented above, $R_n(\theta_3)$ is conceptually defined as a combination of three matrices, as illus-

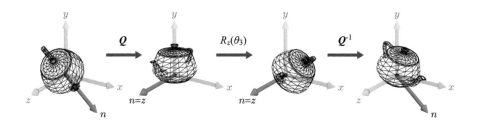

Fig. 11.3: $R_n(\theta_3)$ is defined as a combination of three rotations.

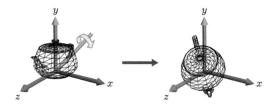

Fig. 11.4: The teapot is rotated about a non-principal axis to have an arbitrary orientation.

trated in Fig. 11.3: (1) The matrix that rotates n onto the z-axis, which we denote by Q. (2) The matrix for rotation about the z-axis by θ_3, i.e., $R_z(\theta_3)$, which we do know. It was defined in Equation (4.31). (3) The inverse of Q.

Let $R_v(\theta_2)R_u(\theta_1)$ be denoted by P. Then, Q equals P^{-1}, and the object-space Euler transform $R_n(\theta_3)R_v(\theta_2)R_u(\theta_1)$ is defined as follows:

$$
\begin{aligned}
R_n(\theta_3)R_v(\theta_2)R_u(\theta_1) &= Q^{-1}R_z(\theta_3)QP \\
&= [P^{-1}]^{-1}R_z(\theta_3)P^{-1}P \\
&= PR_z(\theta_3) \\
&= R_v(\theta_2)R_u(\theta_1)R_z(\theta_3) \\
&= R_x(\theta_1)R_y(\theta_2)R_z(\theta_3)
\end{aligned}
\tag{11.2}
$$

The last line is obtained because $R_v(\theta_2)R_u(\theta_1) = R_x(\theta_1)R_y(\theta_2)$, as presented in Equation (11.1). It is again found that the object-space Euler transform (with the axis order of u, v, and then n) is implemented as if the Euler angles were applied in reverse order to the world-space axes (z, y, and then x).

A more direct method of defining an arbitrary orientation is to use a non-principal axis, as shown in Fig. 11.4. Section 11.3 will give in-depth discussions on this method.

11.2 Euler Transforms for Keyframe Animation

In real-time computer animation, the sequence of motions created by an artist is played back at run time. However, the artist does not define the motions of all frames. For a 60-fps animation, for example, much fewer than 60 frames are defined per second by the artist. Such frames in distinct time steps are called the *keyframes*. The *in-between frames* are automatically filled at run time. This keyframe-based technique originated from traditional hand-drawn cartoon animations, where the senior key artist drew the keyframes and the junior artist filled the in-between frames.

11.2.1 2D Keyframe Animation

In order to generate the in-between frames, the key data assigned to the keyframes are *interpolated*. In theory, any data that change in the time domain can be interpolated. Typical examples include the positions, orientations, and scaling factors of the objects.

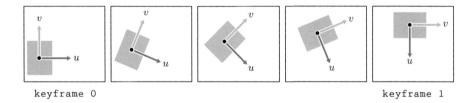

keyframe 0   keyframe 1

Fig. 11.5: The positions and orientations in the keyframes are interpolated to generate the in-between frames. The coordinate system bound to the rectangle represents its object space.

Consider the 2D example in Fig. 11.5. The pose data for **keyframe 0** and **keyframe 1** are $\{p_0, \theta_0\}$ and $\{p_1, \theta_1\}$, respectively, where p_i denotes the position of the rectangle's center and θ_i denotes the rotation angle that defines the orientation. The keyframe data are interpolated to describe the rectangle's poses in the in-between frames.

Consider parameter t in the normalized range $[0, 1]$. Suppose that $t = 0$ for **keyframe 0** and $t = 1$ for **keyframe 1**. The rectangle's position in the frame at t is defined through *linear interpolation*:

$$p(t) = (1 - t)p_0 + tp_1 \tag{11.3}$$

The keyframe orientations are also linearly interpolated:

$$\theta(t) = (1 - t)\theta_0 + t\theta_1 \qquad (11.4)$$

Such $p(t)$ and $\theta(t)$ define the rectangle's pose in the frame with t. If $t = 0.5$, for example, the rectangle's position is $(p_0 + p_1)/2$ and the orientation is defined by $(\theta_0 + \theta_1)/2$. The position and orientation generate the frame in the middle of Fig. 11.5.

11.2.2   3D Keyframe Animation

The linear interpolation also works for 3D keyframe animation. Fig. 11.6-(a) shows teapots in three keyframes. The coordinate system shown in the middle is the world space. The teapot at `keyframe 0` is located on the $-x$ axis and is translated along the axis to define the teapot at `keyframe 1`. No rotation is made between the keyframes.

In Fig. 11.6-(b), the black dots represent the key data, and linear interpolations of the data are illustrated as line segments. The orientation column shows the rotation angles about the principal axes, θ_x, θ_y, and θ_z. They are *Euler angles*. As the teapot does not rotate between `keyframe 0` and `keyframe 1`, the three graphs remain zero in the interval. In contrast, in the position column, x increases between `keyframe 0` and `keyframe 1` but y and z remain zero.

Now consider the transition from `keyframe 1` to `keyframe 2`. The teapot at `keyframe 1` is first rotated about the x-axis by $90°$ and then rotated about the z-axis by $-90°$, i.e., clockwise $90°$. Then, $(\theta_x, \theta_y, \theta_z) = (90°, 0°, -90°)$. The Euler angles are depicted in the orientation column in Fig. 11.6-(b). After being rotated, the teapot is translated on the xy-plane. The position column in Fig. 11.6-(b) shows that the x-coordinate increases whereas the y-coordinate decreases between `keyframe 1` and `keyframe 2`. The z-coordinate remains zero, implying that the teapot slides on the xy-plane.

In order to create an in-between frame, the six graphs in Fig. 11.6-(b) are sampled to obtain the Euler angles $(\theta_x, \theta_y, \theta_z)$ and the position (x, y, z). The interpolated data define the teapot's pose. Fig. 11.6-(c) shows the keyframes and the in-between frames together. It shows that the colors of the teapot can also be interpolated.

In general, the GUI of a modeling and animation package provides the artist with the graphs shown in Fig. 11.6-(b) for interactive editing. The graphs are not limited to piecewise line segments representing linear interpolations. Higher-order interpolations can be chosen, as shown in Fig. 11.7-(a), and the curve can be altered by hand. Fig. 11.7-(b) shows the resulting animation obtained using the curve in Fig. 11.7-(a).

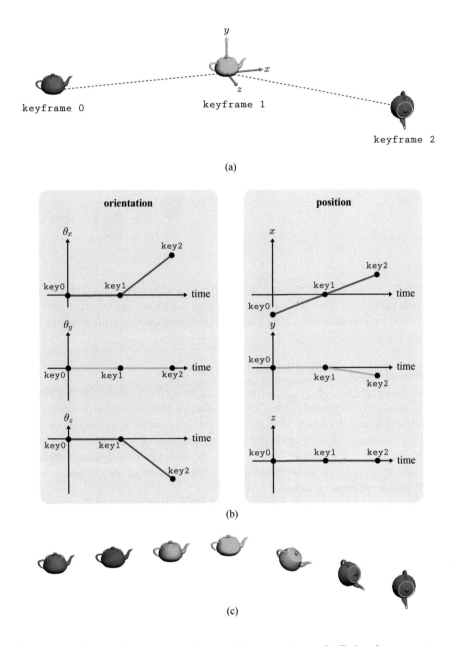

Fig. 11.6: 3D keyframe animation is the extension of 2D keyframe animation. The positions and orientations of the keyframes are interpolated. (a) Keyframes. (b) Graphs defined by the key data. (c) Keyframes and in-between frames.

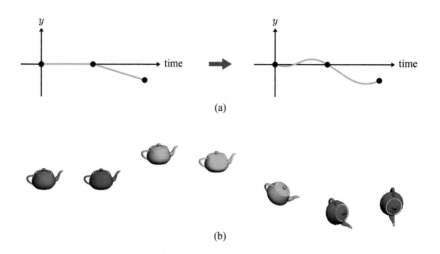

(a)

(b)

Fig. 11.7: Smoother animations may often be obtained using higher-order interpolations. (a) The y-coordinates of key positions are interpolated by a curve, not by line segments. (b) The teapot traverses along a smoother path.

11.2.3 Interpolation of Euler Angles

The Euler angles, $(\theta_x, \theta_y, \theta_z)$, provide an intuitive method for defining an orientation. Unfortunately, they are not always correctly interpolated. Consider the L-shaped object in Fig. 11.8. A successive application of Euler angles is given in Fig. 11.8-(a). The orientation of the object is defined by $(0°, 90°, 0°)$. The object in Fig. 11.8-(b) has the orientation defined by $(90°, 45°, 90°)$. Let us take them as the orientations of keyframe 0 (when $t = 0$) and keyframe 1 (when $t = 1$).

Consider an in-between frame with t 0.5. The orientation obtained by interpolating the Euler angles is $(45°, 67.5°, 45°)$. Fig. 11.8-(c) shows a successive application of the interpolated Euler angles. Observe that the x-coordinates of the object's end points are not zero, i.e., the object does not lie in the yz-plane. It is an unexpected result because both objects in the keyframes lie in the yz-plane and therefore the object at any in-between frame is expected to do so.

This shows that Euler angles are not suitable for keyframe animation because they are not always correctly interpolated. An alternative to Euler angles is *quaternions* [6]. They compactly represent rotations and prove to be correctly interpolated.

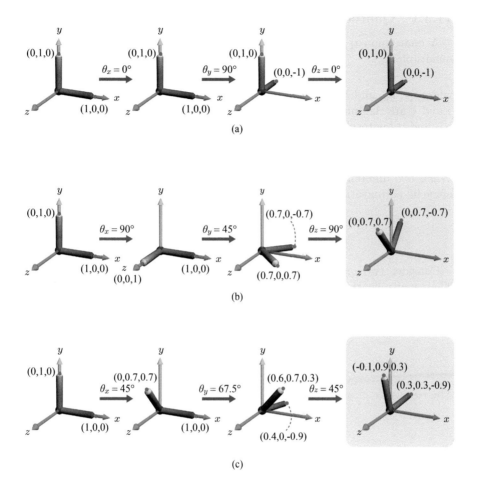

Fig. 11.8: Euler angles are widely used for representing arbitrary orientations but are not always correctly interpolated.

11.3 Quaternions

The theory of quaternions is not simple. This section presents its minimum so that the readers are not discouraged from learning the beauty of quaternions.

11.3.1   Quaternion Representation

A quaternion $\mathbf{q}$ is an extended *complex number* and is represented as a quadruple:

$$(q_x, q_y, q_z, q_w) = q_x i + q_y j + q_z k + q_w \tag{11.5}$$

where q_x, q_y, and q_z represent the *imaginary part*, q_w is the *real part*, and i, j and k are the imaginary units. The imaginary part is often abbreviated to $\mathbf{q}_v$, and a quaternion is denoted by $(\mathbf{q}_v, q_w)$. The imaginary units have the following properties:

$$i^2 = j^2 = k^2 = -1 \tag{11.6}$$

When two different imaginary units are multiplied, the following properties of cyclic permutation are observed:

$$\begin{array}{l} ij = k, ji = -k \\ jk = i, kj = -i \\ ki = j, ik = -j \end{array} \tag{11.7}$$

Consider two quaternions, $\mathbf{p} = (p_x, p_y, p_z, p_w)$ and $\mathbf{q} = (q_x, q_y, q_z, q_w)$. Their multiplication returns another quaternion:

$$\begin{aligned} \mathbf{pq} &= (p_x i + p_y j + p_z k + p_w)(q_x i + q_y j + q_z k + q_w) \\ &= (p_x q_w + p_y q_z - p_z q_y + p_w q_x)i + \\ &\quad (-p_x q_z + p_y q_w + p_z q_x + p_w q_y)j + \\ &\quad (p_x q_y - p_y q_x + p_z q_w + p_w q_z)k + \\ &\quad (-p_x q_x - p_y q_y - p_z q_z + p_w q_w) \end{aligned} \tag{11.8}$$

The *conjugate* of quaternion $\mathbf{q}$ is defined as follows:

$$\begin{aligned} \mathbf{q}^* &= (-\mathbf{q}_v, q_w) \\ &= (-q_x, -q_y, -q_z, q_w) \\ &= -q_x i - q_y j - q_z k + q_w \end{aligned} \tag{11.9}$$

Given two quaternions, $\mathbf{p}$ and $\mathbf{q}$, it is straightforward to show that $(\mathbf{pq})^* = \mathbf{q}^*\mathbf{p}^*$ using Equations (11.8) and (11.9).

The magnitude or norm of a quaternion is calculated in exactly the same way as in an ordinary vector:

$$\|\mathbf{q}\| = \sqrt{q_x^2 + q_y^2 + q_z^2 + q_w^2} \tag{11.10}$$

If $\|\mathbf{q}\| = 1$, $\mathbf{q}$ is called a *unit quaternion*.

11.3.2   Rotations Using Quaternions

Recall 2D rotation presented in Fig. 4.2. If a vector represented as (x, y) is rotated counter-clockwise by θ, the rotated vector is described as follows:

$$\begin{aligned} \begin{pmatrix} x' \\ y' \end{pmatrix} &= \begin{pmatrix} cos\theta & -sin\theta \\ sin\theta & cos\theta \end{pmatrix} \begin{pmatrix} x \\ y \end{pmatrix} \\ &= \begin{pmatrix} xcos\theta - ysin\theta \\ xsin\theta + ycos\theta \end{pmatrix} \end{aligned} \tag{11.11}$$

Given the vector (x, y), devise a complex number, $x + yi$, and denote it by **p**. On the other hand, given the rotation angle θ, devise a unit-length complex number, $cos\theta + sin\theta i$, and denote it by **q**. When **p** and **q** are multiplied, we have the following result:

$$
\begin{aligned}
\mathbf{pq} &= (x + yi)(cos\theta + sin\theta i) \\
&= (xcos\theta - ysin\theta) + (xsin\theta + ycos\theta)i
\end{aligned}
\tag{11.12}
$$

Surprisingly, the real and imaginary parts in Equation (11.12) are identical to x' and y' in Equation (11.11), respectively. It is found that 2D rotations can be described using complex numbers.

As extended complex numbers, quaternions are used to describe 3D rotations. In Fig. 11.9-(a), a 3D vector p is rotated about an axis u by an angle θ to define p'. To implement this rotation, p is represented in a quaternion **p**. The imaginary part of **p** is set to p, and the real part is set to 0:

$$
\begin{aligned}
\mathbf{p} &= (\mathbf{p}_v, p_w) \\
&= (p, 0)
\end{aligned}
\tag{11.13}
$$

On the other hand, u is normalized to **u**, and a *unit quaternion* **q** is defined using **u** and the rotation angle θ:

$$
\begin{aligned}
\mathbf{q} &= (\mathbf{q}_v, q_w) \\
&= (sin\tfrac{\theta}{2}\mathbf{u}, cos\tfrac{\theta}{2})
\end{aligned}
\tag{11.14}
$$

Then, "rotation of p about **u** (or u) by θ" is defined as follows:

$$
\mathbf{p}' = \mathbf{qpq}^*
\tag{11.15}
$$

Two quaternions are multiplied to define a new quaternion, as presented in Equation (11.8), and therefore **qp** is a quaternion. Multiplying it with another quaternion, $\mathbf{q}^*$, also returns a quaternion. It is $\mathbf{p}'$. Its imaginary part corresponds to the rotated vector p' whereas the real part is zero.

[Note: Proof of quaternion-based rotation]

When we denote **p** and **q** by $(\mathbf{p}_v, p_w)$ and $(\mathbf{q}_v, q_w)$, respectively, **pq** in Equation (11.8) can be rewritten as follows:

$$
\begin{aligned}
\mathbf{pq} &= (p_x q_w + p_y q_z - p_z q_y + p_w q_x)i+ \\
&\quad (-p_x q_z + p_y q_w + p_z q_x + p_w q_y)j+ \\
&\quad (p_x q_y - p_y q_x + p_z q_w + p_w q_z)k+ \\
&\quad (-p_x q_x - p_y q_y - p_z q_z + p_w q_w) \\
&= (\mathbf{p}_v \times \mathbf{q}_v + q_w \mathbf{p}_v + p_w \mathbf{q}_v, p_w q_w - \mathbf{p}_v \cdot \mathbf{q}_v)
\end{aligned}
\tag{11.16}
$$

where $\times$ represents the cross product and $\cdot$ represents the dot product.

Using Equations (11.13), (11.14), and (11.16), $\mathbf{qpq}^*$ in Equation (11.15) is expanded as follows:

$$
\begin{aligned}
\mathbf{qpq}^* &= (\mathbf{q}_v \times \mathbf{p}_v + q_w\mathbf{p}_v, -\mathbf{q}_v \cdot \mathbf{p}_v)\mathbf{q}^*\,[1] \\
&= (\mathbf{q}_v \times \mathbf{p}_v + q_w\mathbf{p}_v, -\mathbf{q}_v \cdot \mathbf{p}_v)(-\mathbf{q}_v, q_w) \\
&= ((\mathbf{q}_v \times \mathbf{p}_v + q_w\mathbf{p}_v) \times (-\mathbf{q}_v) + q_w(\mathbf{q}_v \times \mathbf{p}_v + q_w\mathbf{p}_v) + (-\mathbf{q}_v \cdot \mathbf{p}_v)(-\mathbf{q}_v), \\
&\qquad (-\mathbf{q}_v \cdot \mathbf{p}_v)q_w - (\mathbf{q}_v \times \mathbf{p}_v + q_w\mathbf{p}_v) \cdot (-\mathbf{q}_v))\,[2] \\
&= ((\mathbf{q}_v \cdot \mathbf{p}_v)\mathbf{q}_v - (\mathbf{q}_v \cdot \mathbf{q}_v)\mathbf{p}_v + 2q_w(\mathbf{q}_v \times \mathbf{p}_v) + q_w^2\mathbf{p}_v + (\mathbf{q}_v \cdot \mathbf{p}_v)\mathbf{q}_v, 0)\,[3] \\
&= (2(\mathbf{q}_v \cdot \mathbf{p}_v)\mathbf{q}_v + (q_w^2 - \|\mathbf{q}_v\|^2)\mathbf{p}_v + 2q_w(\mathbf{q}_v \times \mathbf{p}_v), 0) \\
&= (2sin^2\tfrac{\theta}{2}(\mathbf{u} \cdot \mathbf{p}_v)\mathbf{u} + (cos^2\tfrac{\theta}{2} - sin^2\tfrac{\theta}{2})\mathbf{p}_v + 2cos\tfrac{\theta}{2}sin\tfrac{\theta}{2}(\mathbf{u} \times \mathbf{p}_v), 0)\,[4] \\
&= ((1 - cos\theta)(\mathbf{u} \cdot \mathbf{p}_v)\mathbf{u} + cos\theta\mathbf{p}_v + sin\theta(\mathbf{u} \times \mathbf{p}_v), 0)\,[5] \\
&= ((\mathbf{u} \cdot \mathbf{p}_v)\mathbf{u} + cos\theta(\mathbf{p}_v - (\mathbf{u} \cdot \mathbf{p}_v)\mathbf{u}) + sin\theta(\mathbf{u} \times \mathbf{p}_v), 0)\,[6]
\end{aligned}
$$

$$(11.17)$$

where [1] is obtained as $p_w = 0$, [2] follows from Equation (11.16), the imaginary part in [3] follows from the theorem of vector triple product that asserts $\mathbf{a} \times (\mathbf{b} \times \mathbf{c}) = (\mathbf{a} \cdot \mathbf{c})\mathbf{b} - (\mathbf{a} \cdot \mathbf{b})\mathbf{c}$, the real part in [3] becomes 0 because $(\mathbf{q}_v \times \mathbf{p}_v) \cdot \mathbf{q}_v = 0$, [4] uses the definition, $\mathbf{q} = (sin\tfrac{\theta}{2}\mathbf{u}, cos\tfrac{\theta}{2})$, [5] follows from the theorems of trigonometry, $sin^2\tfrac{\theta}{2} = \tfrac{1-cos\theta}{2}$, $cos^2\tfrac{\theta}{2} = \tfrac{1+cos\theta}{2}$, and $sin2\theta = 2sin\theta cos\theta$, and [6] is obtained simply by rearranging [5].

In Fig. 11.9-(b), consider the circumference of the circle along which p is rotated to p'. The vector connecting the origin $\mathbf{O}$ to the circle's center is $(\mathbf{u} \cdot \mathbf{p}_v)\mathbf{u}$. Consider the orthogonal vectors on the circle. One is $\mathbf{u} \times \mathbf{p}_v$, and the other is $\mathbf{p}_v - (\mathbf{u} \cdot \mathbf{p}_v)\mathbf{u}$ that connects the circle's center to p. Fig. 11.9-(c) shows the circle seen from above. On the circle, p' is the sum of $cos\theta(\mathbf{p}_v - (\mathbf{u} \cdot \mathbf{p}_v)\mathbf{u})$ and $sin\theta(\mathbf{u} \times \mathbf{p}_v)$. When the displacement of the circle, $(\mathbf{u} \cdot \mathbf{p}_v)\mathbf{u}$, is added to the sum, we obtain p'. It is the imaginary part of [6] in Equation (11.17).

In Equation (11.15), $\mathbf{p}'$ represents the rotated vector p'. Consider rotating p' by another quaternion $\mathbf{r}$. It is defined and rephrased as follows:

$$
\begin{aligned}
\mathbf{rp}'\mathbf{r}^* &= \mathbf{r}(\mathbf{qpq}^*)\mathbf{r}^* \\
&= (\mathbf{rq})\mathbf{p}(\mathbf{q}^*\mathbf{r}^*) \\
&= (\mathbf{rq})\mathbf{p}(\mathbf{rq})^*
\end{aligned}
$$

$$(11.18)$$

This shows that $\mathbf{rq}$ represents the combined rotation.

As shown in Fig. 11.10, "rotation about $\mathbf{u}$ by θ" is identical to "rotation about $-\mathbf{u}$ by $-\theta$." Let us denote them by $\mathbf{q}$ and $\mathbf{r}$, respectively: $\mathbf{q}$ is defined as follows:

$$\mathbf{q} = (sin\tfrac{\theta}{2}\mathbf{u}, cos\tfrac{\theta}{2})$$

$$(11.19)$$

whereas $\mathbf{r}$ is defined and rephrased as follows:

$$
\begin{aligned}
\mathbf{r} &= (sin\tfrac{-\theta}{2}(-\mathbf{u}), cos\tfrac{-\theta}{2}) \\
&= (sin\tfrac{\theta}{2}\mathbf{u}, cos\tfrac{\theta}{2})
\end{aligned}
$$

$$(11.20)$$

This confirms that $\mathbf{q}$ and $\mathbf{r}$ are identical.

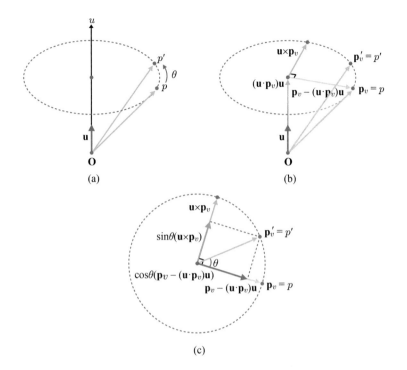

Fig. 11.9: 3D rotation: (a) Rotation of p about u by θ. (b) Two orthogonal vectors on the circle. (c) Computing p' using the orthogonal vectors.

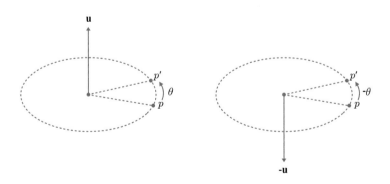

Fig. 11.10: "Rotation about $\mathbf{u}$ by θ" equals "rotation about $-\mathbf{u}$ by $-\theta$."

While $\mathbf{q}$ denotes "rotation about $\mathbf{u}$ by θ," i.e., $\mathbf{q} = (sin\frac{\theta}{2}\mathbf{u}, cos\frac{\theta}{2})$, let $\mathbf{s}$ denote "rotation about $\mathbf{u}$ by $2\pi + \theta$." Obviously $\mathbf{s} = \mathbf{q}$, and $\mathbf{s}$ is rephrased as follows:

$$\begin{aligned}\mathbf{s} &= (sin\tfrac{2\pi+\theta}{2}\mathbf{u}, cos\tfrac{2\pi+\theta}{2})\\ &= (sin(\pi+\tfrac{\theta}{2})\mathbf{u}, cos(\pi+\tfrac{\theta}{2}))\\ &= (-sin\tfrac{\theta}{2}\mathbf{u}, -cos\tfrac{\theta}{2})\end{aligned} \qquad (11.21)$$

This is $-\mathbf{q}$ in that all components of $\mathbf{q}$ are negated, i.e., $\mathbf{s} = -\mathbf{q}$. It is concluded that $\mathbf{q} = -\mathbf{q}$, i.e., $\mathbf{q}$ and $-\mathbf{q}$ represent the same rotation.

11.3.3 Interpolation of Quaternions

Consider two unit quaternions, $\mathbf{q}$ and $\mathbf{r}$, which represent rotations. They can be interpolated using the parameter t in the range of $[0, 1]$:

$$\frac{sin(\phi(1-t))}{sin\phi}\mathbf{q} + \frac{sin(\phi t)}{sin\phi}\mathbf{r} \qquad (11.22)$$

where ϕ denotes the angle between $\mathbf{q}$ and $\mathbf{r}$. The dot product of $\mathbf{q}$ and $\mathbf{r}$, $\mathbf{q} \cdot \mathbf{r}$, is defined either as $(q_x, q_y, q_z, q_w) \cdot (r_x, r_y, r_z, r_w) = q_x r_x + q_y r_y + q_z r_z + q_w r_w$ or as $\|\mathbf{q}\|\|\mathbf{r}\|cos\phi$, which is reduced to $cos\phi$ because $\|\mathbf{q}\| = \|\mathbf{r}\| = 1$. Then, $cos\phi = q_x r_x + q_y r_y + q_z r_z + q_w r_w$ and $\phi = arccos(q_x r_x + q_y r_y + q_z r_z + q_w r_w)$. Equation (11.22) is a variant of liner interpolation and is called the *spherical linear interpolation* (slerp).

[Note: Proof of spherical linear interpolation]

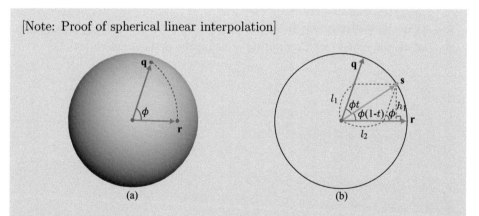

(a)   (b)

Fig. 11.11: Spherical linear interpolation on the 4D unit sphere: (a) Shortest arc between $\mathbf{q}$ and $\mathbf{r}$. (b) Spherical linear interpolation of $\mathbf{q}$ and $\mathbf{r}$ returns $\mathbf{s}$.

The set of all possible quaternions makes up a 4D unit sphere. Fig. 11.11-(a) illustrates $\mathbf{q}$ and $\mathbf{r}$ on the sphere. Note that the interpolated quaternion must lie on the shortest arc connecting $\mathbf{q}$ and $\mathbf{r}$. Fig. 11.11-(b) shows the cross section of the unit sphere. It is in fact the great circle defined by $\mathbf{q}$ and $\mathbf{r}$. The interpolated quaternion is denoted by **s** and is defined by the parallelogram rule:

$$\mathbf{s} = l_1\mathbf{q} + l_2\mathbf{r} \tag{11.23}$$

In Fig. 11.11-(b), $sin\phi = \frac{h_1}{l_1}$, and therefore $l_1 = \frac{h_1}{sin\phi}$. As $h_1 = sin(\phi(1-t))$, we can compute l_1 as follows:

$$l_1 = \frac{sin(\phi(1-t))}{sin\phi} \tag{11.24}$$

Similarly, l_2 is computed as follows:

$$l_2 = \frac{sin(\phi t)}{sin\phi} \tag{11.25}$$

When we insert Equations (11.24) and (11.25) into Equation (11.23), we obtain the slerp function presented in Equation (11.22).

11.3.4 Conversion between Quaternion and Rotation Matrix

A quaternion representing a rotation can be converted into a matrix form. If $\mathbf{q} = (q_x, q_y, q_z, q_w)$, the rotation matrix is defined as follows:

$$\mathbf{M} = \begin{pmatrix} 1 - 2(q_y^2 + q_z^2) & 2(q_xq_y - q_wq_z) & 2(q_xq_z + q_wq_y) & 0 \\ 2(q_xq_y + q_wq_z) & 1 - 2(q_x^2 + q_z^2) & 2(q_yq_z - q_wq_x) & 0 \\ 2(q_xq_z - q_wq_y) & 2(q_yq_z + q_wq_x) & 1 - 2(q_x^2 + q_y^2) & 0 \\ 0 & 0 & 0 & 1 \end{pmatrix} \tag{11.26}$$

Conversely, given a rotation matrix, we can compute the corresponding quaternion. Read the following notes.

[Note: Conversion from a quaternion to a rotation matrix]

Notice that each component of **pq** presented in Equation (11.8) is a linear combination of p_x, p_y, p_z and p_w. Therefore, **pq** can be represented by a matrix-vector multiplication form:

$$\mathbf{pq} = \begin{pmatrix} q_w & q_z & -q_y & q_x \\ -q_z & q_w & q_x & q_y \\ q_y & -q_x & q_w & q_z \\ -q_x & -q_y & -q_z & q_w \end{pmatrix} \begin{pmatrix} p_x \\ p_y \\ p_z \\ p_w \end{pmatrix} = M_{\mathbf{q}}\mathbf{p} \tag{11.27}$$

where $M_{\mathbf{q}}$ is a 4×4 matrix built upon the components of **q**. Each component of **pq** in Equation (11.8) is also a linear combination of q_x, q_y, q_z and q_w, and therefore **pq** can be represented by another matrix-vector multiplication

form:
$$\mathbf{pq} = \begin{pmatrix} p_w & -p_z & p_y & p_x \\ p_z & p_w & -p_x & p_y \\ -p_y & p_x & p_w & p_z \\ -p_x & -p_y & -p_z & p_w \end{pmatrix} \begin{pmatrix} q_x \\ q_y \\ q_z \\ q_w \end{pmatrix} = N_\mathbf{p} \mathbf{q} \tag{11.28}$$

where $N_\mathbf{p}$ is a 4×4 matrix built upon the components of $\mathbf{p}$.

Then, $\mathbf{qpq}^*$ in Equation (11.15) is expanded as follows:

$$\begin{aligned} \mathbf{qpq}^* &= (\mathbf{qp})\mathbf{q}^* \\ &= M_{\mathbf{q}^*}(\mathbf{qp}) \\ &= M_{\mathbf{q}^*}(N_\mathbf{q}\mathbf{p}) \\ &= (M_{\mathbf{q}^*}N_\mathbf{q})\mathbf{p} \\ &= \begin{pmatrix} q_w & -q_z & q_y & -q_x \\ q_z & q_w & -q_x & -q_y \\ -q_y & q_x & q_w & -q_z \\ q_x & q_y & q_z & q_w \end{pmatrix} \begin{pmatrix} q_w & -q_z & q_y & q_x \\ q_z & q_w & -q_x & q_y \\ -q_y & q_x & q_w & q_z \\ -q_x & -q_y & -q_z & q_w \end{pmatrix} \begin{pmatrix} p_x \\ p_y \\ p_z \\ p_w \end{pmatrix} \end{aligned} \tag{11.29}$$

$M_{\mathbf{q}^*}N_\mathbf{q}$ returns a 4×4 matrix. Consider its first element, $(q_w^2 - q_z^2 - q_y^2 + q_x^2)$. As $\mathbf{q}$ is a unit quaternion, $q_x^2 + q_y^2 + q_z^2 + q_w^2 = 1$. The first element is rewritten as $(1 - 2(q_y^2 + q_z^2))$. When all of the 4×4 elements are processed in similar manners, $M_{\mathbf{q}^*}N_\mathbf{q}$ is proven to be $\mathbf{M}$ in Equation (11.26).

[Note: Conversion from a rotation matrix to a quaternion]

Converting a rotation matrix into a quaternion is equivalent to extracting q_x, q_y, q_z, and q_w from the matrix $\mathbf{M}$ in Equation (11.26). Let us first compute the *trace* of $\mathbf{M}$, $tr(\mathbf{M})$, which is defined as the sum of all diagonal elements:

$$\begin{aligned} tr(\mathbf{M}) &= 4 - 4(q_x^2 + q_y^2 + q_z^2) \\ &= 4 - 4(1 - q_w^2) \\ &= 4q_w^2 \end{aligned} \tag{11.30}$$

The real part, q_w, is $\pm\sqrt{tr(\mathbf{M})}/2$. Now consider two elements in $\mathbf{M}$: $m_{21} = 2(q_xq_y + q_wq_z)$ and $m_{12} = 2(q_xq_y - q_wq_z)$. Let us subtract m_{12} from m_{21}:

$$\begin{aligned} m_{21} - m_{12} &= 2(q_xq_y + q_wq_z) - 2(q_xq_y - q_wq_z) \\ &= 4q_wq_z \end{aligned} \tag{11.31}$$

Since we know q_w, we can compute q_z. It is $\frac{m_{21}-m_{12}}{4q_w}$. In the same manner, q_x and q_y can be computed: $q_x = \frac{m_{32}-m_{23}}{4q_w}$ and $q_y = \frac{m_{13}-m_{31}}{4q_w}$. As we have two values for q_w, which are $\pm\sqrt{tr(\mathbf{M})}/2$, we obtain two quaternions: when one is denoted by $\mathbf{q}$, the other is $-\mathbf{q}$. Section 11.3.2 showed that $\mathbf{q}$ and $-\mathbf{q}$ represent the same rotation.

Exercises

1. Shown below are teapots at three keyframes and the position graphs for keyframe animation. Draw the orientation graphs.

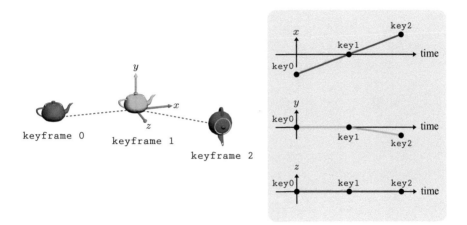

2. Let $\{u, v, n\}$ represent the object-space basis. Suppose that an object is rotated about the n-axis by θ_n and then rotated about the u-axis by θ_u. Describe the object-space Euler transform, $R_u(\theta_u)R_n(\theta_n)$, as a combination of world-space rotation matrices. (The rotation matrices about the world-space x-, y-, and z-axes are denoted as R_x, R_y, and R_z, respectively.)

3. Consider rotating $(0, 1, 0)$ about $(1, 0, 1)$ by $90°$.

   (a) Write the quaternion that represents "rotation about $(1, 0, 1)$ by $90°$." [Hint: The imaginary part of a quaternion contains the sine function and the real part contains the cosine function.]

   (b) In order to rotate $(0, 1, 0)$ using the above quaternion, $(0, 1, 0)$ should also be represented in a quaternion. Write it.

   (c) When $\mathbf{q}$ and $\mathbf{p}$ denote the quaternions in (a) and (b), respectively, $\mathbf{qpq}^*$ defines the rotation of $(0, 1, 0)$ about $(1, 0, 1)$ by $90°$. Compute $\mathbf{qp}$ and $\mathbf{q}^*$. [Hint: $ij = k$.]

4. Let $\mathbf{q}$ denote the quaternion for "rotation about a unit vector $\mathbf{u}$ by θ." Prove that $-\mathbf{q}$ represents the same rotation.

Chapter 12

Screen-space Object Manipulation

An operation frequently used in 3D graphics applications is to pick or select an object from the screen. Another is to rotate an object, for example, by sliding a finger on a touchscreen. Such object picking and rotating algorithms are seemingly complicated but are implemented by combining the transforms we have learned so far.

12.1 Picking an Object

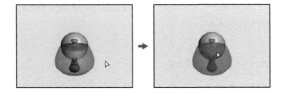

Fig. 12.1: On the 2D screen, both the teapot and sphere are at the position clicked by mouse. The teapot in front of the sphere is selected.

On a touchscreen, an object can be picked by tapping it with a finger. On a PC screen, mouse clicking is popularly used for the same purpose, as shown in Fig. 12.1. The screen-space image is an array of pixels, and each pixel is not associated with any object information. A screen touch or mouse click simply returns the 2D pixel coordinates (x_s, y_s), and we need a procedure to identify the selected object using (x_s, y_s).

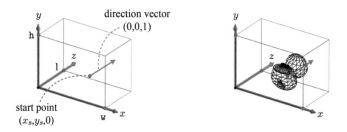

Fig. 12.2: Clicking on (x_s, y_s) returns a 3D ray starting from $(x_s, y_s, 0)$.

12.1.1   Screen-space Ray

A 3D viewport is defined by six parameters: (minX, minY) for the lower-left corner's coordinates, w×h for the resolution, and [minZ, maxZ] for the depth range. Consider a viewport shown in Fig. 12.2, where both minX and minY are zero, and minZ and maxZ are 0.0 and 1.0, respectively.

Given the pixel position (x_s, y_s), we can define a 3D screen-space *ray* with the *start point*, $(x_s, y_s, 0)$, and the *direction vector*, $(0, 0, 1)$. We need ray-object intersection tests to find the object that is *first* hit by the ray. It is the teapot in our example. However, it is not good to compute the intersections in the screen space because the screen-space information available to us is about the pixels or fragments, not about the objects. Our solution is to transform the screen-space ray back to the object spaces and do the intersection tests in the object spaces. Section 12.1.2 presents the back-transform from the screen space to the camera space and Section 12.1.3 presents that from the camera space to the object space.

12.1.2   Camera-space Ray

Fig. 12.3 shows the flow from the camera space to the screen space. Conceptually, we will go up-stream to compute the start point and direction vector of the ray in the camera space. Note that the near plane of the view frustum is transformed to the xy-plane of the screen space, where the screen-space ray starts. Thus, the camera-space ray's start point is represented by $(x_c, y_c, -n)$. Its z-coordinate is fixed to $-n$. We need to compute x_c and y_c.

The projection matrix presented in Equation (5.12) is applied to $(x_c, y_c, -n)$.

$$\begin{pmatrix} m_{11} & 0 & 0 & 0 \\ 0 & m_{22} & 0 & 0 \\ 0 & 0 & -\frac{f+n}{f-n} & -\frac{2nf}{f-n} \\ 0 & 0 & -1 & 0 \end{pmatrix} \begin{pmatrix} x_c \\ y_c \\ -n \\ 1 \end{pmatrix} = \begin{pmatrix} m_{11}x_c \\ m_{22}y_c \\ -n \\ n \end{pmatrix} \rightarrow \begin{pmatrix} \frac{m_{11}x_c}{n} \\ \frac{m_{22}y_c}{n} \\ -1 \\ 1 \end{pmatrix} \qquad (12.1)$$

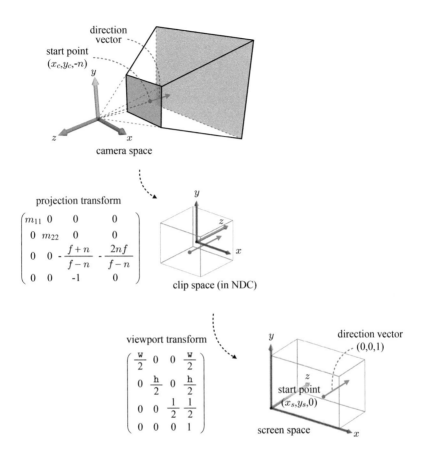

Fig. 12.3: The camera-space ray's start point, $(x_c, y_c, -n)$, can be computed using the projection and viewport transforms. The direction vector of the ray is obtained by connecting the origin and the start point.

where m_{11} and m_{22} represent $\frac{cot\frac{fovy}{2}}{aspect}$ and $cot\frac{fovy}{2}$, respectively, and $\rightarrow$ implies perspective division. The point is then transformed to the screen space by the viewport matrix presented in Equation (7.4):

$$\begin{pmatrix} \frac{w}{2} & 0 & 0 & \frac{w}{2} \\ 0 & \frac{h}{2} & 0 & \frac{h}{2} \\ 0 & 0 & \frac{1}{2} & \frac{1}{2} \\ 0 & 0 & 0 & 1 \end{pmatrix} \begin{pmatrix} \frac{m_{11}x_c}{n} \\ \frac{m_{22}y_c}{n} \\ -1 \\ 1 \end{pmatrix} = \begin{pmatrix} \frac{w}{2}\left(\frac{m_{11}x_c}{n} + 1\right) \\ \frac{h}{2}\left(\frac{m_{22}y_c}{n} + 1\right) \\ 0 \\ 1 \end{pmatrix} \tag{12.2}$$

In Equation (12.2), the x- and y-coordinates of the screen-space ray should be identical to x_s and y_s, respectively. Then, x_c and y_c are computed, and we obtain the start point of the camera-space ray:

$$
\begin{pmatrix} x_c \\ y_c \\ -n \\ 1 \end{pmatrix} = \begin{pmatrix} \frac{n}{m_{11}}\left(\frac{2x_s}{w} - 1\right) \\ \frac{n}{m_{22}}\left(\frac{2y_s}{h} - 1\right) \\ -n \\ 1 \end{pmatrix}
\tag{12.3}
$$

It is simple to compute the direction vector of the camera-space ray. Recall that the view frustum is considered to be a pencil of projection lines converging on the origin of the camera space. Therefore, if we extend the camera-space ray backward, it reaches the origin, as illustrated in Fig. 12.3. The direction vector is obtained by connecting the origin and the start point:

$$
\begin{pmatrix} \frac{n}{m_{11}}\left(\frac{2x_s}{w} - 1\right) \\ \frac{n}{m_{22}}\left(\frac{2y_s}{h} - 1\right) \\ -n \\ 1 \end{pmatrix} - \begin{pmatrix} 0 \\ 0 \\ 0 \\ 1 \end{pmatrix} = \begin{pmatrix} \frac{n}{m_{11}}\left(\frac{2x_s}{w} - 1\right) \\ \frac{n}{m_{22}}\left(\frac{2y_s}{h} - 1\right) \\ -n \\ 0 \end{pmatrix} \rightarrow \begin{pmatrix} \frac{1}{m_{11}}\left(\frac{2x_s}{w} - 1\right) \\ \frac{1}{m_{22}}\left(\frac{2y_s}{h} - 1\right) \\ -1 \\ 0 \end{pmatrix}
\tag{12.4}
$$

As all coordinates of the direction vector contain n, division by n, denoted by $\rightarrow$, leads to a simplified vector.

12.1.3　Object-space Ray

We have computed the camera-space ray. It will be transformed back to the world space and then to the object space. Obviously, the back-transform from the camera space to the world space is done by the *inverse* of the view transform. Note that, as presented in Equation (5.10), the view transform M_{view} is a translation followed by a rotation, which we denote by RT. Then, its inverse, M_{view}^{-1}, is $T^{-1}R^{-1}$. T is a translation by $-\mathbf{EYE}$, and therefore T^{-1} is a translation by $\mathbf{EYE}$. The inverse of a rotation is simply its transpose. Then, M_{view}^{-1} is defined as follows:

$$
\begin{aligned}
M_{view}^{-1} &= (RT)^{-1} \\
&= T^{-1}R^{-1} \\
&= \begin{pmatrix} 1 & 0 & 0 & \mathbf{EYE}_x \\ 0 & 1 & 0 & \mathbf{EYE}_y \\ 0 & 0 & 1 & \mathbf{EYE}_z \\ 0 & 0 & 0 & 1 \end{pmatrix} \begin{pmatrix} u_x & v_x & n_x & 0 \\ u_y & v_y & n_y & 0 \\ u_z & v_z & n_z & 0 \\ 0 & 0 & 0 & 1 \end{pmatrix} \\
&= \begin{pmatrix} u_x & v_x & n_x & \mathbf{EYE}_x \\ u_y & v_y & n_y & \mathbf{EYE}_y \\ u_z & v_z & n_z & \mathbf{EYE}_z \\ 0 & 0 & 0 & 1 \end{pmatrix}
\end{aligned}
\tag{12.5}
$$

This transforms the camera-space ray to the world space. The first step shown in Fig. 12.4 is completed.

Note that, in Fig. 12.4, the teapot and sphere have their own world transforms. Their inverses are applied to the world-space ray. We then have a

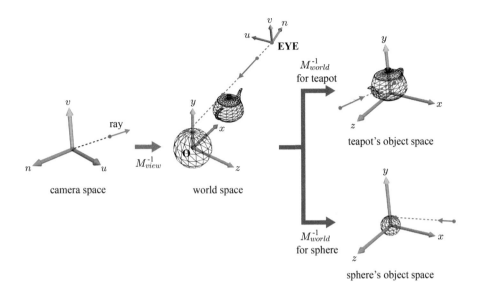

Fig. 12.4: The camera-space ray is transformed into the world space using the inverse view transform. Then, the world-space ray is transformed to the object spaces of the teapot and sphere using the inverse world transforms.

distinct ray in each object space. The parametric equation of a ray is defined as follows:

$$p(t) = s + td \qquad (12.6)$$

where s denotes the start point, t is the parameter in the range of $[0, \infty]$, and d is the direction vector. See Fig. 12.5. Obviously, the coordinates of s in the teapot's object space are different from those in the sphere's. This is also the case for d. The next subsections present how to use these object-space rays to identify the first-hit object.

12.1.4 Intersection between Ray and Bounding Volume

In order to determine if a ray hits an object represented in a polygon mesh, we have to perform a ray-triangle intersection test for *every* triangle of the object. If there exists at least one triangle intersecting the ray, the object is judged to be hit by the ray. Unfortunately, processing every triangle is costly. A less accurate but faster method is to approximate a polygon mesh with a *bounding volume* (BV) that completely contains the polygon mesh and then do the ray-BV intersection test.

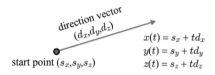

$$x(t) = s_x + td_x$$
$$y(t) = s_y + td_y$$
$$z(t) = s_z + td_z$$

Fig. 12.5: A 3D ray is represented as a parametric equation.

Fig. 12.6: The most popular bounding volumes are the AABB and bounding sphere.

Fig. 12.6 shows two popular BVs: *axis-aligned bounding box* (AABB) and *bounding sphere*. The geometry of a BV is usually much simpler than that of the input polygon mesh. An AABB is represented by the extents along the principal axes, i.e., $[x_{min}, x_{max}]$, $[y_{min}, y_{max}]$, and $[z_{min}, z_{max}]$. A bounding sphere is represented by its center and radius.

Fig. 12.7 shows in 2D space how to construct the AABB and bounding sphere. The AABB is the simplest BV to create. Its extents are initialized by the coordinates of a vertex in the input polygon mesh. Then, the remaining vertices are visited one at a time to update the extents.

A brute-force method to create a bounding sphere is to use the AABB. The center and diagonal of the AABB determine the center and diameter of the bounding sphere, respectively. Fig. 12.7-(c) shows the bounding sphere constructed from the AABB of Fig. 12.7-(b). Unfortunately, such an AABB-based bounding sphere is often too large to tightly bound the polygon mesh. In contrast, Fig. 12.7-(d) shows a tight bounding sphere. There are many algorithms to create a tight or an optimal bounding sphere.

Fig. 12.8 compares the intersection tests: one with the original polygon mesh and the other with its bounding sphere. The coordinates of the intersection points would be different. Let us consider the bounding sphere for the intersection test with the ray.

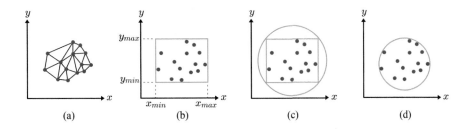

Fig. 12.7: AABB and bounding sphere construction: (a) Input polygon mesh. (b) A 2D AABB is described by $[x_{min}, x_{max}]$ and $[y_{min}, y_{max}]$. (c) A poor-fit bounding sphere. (d) A tighter bounding sphere.

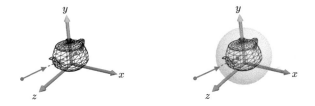

Fig. 12.8: The ray-triangle intersection tests (shown on the left) produce an accurate result but would be costly. The ray-BV intersection test (shown on the right) is cheap but may produce an inaccurate result. The intersection point on the left is located on a triangle whereas that on the right is on the sphere's surface.

As shown in Fig. 12.5, the 3D ray is defined as three parametric equations:

$$p(t) = \begin{pmatrix} x(t) \\ y(t) \\ z(t) \end{pmatrix} = \begin{pmatrix} s_x + td_x \\ s_y + td_y \\ s_z + td_z \end{pmatrix} \tag{12.7}$$

On the other hand, the bounding sphere is defined as follows:

$$(x - C_x)^2 + (y - C_y)^2 + (z - C_z)^2 = r^2 \tag{12.8}$$

where (C_x, C_y, C_z) represent the center and r is the radius. If we insert $x(t)$, $y(t)$, and $z(t)$ of Equation (12.7) into x, y, and z of Equation (12.8), respectively, we obtain a quadratic equation of the following form:

$$at^2 + bt + c = 0 \tag{12.9}$$

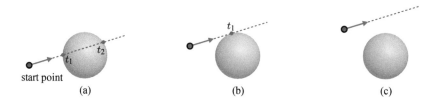

Fig. 12.9: Intersections between the ray and BV: (a) Between two roots, the smaller, t_1, is the parameter at the first intersection. (b) The double root t_1 implies that the ray is tangent to the BV. (c) The ray does not hit the BV, and there is no real root.

where a, b, and c are known and t is an unknown. Solving Equation (12.9) for parameter t amounts to finding the roots by the quadratic formula:

$$t = \frac{-b \pm \sqrt{b^2 - 4ac}}{2a} \qquad (12.10)$$

The roots are the parameters at the intersection points between the ray and the BV.

In Equation (12.10), the expression underneath the square root sign is the *discriminant*. If it is positive, we have two distinct roots, t_1 and t_2. Assuming $t_1 < t_2$, Fig. 12.9-(a) shows the geometric interpretation. The ray enters the BV at t_1 and exits at t_2. Between them, we take the smaller, t_1, which represents the first intersection[1]. If the discriminant is zero, we have a distinct real root called a double root. It implies that, as shown in Fig. 12.9-(b), the ray is tangent to the BV. If the discriminant is negative, there are no real roots. Its geometric interpretation is illustrated in Fig. 12.9-(c). The BV is excluded from further consideration.

In Fig. 12.10, which redraws part of Fig. 12.4, two BVs (for the teapot and sphere) are independently tested, and the ray is found to hit both. Between two parameters, t_a for the teapot and t_b for the sphere, t_a is smaller. It indicates that the teapot's BV is hit *first* by the ray.

A ray may not intersect a polygon mesh even though it intersects its BV. See Fig. 12.11-(a). If accurate results are required, we have to resort to the ray-triangle intersection tests. Even when we run the ray-triangle tests, the ray-BV intersection test is usually done at the preprocessing step. If the ray does not intersect the BV, it is guaranteed not to intersect the polygon mesh. See Fig. 12.11-(b). Through a simple preprocessing step, time-consuming iterations of the ray-triangle test can be avoided. If the ray intersects a polygon

---

[1] Inserting t_1 into Equation (12.7), we obtain the 3D coordinates of the intersection point. However, our goal is not to compute such coordinates but to identify the intersected object.

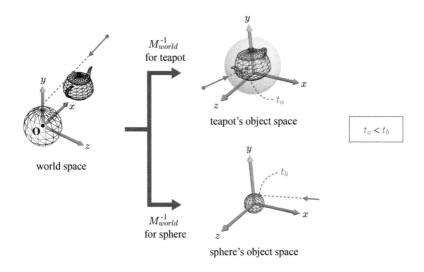

Fig. 12.10: Intersections between the ray and BVs in the object spaces.

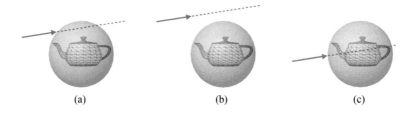

Fig. 12.11: Ray-BV intersection test as a preprocessing step: (a) The ray intersects the BV but does not intersect the mesh. (b) The ray does not intersect the BV, and the ray-triangle test is not invoked at all. (c) The ray intersects both the BV and the mesh.

mesh, the ray always intersects its BV, as shown in Fig. 12.11-(c), and the preprocessing step directs us to the ray-triangle tests.

12.1.5 Intersection between Ray and Triangle

The ray-triangle intersection test is made with every triangle of the polygon mesh. Suppose that a triangle $\langle a, b, c \rangle$ is hit by the ray at p. See Fig. 12.12-(a). The triangle is divided by p into three sub-triangles. [Note: Triangle area] presents how to compute the area of a 3D triangle. Let u denote the ratio of

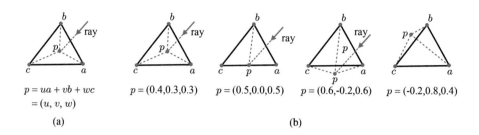

$$p = ua + vb + wc$$
$$= (u, v, w)$$

(a)

$$p = (0.4, 0.3, 0.3) \quad p = (0.5, 0.0, 0.5) \quad p = (0.6, -0.2, 0.6) \quad p = (-0.2, 0.8, 0.4)$$

(b)

Fig. 12.12: Ray-triangle intersection: (a) A point in the triangle is defined by the weights (u, v, w), which are called the barycentric coordinates. (b) The intersection of the ray and a triangle's *plane* may fall outside of the triangle.

the area of $\langle p, b, c \rangle$ to that of $\langle a, b, c \rangle$. It describes how close p is to a. If p is on the edge connecting b and c, $u = 0$. When p gets closer to a, u becomes larger. If $p = a$, $u = 1$.

[Note: Triangle area]
  Given a 3D triangle $\langle v_0, v_1, v_2 \rangle$, where v_i's coordinates are (x_i, y_i, z_i), we project its vertices to either xy-, yz-, or zx-plane of the coordinate system. Any plane can be selected unless the area of the projected triangle becomes zero. Suppose that the triangle is projected to the xy-plane. Then, its area is computed using the determinant:

$$\frac{1}{2} \begin{vmatrix} x_0 & x_1 & x_2 \\ y_0 & y_1 & y_2 \\ 1 & 1 & 1 \end{vmatrix}$$

  Similarly, let v denote the ratio of the area of $\langle p, c, a \rangle$ to that of $\langle a, b, c \rangle$, and w denote the ratio of $\langle p, a, b \rangle$ to that of $\langle a, b, c \rangle$. Then, p is defined as a weighted sum of the vertices:

$$p = ua + vb + wc \tag{12.11}$$

The weights (u, v, w) are called the *barycentric coordinates* of p with respect to $\langle a, b, c \rangle$. Obviously, $u + v + w = 1$, and therefore w can be replaced by $(1 - u - v)$ so that Equation (12.11) is rewritten as follows:

$$p = ua + vb + (1 - u - v)c \tag{12.12}$$

  Computing the intersection between a ray, represented in $s + td$, and a triangle, $\langle a, b, c \rangle$, is equivalent to solving the following equation:

$$s + td = ua + vb + (1 - u - v)c \tag{12.13}$$

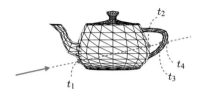

Fig. 12.13: The ray may intersect an object multiple times. Then, the smallest t, t_1 in this example, is chosen.

It is rearranged as follows:

$$td + u(c - a) + v(c - b) = c - s \tag{12.14}$$

Let A, B, and S denote $(c - a)$, $(c - b)$, and $(c - s)$, respectively:

$$td + uA + vB = S \tag{12.15}$$

Because d, A, B, and S all have 3D coordinates, Equation (12.15) is rewritten into a system of linear equations:

$$
\begin{aligned}
td_x + uA_x + vB_x &= S_x \\
td_y + uA_y + vB_y &= S_y \\
td_z + uA_z + vB_z &= S_z
\end{aligned} \tag{12.16}
$$

The solution to this system is obtained using *Cramer's rule*:

$$
t = \frac{\begin{vmatrix} S_x & A_x & B_x \\ S_y & A_y & B_y \\ S_z & A_z & B_z \end{vmatrix}}{\begin{vmatrix} d_x & A_x & B_x \\ d_y & A_y & B_y \\ d_z & A_z & B_z \end{vmatrix}}, u = \frac{\begin{vmatrix} d_x & S_x & B_x \\ d_y & S_y & B_y \\ d_z & S_z & B_z \end{vmatrix}}{\begin{vmatrix} d_x & A_x & B_x \\ d_y & A_y & B_y \\ d_z & A_z & B_z \end{vmatrix}}, v = \frac{\begin{vmatrix} d_x & A_x & S_x \\ d_y & A_y & S_y \\ d_z & A_z & S_z \end{vmatrix}}{\begin{vmatrix} d_x & A_x & B_x \\ d_y & A_y & B_y \\ d_z & A_z & B_z \end{vmatrix}} \tag{12.17}
$$

We obtain t. Note however that it is in fact for the intersection point between the triangle's *plane* and the ray. The intersection point is not guaranteed to be located inside the triangle. Fig. 12.12-(b) shows some examples of the barycentric coordinates, (u, v, w), for the intersection points. In order for the intersection point to be confined to the triangle, the following conditions should be satisfied: $u \geq 0$, $v \geq 0$, and $w \geq 0$. As $w = 1 - u - v$, the last condition is equivalent to $u + v \leq 1$.

When every triangle of a mesh is tested for intersection with the ray, multiple intersections can be found, as illustrated in Fig. 12.13. Then, we choose the point with the smallest t, e.g., t_1 in Fig. 12.13.

12.2   Rotating an Object

Rotating an object is used as frequently as picking an object. As illustrated in Fig. 12.14-(a), an object in a touchscreen can spin by placing a finger on the screen and sliding it. To implement this, we use what is called an *arcball*. It is a virtual ball that is located behind the screen and stuck to the object. Conceptually, the sliding finger rotates the arcball so that the object is accordingly rotated.

On the 2D screen, the sliding finger's positions, $\{p_1, p_2, \ldots, p_n\}$, are tracked. For each pair of successive finger positions, p_i and p_{i+1} shown in Fig. 12.14-(b), a 3D rotation is computed and applied to the object. For efficient implementation, the 2D screen with dimensions w×h is normalized to the square shown in Fig. 12.14-(c), and the 2D coordinates, (x, y), of the finger's position are accordingly normalized:

$$\begin{aligned} x' &= 2x/\text{w} - 1 \\ y' &= 2y/\text{h} - 1 \end{aligned} \qquad (12.18)$$

where x is in [0, w], y is in [0, h], and both x' and y' are in $[-1, 1]$. Now we can consider the arcball as a unit sphere (of radius one). It is contained in a cube behind the normalized screen. The dimensions of the cube are 2×2×2 and its center is located at $(0, 0, 0)$.

Equation (12.18) maps p_i and p_{i+1} in Fig. 12.14-(b) into q_i and q_{i+1} in Fig. 12.14-(c), respectively. Consider a point q in the normalized screen. As depicted in Fig. 12.14-(d), q is orthographically projected along $-z$ onto the surface of the arcball. Let v denote the vector connecting the arcball's center and the projected point. Obviously, its x- and y-coordinates are identical to those of q, i.e., $v_x = q_x$ and $v_y = q_y$. On the other hand, $v_z = \sqrt{1 - v_x^2 - v_y^2}$ because the arcball is a unit sphere and v is a unit vector.

Note that q may not be projected onto the arcball's surface if $q_x^2 + q_y^2 > 1$. In such a case, we first project q onto the xy-plane of the 3D space. Its coordinates are $(q_x, q_y, 0)$, as illustrated in Fig. 12.14-(e), which shows the front view of the arcball. Then, we normalize it to obtain v. This is equivalent to projecting $(q_x, q_y, 0)$ to the nearest point on the arcball's surface.

Let v_i and v_{i+1} denote the vectors obtained from q_i and q_{i+1}, respectively. See Fig. 12.14-(f). The arcball will spin such that v_i is rotated onto v_{i+1}. For this, we need the *rotation angle*, θ, between v_i and v_{i+1}, and the *rotation axis* that is orthogonal to both v_i and v_{i+1}. As $v_i \cdot v_{i+1} = \|v_i\|\|v_{i+1}\|\cos\theta = \cos\theta$, $\theta = arccos(v_i \cdot v_{i+1})$. On the other hand, the rotation axis is obtained by taking the cross product of v_i and v_{i+1}.

The object will be rotated and then displayed on the screen. For this, the rotation axis should be redefined in the object space so that the rotation is made prior to the original world transform. We computed the rotation axis in the arcball's space. It is a temporarily devised coordinate system, which we have not encountered in the rendering pipeline. Our strategy is then to

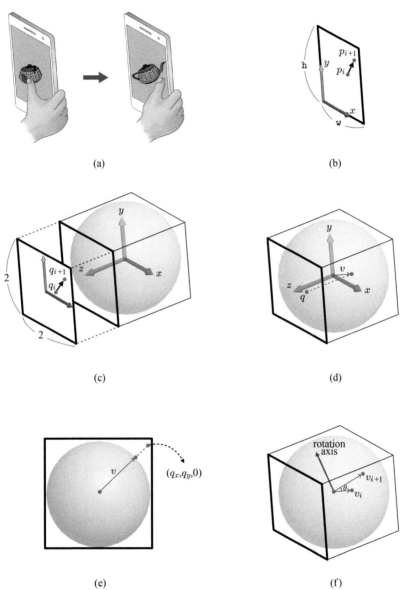

Fig. 12.14: Object rotation implemented using an arcball.

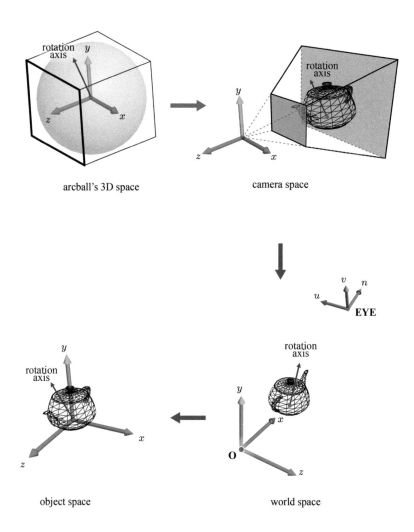

arcball's 3D space

camera space

object space

world space

Fig. 12.15: The rotation axis is transformed into the object space.

take the rotation axis *as is* into the camera space of the rendering pipeline, as shown on the top of Fig. 12.15. The camera-space axis will be transformed back to the world space and then to the object space using the inverses of the view and world transforms, as presented in Section 12.1.3. Observe that the rotation axis, as a vector, can be thought of as passing through the object in the camera space, and such a configuration is preserved in the object space, as illustrated in Fig. 12.15.

Given the rotation angle and axis, we need to compute a rotation matrix. If we use `glm` introduced in Section 6.4.1, the rotation matrix is obtained simply by invoking `glm::rotate(angle, axis)`. Otherwise, we can define a quaternion using Equation (11.14) and then convert it into a matrix, as presented in Equation (11.26).

Initially, the finger is at p_1 on the screen. Let M denote the current world matrix. When the finger moves to p_2, the rotation axis is computed using p_1 and p_2, as presented above, and is finally transformed from the world space to the object space using the inverse of M. Let R_1 denote the rotation matrix determined by the rotation axis. Then, MR_1 will be provided for the vertex shader as the world matrix, making the object slightly rotated in the screen. Let M' denote the new world matrix, MR_1.

When the finger moves from p_2 to p_3, the rotation matrix is computed using the inverse of M'. Let R_2 denote the rotation matrix. Then, the world matrix is updated to $M'R_2$ and is passed to the vertex shader. This process is repeated while the finger remains on the screen.

Exercises

1. In Fig. 12.3, the screen-space ray starts from $(x_s, y_s, 0)$ and the camera-space ray starts from $(x_c, y_c, -n)$.

   (a) Using the *inverse* of the viewport transform, compute the clip-space ray's start point in NDC.

   (b) Using the fact that the answer in (a) is identical to the point in Equation (12.1), compute x_c and y_c.

2. Suppose that, for object picking, the user clicks exactly the center of the viewport.

   (a) The view-frustum parameters are given as follows: $n = 12$, $f = 18$, $fovy = 120°$, and $aspect = 1$. Represent the camera-space ray in a parametric equation of t. [Hint: No transform between the screen and camera spaces is needed. The camera-space ray can be intuitively defined.]

   (b) Imagine a camera-space bounding sphere. Its radius is 2 and center is at $(0, -1, -14)$. Compute the parameter t at the first intersection between the ray and the bounding sphere, and also compute the 3D coordinates of the intersection point.

3. Shown below is a screen-space triangle, each vertex of which is associated with $\{(R, G, B), z\}$.

   (a) Compute the barycentric coordinates of the red dot at $(5.5, 3.5)$ in terms of v_1, v_2, and v_3.

   (b) Using the barycentric coordinates, compute R and z at $(5.5, 3.5)$.

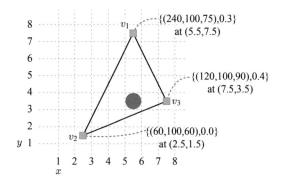

4. The last step in Fig. 12.15 is the *inverse* of the world transform. Suppose that the original world matrix is a rotation (denoted as R_0) followed by a translation (denoted as T) and $\{p_1, p_2, p_3, \ldots, p_n\}$ represents the finger's trajectory.

(a) Let R_1 denote the rotation matrix computed using p_1 and p_2. Define the inverse world transform used to compute R_1.

(b) Let R_2 denote the rotation matrix computed using p_2 and p_3. Define the inverse world transform used to compute R_2.

Chapter 13

Character Animation

The most important objects to be animated are definitely the characters. Making a character move in a realistic way is an everlasting goal in computer animation, and a variety of techniques have been developed toward achieving that goal. This chapter presents the fundamental algorithms for character animation, upon which various state-of-the-art techniques are built.

13.1 Skeleton and Space Change

The most popular method to animate a character is to use a *skeleton*. It is an instance of an *articulated body* and is composed of a set of connected rigid components, *bones*.

13.1.1 Skeleton

Suppose that an artist uses an interactive 3D modeling package and creates a character represented in the polygon mesh shown in Fig. 13.1-(a). The initial pose of a character has many synonyms: default pose, rest pose, dress pose, bind pose, etc. This chapter uses the first term, *default pose*.

In general, 3D modeling packages provide a few skeleton *templates* for a human character. Fig. 13.1-(b) shows a 3ds Max template named 'biped.'

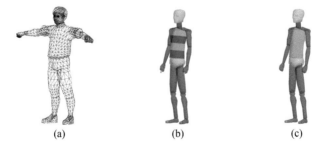

(a)   (b)   (c)

Fig. 13.1: Polygon mesh and skeleton for character animation.

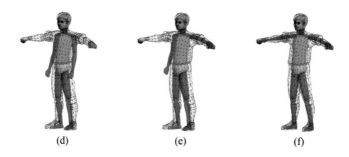

(d)   (e)   (f)

Fig. 13.1: Polygon mesh and skeleton for character animation (*continued*).

Such a template can be edited. Fig. 13.1-(c) shows a simplified skeleton, where several bones are deleted and four spines are combined into one. The skeleton is embedded into the character mesh (Fig. 13.1-(d)) and is then made to fit to the default pose. For example, the left arm is stretched so as to fit to the mesh (Fig. 13.1-(e)). The other bones are similarly processed. Fig. 13.1-(f) shows the result. Now the vertices of the character mesh are ready to be animated according to the skeletal motion.

The bones are illustrated as if they were solids. However, they are not geometric entities. The solid look is provided for user-interface purposes. When the skeleton is made to fit to the default pose, a *matrix* is automatically computed per bone. The skeletal motion will be described using such matrices. The rest of this section presents the matrices obtained from the default pose.

13.1.2   Space Change between Bones

In a skeleton, the bones form a *hierarchical structure* with parent-child relationships. Fig. 13.2 shows the bones of our simplified skeleton and their hierarchy. The pelvis is normally taken as the root node of the hierarchy.

The bones are connected at *rotary joints*, which allow the rigid skeleton to animate in an articulated fashion. Fig. 13.3 shows a part of the skeleton, which consists of three bones (upper arm, forearm, and hand) and three joints (shoulder, elbow, and wrist). To simply the presentation, we will use the 2D illustration of the bones.

In the character mesh, consider the vertices, v_u, v_f, and v_h, which belong to the upper arm, forearm, and hand, respectively. When the forearm moves, for example, v_f has to move accordingly. It can be achieved if v_f is defined in the forearm's *object space*. The forearm and its object space always move together, and therefore v_f moves together with the forearm.

Initially, all vertices of the default pose are defined in a single space. It is the "object space of the character," and we simply call it the *character space*. For character animation, each character-space vertex is required to

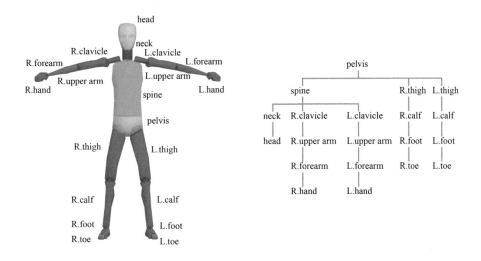

Fig. 13.2: In our example, the character has a skeleton composed of 20 bones.

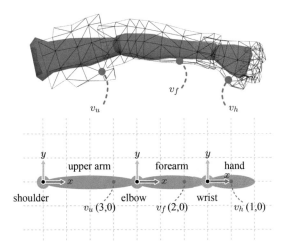

Fig. 13.3: The character's upper arm, forearm, and hand. (The dotted 2D grid in the background may help you estimate the coordinates of v_u, v_f, and v_h.)

be transformed into the "object space of the bone" to which it belongs. We simply call it the *bone space*. For example, v_f in Fig. 13.3 is initially defined in the character space but will be transformed into the forearm's bone space, where its coordinates are $(2, 0)$. For now, consider the opposite direction, i.e., transforming a bone-space vertex to the character space. Once it is computed, we will use its inverse to convert a character-space vertex into the bone space.

Given the default pose, each bone's position and orientation relative to its parent are immediately determined. A bone has its own length and is conventionally aligned along the x-axis of its bone space. Suppose that, in Fig. 13.3, the upper arm's length is four. Then, the forearm's joint, elbow, is located at $(4, 0)$ in the upper arm's bone space. The *space change* from the forearm's bone space to the upper arm's is represented in the matrix that superimposes the upper arm's space onto the forearm's. (If this is unclear, review Section 5.2.2.) In Fig. 13.3, the space-change matrix is a translation along the x-axis by four units. We call it the *to-parent transform* of the forearm in the sense that it transforms the forearm's vertex to the bone space of its *parent*, the upper arm. The forearm's to-parent matrix is denoted by $M_{f,p}$:

$$M_{f,p} = \begin{pmatrix} 1 & 0 & 4 \\ 0 & 1 & 0 \\ 0 & 0 & 1 \end{pmatrix} \tag{13.1}$$

The coordinates of v_f are $(2, 0)$ in the forearm's space, and those in the upper arm's space are $(6, 0)$:

$$\begin{aligned} M_{f,p} v_f &= \begin{pmatrix} 1 & 0 & 4 \\ 0 & 1 & 0 \\ 0 & 0 & 1 \end{pmatrix} \begin{pmatrix} 2 \\ 0 \\ 1 \end{pmatrix} \\ &= \begin{pmatrix} 6 \\ 0 \\ 1 \end{pmatrix} \end{aligned} \tag{13.2}$$

Now consider the to-parent matrix of the hand:

$$M_{h,p} = \begin{pmatrix} 1 & 0 & 3 \\ 0 & 1 & 0 \\ 0 & 0 & 1 \end{pmatrix} \tag{13.3}$$

It transforms v_h, whose coordinates in the hand's space are $(1, 0)$, into the forearm's space as follows:

$$\begin{aligned} v'_h &= M_{h,p} v_h \\ &= \begin{pmatrix} 1 & 0 & 3 \\ 0 & 1 & 0 \\ 0 & 0 & 1 \end{pmatrix} \begin{pmatrix} 1 \\ 0 \\ 1 \end{pmatrix} \\ &= \begin{pmatrix} 4 \\ 0 \\ 1 \end{pmatrix} \end{aligned} \tag{13.4}$$

Note that v'_h in Equation (13.4) can be again transformed into the upper arm's space by $M_{f,p}$ defined in Equation (13.1):

$$
\begin{aligned}
M_{f,p}v'_h &= \begin{pmatrix} 1 & 0 & 4 \\ 0 & 1 & 0 \\ 0 & 0 & 1 \end{pmatrix}\begin{pmatrix} 4 \\ 0 \\ 1 \end{pmatrix} \\
&= \begin{pmatrix} 8 \\ 0 \\ 1 \end{pmatrix}
\end{aligned} \tag{13.5}
$$

Equation (13.5) can be rephrased as follows:

$$
\begin{aligned}
M_{f,p}v'_h &= M_{f,p}M_{h,p}v_h \\
&= \begin{pmatrix} 1 & 0 & 4 \\ 0 & 1 & 0 \\ 0 & 0 & 1 \end{pmatrix}\begin{pmatrix} 1 & 0 & 3 \\ 0 & 1 & 0 \\ 0 & 0 & 1 \end{pmatrix}\begin{pmatrix} 1 \\ 0 \\ 1 \end{pmatrix} \\
&= \begin{pmatrix} 8 \\ 0 \\ 1 \end{pmatrix}
\end{aligned} \tag{13.6}
$$

i.e., $M_{f,p}$ and $M_{h,p}$ are concatenated to transform a vertex of the hand to the bone space of its *grandparent*, upper arm.

This observation can be generalized. Given a vertex that belongs to a bone, we can concatenate the to-parent matrices so as to transform the vertex into the bone space of any ancestor in the skeleton hierarchy. The ancestor can be of course the root node, pelvis.

13.1.3   Character Space to Bone Space

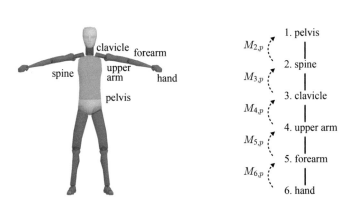

Fig. 13.4: To-parent transforms.

Fig. 13.4 shows the parent-child relationships on a part of the skeleton. To simplify the discussion, the bones are numbered: 1 for pelvis, 2 for spine, 3 for clavicle, and so on. Their to-parent matrices are denoted using the numbers. For example, $M_{3,p}$ is the to-parent transform from the bone space of the clavicle to that of the spine.

Given the default pose, we can establish the transform from each bone space to the character space. It is denoted by $M_{i,d}$, where i and d stand for the i-th bone and default pose, respectively. The root node is the pelvis, and its bone space is taken as the character space. Then, $M_{1,d}$ is the identity matrix.

Consider $M_{2,d}$ from the spine's bone space to the character space. It is defined as follows:

$$M_{2,d} = M_{1,d}M_{2,p} \qquad (13.7)$$

i.e., a vertex of the spine is transformed first into the bone space of its parent, the pelvis, by the to-parent matrix $M_{2,p}$, and then transformed into character space by $M_{1,d}$. The dotted arrows in Fig. 13.5-(a) show the path.

The same applies to the other bones. See Fig. 13.5-(b). The clavicle's vertex is transformed into the character space using three matrices:

$$M_{3,d} = M_{1,d}M_{2,p}M_{3,p} \qquad (13.8)$$

Note that $M_{1,d}M_{2,p}$ equals $M_{2,d}$, as presented in Equation (13.7). Equation (13.8) can then be simplified as follows:

$$\begin{aligned} M_{3,d} &= M_{1,d}M_{2,p}M_{3,p} \\ &= M_{2,d}M_{3,p} \end{aligned} \qquad (13.9)$$

This asserts that the path followed by the clavicle's vertex in Fig. 13.5-(b) includes the path of the spine's vertex in Fig. 13.5-(a).

Equations (13.7) and (13.9) can be generalized as follows:

$$M_{i,d} = M_{i-1,d}M_{i,p} \qquad (13.10)$$

The horizontal arrows in Fig. 13.5-(c) enumerate the transforms.

To this point, we have considered $M_{i,d}$ from the bone space to the character space. What is needed in an articulated-body animation is its *inverse*, $M_{i,d}^{-1}$, which transforms a character-space vertex into the space of the bone the vertex belongs to:

$$M_{i,d}^{-1} = M_{i,p}^{-1}M_{i-1,d}^{-1} \qquad (13.11)$$

The horizontal arrows in Fig. 13.5-(d) enumerate $M_{i,d}^{-1}$ for each bone. Given the default pose, the to-parent transform of each bone, $M_{i,p}$, is immediately determined, and so is its inverse, $M_{i,p}^{-1}$. Therefore, computing $M_{i,d}^{-1}$ in Equation (13.11) simply requires $M_{i-1,d}^{-1}$ to be computed in advance. The skeleton hierarchy implies that we eventually need $M_{1,d}^{-1}$. We know $M_{1,d}^{-1} = I$. Then, we can compute $M_{i,d}^{-1}$ for every bone through the top-down traversal of the skeleton hierarchy.

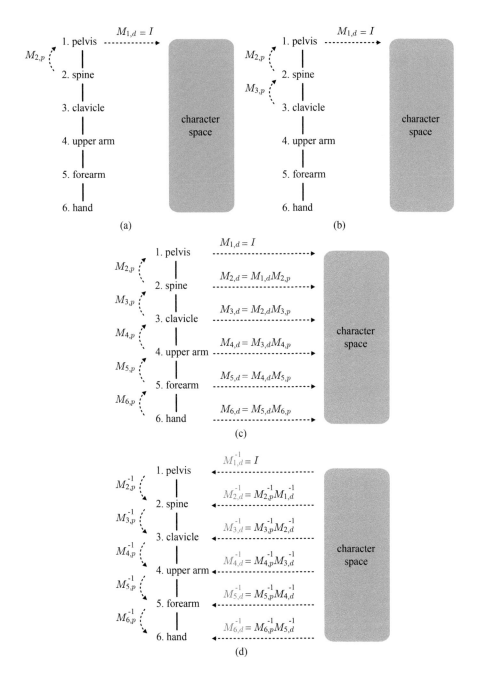

Fig. 13.5: Transforms between the character space and the bone spaces for the default pose: (a) From the spine's bone space to the character space. (b) From the clavicle's bone space to the character space. (c) Transforms from the bone spaces to the character space. (d) Transforms from the character space to the bone spaces.

13.2　Forward Kinematics

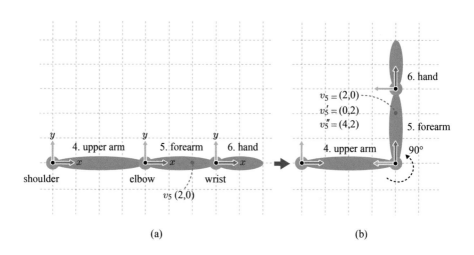

(a)　　　　　　　　　　　　　　　(b)

Fig. 13.6: Forward kinematics: (a) Default pose. (b) Animated pose.

The previous section presented $M_{i,d}^{-1}$ that transforms a character-space vertex into the i-th bone's space in the "default pose." For example, v_5 in Fig. 13.6-(a) was originally defined in the character space but has been transformed by $M_{5,d}^{-1}$ to have the coordinates $(2,0)$ in the forearm's space.

When the skeleton is animated in an articulated fashion, every vertex is animated by its bone's motion. In Fig. 13.6-(b), the forearm is rotated and so is v_5. For rendering a character in such an "animated pose," all of its vertices should be transformed back to the character space so that they can enter the rendering pipeline. In the example of Fig. 13.6-(b), we need a matrix that animates v_5 and transforms "animated v_5" back to the character space. We denote the matrix by $M_{5,a}$, where a stands for the animated pose.

In Fig. 13.6-(b), the forearm is rotated by $90°$. The rotation is about its *local* joint, elbow, and is generally named the *local transform*. The forearm's local transform is denoted by $M_{5,l}$. In the homogeneous coordinates, 2D rotation is defined as

$$\begin{pmatrix} cos\theta & -sin\theta & 0 \\ sin\theta & cos\theta & 0 \\ 0 & 0 & 1 \end{pmatrix} \qquad (13.12)$$

and therefore $M_{5,l}$ (rotation by $90°$) is determined as follows:

$$M_{5,l} = \begin{pmatrix} 0 & -1 & 0 \\ 1 & 0 & 0 \\ 0 & 0 & 1 \end{pmatrix} \tag{13.13}$$

$M_{5,l}$ is applied to v_5:

$$\begin{aligned} v_5' &= M_{5,l}v_5 \\ &= \begin{pmatrix} 0 & -1 & 0 \\ 1 & 0 & 0 \\ 0 & 0 & 1 \end{pmatrix} \begin{pmatrix} 2 \\ 0 \\ 1 \end{pmatrix} \\ &= \begin{pmatrix} 0 \\ 2 \\ 1 \end{pmatrix} \end{aligned} \tag{13.14}$$

Fig. 13.6-(b) compares v_5 and v_5'. With respect to the forearm's bone space, which is stuck to the forearm and rotates together with it, v_5 is fixed to $(2,0)$. In contrast, v_5' represents the coordinates with respect to the original bone space of the forearm "before rotation." The bone spaces of the upper arm and forearm "before rotation" are related by the to-parent matrix $M_{5,p}$ ($M_{f,p}$) presented in Equation (13.1), and therefore the coordinates of v_5' "in the upper arm's space" are computed as follows:

$$\begin{aligned} v_5'' &= M_{5,p}v_5' \\ &= \begin{pmatrix} 1 & 0 & 4 \\ 0 & 1 & 0 \\ 0 & 0 & 1 \end{pmatrix} \begin{pmatrix} 0 \\ 2 \\ 1 \end{pmatrix} \\ &= \begin{pmatrix} 4 \\ 2 \\ 1 \end{pmatrix} \end{aligned} \tag{13.15}$$

The dotted grid in the background of Fig. 13.6-(b) may help you understand that v_5'' has the coordinates $(4,2)$ in the upper arm's bone space. Equations (13.14) and (13.15) can be combined:

$$\begin{aligned} v_5'' &= M_{5,p}M_{5,l}v_5 \\ &= \begin{pmatrix} 1 & 0 & 4 \\ 0 & 1 & 0 \\ 0 & 0 & 1 \end{pmatrix} \begin{pmatrix} 0 & -1 & 0 \\ 1 & 0 & 0 \\ 0 & 0 & 1 \end{pmatrix} \begin{pmatrix} 2 \\ 0 \\ 1 \end{pmatrix} \\ &= \begin{pmatrix} 4 \\ 2 \\ 1 \end{pmatrix} \end{aligned} \tag{13.16}$$

The forearm's parent (the upper arm) can also be animated. Let $M_{4,a}$ denote the matrix that animates the upper arm's vertex and transforms it into the character space. Then, $M_{5,a}$ is defined in terms of $M_{4,a}$ together with $M_{5,p}M_{5,l}$ presented in Equation (13.16):

$$M_{5,a} = M_{4,a}M_{5,p}M_{5,l} \tag{13.17}$$

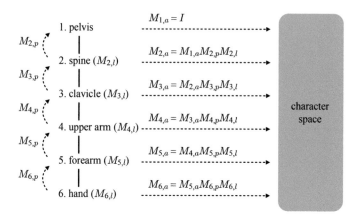

Fig. 13.7: The transforms from the animated bone spaces to the character space.

Considering the hierarchical structure of the skeleton, Equation (13.17) is generalized into

$$M_{i,a} = M_{i-1,a}M_{i,p}M_{i,l} \qquad (13.18)$$

Once the artist defines the animated pose of a character, each bone's $M_{i,l}$ is immediately determined. If we have 20 bones, for example, 20 instances of $M_{i,l}$ are immediately available. An example is $M_{5,l}$ in Equation (13.13). Recall that, given the default pose, $M_{i,p}$ of each bone is immediately determined, as illustrated in Fig. 13.4. Therefore, computing $M_{i,a}$ in Equation (13.18) simply requires $M_{i-1,a}$ to be computed in advance. The skeleton hierarchy implies that we eventually need $M_{1,a}$.

In the same manner as $M_{4,a}$ and $M_{5,a}$, $M_{1,a}$ is defined to be the matrix that animates the vertices of the root node, pelvis, and transforms them into the character space. However, the transform to the character space is not needed because the character space is identical to the pelvis' bone space. Furthermore, the pelvis itself is not animated in general. Its animation is usually replaced by the world transform of the character. Consequently, $M_{1,a}$ is reduced to the identity matrix. Then, we can compute $M_{i,a}$ for every bone through the top-down traversal of the skeleton hierarchy. The horizontal arrows in Fig. 13.7 show $M_{i,a}$ for each bone.

Given the default pose, the skeleton hierarchy is traversed to compute $M_{i,d}^{-1}$ for each bone, as illustrated in Fig. 13.5-(d). It is computed once and remains fixed during animation. For each frame of animation, the skeleton hierarchy is traversed to compute $M_{i,a}$ for each bone, as illustrated in Fig. 13.7. A character-space vertex in the default pose, which we denote by v, is trans-

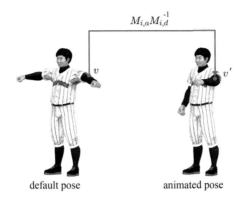

Fig. 13.8: Both v and v' are defined in the character space. For each frame of animation, v' is updated, and the polygon mesh composed of v' is rendered.

formed to the bone space by $M_{i,d}^{-1}$. Then, it is animated and transformed back to the character space by $M_{i,a}$:

$$v' = M_{i,a}M_{i,d}^{-1}v \qquad (13.19)$$

where v' denotes the character-space vertex in the animated pose. The polygon mesh composed of v' is rendered through the GPU pipeline. See Fig. 13.8.

Kinematics is a field of mechanics that describes the motion of objects without consideration of mass or force[1]. Determining the pose of an articulated body by specifying all of its bones' transforms is called the *forward kinematics*. In Section 13.4, we will see a different method named the *inverse kinematics*. It determines the bone transforms of an articulated body in order to achieve a desired pose of the leaf node, such as a hand in our hierarchy.

13.3 Skinning

In character animation, the polygon mesh defined by the skeletal motion is often called a *skin*. This section presents how to obtain a smoothly deformed skin.

---

[1] In contrast, dynamics is another field devoted to studying the forces required to cause motions.

13.3.1 Vertex Blending

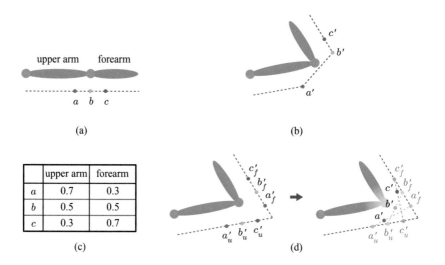

upper arm   forearm

a b c

(a)

(b)

	upper arm	forearm
a	0.7	0.3
b	0.5	0.5
c	0.3	0.7

(c)

(d)

Fig. 13.9: Skinning animation: (a) Vertices on the polygon mesh. (b) No blending. (c) Blend weights. (d) Blending.

In Equation (13.19), we implicitly assumed that a vertex belongs to a single bone. This often leads to unnatural skin deformations. Fig. 13.9-(a) illustrates the upper arm and forearm connected at the elbow, along with three vertices of the mesh (a, b, and c) near the elbow. Suppose that vertex a belongs to the upper arm whereas b and c belong to the forearm. Fig. 13.9-(b) shows the change made when the upper arm and forearm are both animated. The deformed skin is not smooth.

The problem can be alleviated by making multiple bones affect a vertex and then blending the results, instead of binding a vertex to a single bone. For this, each bone affecting a vertex is assigned a blend weight, which describes how much the bone contributes to the position of the vertex in the animated pose. Fig. 13.9-(c) shows an example, where the upper arm contributes 70% to vertex a and the forearm contributes 30%. It looks reasonable because vertex a is closer to the upper arm than to the forearm and therefore is affected more by the upper arm. Similar estimations can be made for the weights given to b and c.

Fig. 13.9-(d) illustrates the blending process, where a'_u, b'_u, and c'_u represent the vertices animated by the upper arm, and a'_f, b'_f, and c'_f represent those by the forearm. Using the blend weights given in Fig. 13.9-(c), a'_u and a'_f are linearly interpolated to generate a'. Similarly, b' and c' are generated.

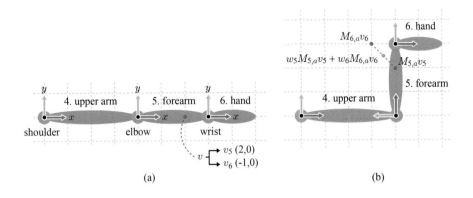

Fig. 13.10: Linear blend skinning: (a) A single character-space vertex leads to two distinct bone-space vertices, v_5 and v_6. (b) They are independently animated to have their own character-space positions, which are then blended.

Connecting a', b', and c' results in a smoother skin. This technique is called *linear blend skinning* or simply *skinning*.

In the default pose of Fig. 13.9-(a), vertex a is initially defined in the character space. It is transformed to the upper arm's bone space, animated by the upper arm's motion, and transformed back to the character space to define a'_u. This is implemented by Equation (13.19). In exactly the same manner, vertex a is also transformed to the forearm's bone space, animated by the forearm's motion, and transformed back to the character space to define a'_f, which is then blended with a'_u.

In the default pose shown in Fig. 13.10-(a), consider a character-space vertex v. It is transformed by $M_{5,d}^{-1}$ into the bone space of the forearm to define v_5:

$$v_5 = M_{5,d}^{-1}v \qquad (13.20)$$

Suppose that v is affected not only by the forearm but also by the hand. Then, it should be also transformed to the hand's bone space by $M_{6,d}^{-1}$:

$$v_6 = M_{6,d}^{-1}v \qquad (13.21)$$

Compare the coordinates of v_5 and v_6 in Fig. 13.10-(a): $(2,0)$ in the forearm's bone space and $(-1,0)$ in the hand's.

Suppose that the forearm is rotated by $90°$ and the hand is rotated by $-90°$ (clockwise $90°$), leading to the animated pose shown in Fig. 13.10-(b). Then, v_5 and v_6 are animated and transformed to the character space by $M_{5,a}$ and $M_{6,a}$, respectively, and are blended using the pre-defined weights, w_5 and w_6:

$$v' = w_5 M_{5,a} v_5 + w_6 M_{6,a} v_6 \qquad (13.22)$$

Equations (13.20) and (13.21) are inserted into Equation (13.22):

$$v' = w_5 M_{5,a} M_{5,d}^{-1} v + w_6 M_{6,a} M_{6,d}^{-1} v \qquad (13.23)$$

In general, the set of bones affecting a vertex and their blend weights are fixed through the entire animation. Suppose that m bones affect a vertex and their weights sum to one. Then, Equation (13.23) is generalized as follows:

$$v' = \sum_{i=1}^{m} w_i M_{i,a} M_{i,d}^{-1} v \qquad (13.24)$$

When $M_{i,a} M_{i,d}^{-1}$ is abbreviated to M_i, Equation (13.24) is simplified:

$$v' = \sum_{i=1}^{m} w_i M_i v \qquad (13.25)$$

In real-time 3D applications such as games, m is typically limited to four for programming efficiency.

Fig. 13.11 sketches how Equation (13.25) is implemented. Our character has 20 bones, and therefore we update 20 instances of M_i for each frame of animation. They are stored in a table, which is often called the *matrix palette*. Consider v that represents a vertex of the character mesh in the default pose. In Fig. 13.11, the indices of the matrices affecting v are 0, 2, 7, and 18, and v is multiplied by M_0, M_2, M_7, and M_{18} (through *mul* for matrix-vertex multiplication). The results are combined using the blend weights, 0.2, 0.3, 0.4, and 0.1, to produce v'.

In general, the skinning algorithm is implemented by the vertex shader, for which the matrix palette is provided as a 'uniform.' In contrast, the palette indices and the blend weights are stored in the vertex array such that they can be passed to the vertex shader as 'attributes' along with the position, normal, and texture coordinates. In the example of Fig. 13.11, the vertex array elements for v include the palette indices, $(0, 2, 7, 18)$, and the blend weights, $(0.2, 0.3, 0.4, 0.1)$.

13.3.2 Integration with Keyframe Animation*

Recall that $M_{i,a}$ in Equation (13.24) is updated "for every frame of animation" whereas $M_{i,d}^{-1}$ is computed once for the default pose and remains fixed. If the skinning algorithm is integrated with keyframe animation, $M_{i,a}$ for an in-between frame is updated by interpolating $M_{i,a}$ in the keyframes.

As presented in Equation (13.18), $M_{i,a} = M_{i-1,a} M_{i,p} M_{i,l}$, where $M_{i,l}$ is (almost always!) a rotation, and $M_{i,p}$ is a space-change matrix composed of a translation and a rotation. Let $M_{i,p,l}$ denote $M_{i,p} M_{i,l}$. Its upper-left 3×3 sub-matrix represents the 'combined' rotation, and the fourth column represents the 'combined' translation. (If this is unclear, review Sections 4.2

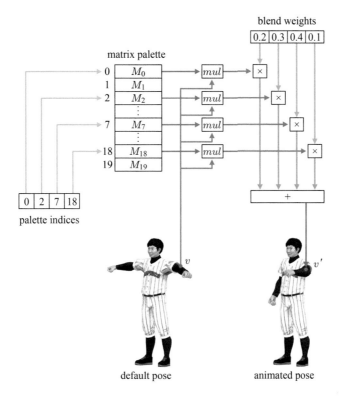

Fig. 13.11: The skinning algorithm operates on each vertex v of the character's polygon mesh in the default pose to transform it into v' of the animated pose. Through the entire animation, the palette indices and blend weights are fixed for a vertex. In contrast, the matrix palette is updated for each frame of animation.

and 4.4.) For each keyframe, the rotation component of $M_{i,p,l}$ is stored as a quaternion, and the translation component is stored as a 3D vector. They form the key data of a bone. If we have 20 bones, for example, a keyframe contains 20 quaternion and translation pairs.

For each in-between frame of animation, the skeleton hierarchy is traversed in a top-down fashion to compute $M_{i,a}$ for each bone. The quaternions and translational vectors stored in the keyframes are independently interpolated. The interpolated quaternion is converted into the matrix presented in Equation (11.26), and the interpolated translation vector fills the fourth column of the matrix. This matrix is combined with $M_{i-1,a}$ to complete $M_{i,a}$.

Sample code 13-1 presents how skinning is integrated with keyframe animation. The first `for` loop computes `Md-` (denoting $M_{i,d}^{-1}$) for each bone. It is computed just once. The second `for` loop is run for each frame of animation.

Sample code 13-1 Pseudocode for skinning + keyframe animation

---

```
 1: for each bone // default pose
 2:     compute Md-
 3:
 4: for each frame
 5:     for each bone i // animated pose
 6:         interpolate key data
 7:         compute Ma
 8:         combine Ma with Md- to define Mi
 9:         store Mi in the matrix palette
10:         invoke vertex shader for skinning
```

(a)   (b)

Fig. 13.12: Skinning + keyframe animation: (a) Keyframes and in-between frames. (b) Superimposed frames.

First of all, the key data are interpolated and Ma (denoting $M_{i,a}$) is computed. Then, Ma is combined with Md- to make a single matrix, Mi (denoting M_i in Equation (13.25)). It is stored in the matrix palette to be passed to the vertex shader. Fig. 13.12-(a) shows two keyframes (on the left and right) and three in-between frames of the skin-animated character. In Fig. 13.12-(b), the frames are superimposed.

13.4 Inverse Kinematics

In robotics, an *end effector* refers to the device located at the end of a robotic arm. A good example is a jaw gripper, designed to grasp an object. *Forward kinematics* computes the pose of the end effector as a function of the joint angles of the robotic arm. The reverse process is called the *inverse kinematics* (IK). Given the desired pose of the end effector along with the initial pose of the robotic arm, the joint angles of the final pose are calculated.

Even though IK was developed in robotics, it is quite relevant to character animation. For example, it is used to compute the leg joints' angles which make the feet land firmly on top of an irregular terrain surface. By solving IK in real time, the character is able to react spontaneously to an unpredictable environment.

The IK solutions adopted in the robotics community are largely based on solving a linear system, but it is computationally expensive. This section presents two cheaper algorithms used in real-time applications.

13.4.1 Analytic Solution

(a)   (b)

Fig. 13.13: Joints and degrees of freedom: (a) The 1-DOF elbow works like a hinge joint. (b) The 3-DOF shoulder works like a ball joint.

The number of independent variables defining the state of an object is called the *degrees of freedom* (DOF). Consider the elbow in Fig. 13.13-(a), which is illustrated as a mechanical joint called a *hinge joint*. It allows the forearm up-and-down movement only. It is a 1-DOF joint. In contrast, the shoulder shown in Fig. 13.13-(b) works like a *ball joint* and provides three DOF for the upper arm. The upper arm may have an arbitrary orientation through up-and-down and left-to-right movements, which are often called *pitch* and *yaw*, respectively. We can also rotate the upper arm as if we were using it as a screwdriver. This is called *roll*.

Consider the two-joint arm shown in Fig. 13.14-(a). Given the goal position, G, and the initial pose of the arm, the *joint angles* of the shoulder and elbow will be analytically calculated. When the upper arm and forearm are rotated by those angles, the forearm's tip, T, will reach G.

The elbow is a 1-DOF joint, and thus it is straightforward to compute its joint angle. See Fig. 13.14-(b), where the upper arm and forearm are illustrated in 2D. The elbow's joint angle is denoted by θ. The lengths of the upper arm and forearm are fixed and are denoted by l_u and l_f, respectively. Given the goal position G, the distance, l_g, between the shoulder and G is also fixed. The *law of cosines* asserts that

$$l_g^2 = l_u^2 + l_f^2 - 2l_u l_f cos\theta \tag{13.26}$$

Then, θ is computed directly from Equation (13.26):

$$\theta = arccos\frac{l_u^2 + l_f^2 - l_g^2}{2l_u l_f} \tag{13.27}$$

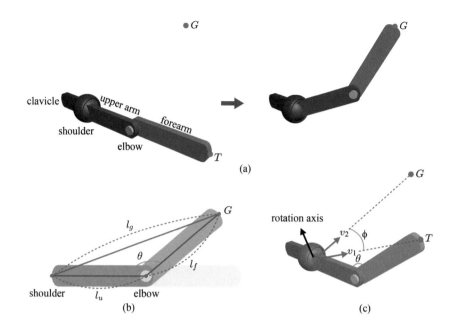

Fig. 13.14: Analytic solution for IK: (a) The final pose of a two-joint arm is computed given its initial pose and the end effector's goal position G. (b) The joint angle θ of the 1-DOF elbow is computed. (c) The rotation angle ϕ and the rotation axis are computed for the 3-DOF shoulder.

Fig. 13.14-(c) shows the result of rotating the forearm. Now the upper arm is rotated such that the forearm is accordingly moved to make T reach G. Consider the unit vector, v_1, connecting the shoulder and T, and another unit vector, v_2, connecting the shoulder and G. If v_1 is rotated by ϕ to be aligned with v_2, T will reach G. As $v_1 \cdot v_2 = \|v_1\|\|v_2\|\cos\phi = \cos\phi$, $\phi = arccos(v_1 \cdot v_2)$. In addition, we need the rotation axis. It should be orthogonal to both v_1 and v_2 and therefore is obtained by taking their cross product.

13.4.2   Cyclic Coordinate Descent

In some applications, analytic solutions are desirable due to their speed and accuracy. For a complex chain of bones with many joints, however, an analytic solution may not be feasible. An alternative is named *Cyclic Coordinate Descent* (CCD). It is an optimization-based IK algorithm that is simple and robust. It works in an iterative fashion, starting from the end effector and moving upward along the connected bones.

Consider the chain of bones in Fig. 13.15-(a). Our goal is to make T reach G. The CCD algorithm first rotates the hand such that it points directly at

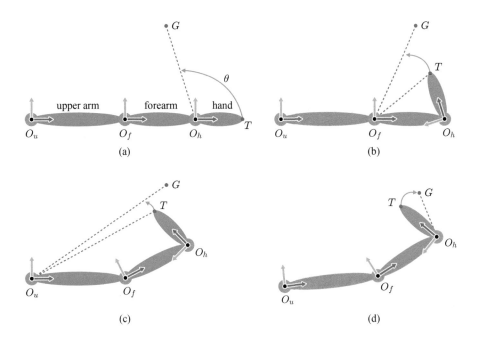

Fig. 13.15: The CCD algorithm processes one bone at a time. (a) Initial pose. (b) The hand has been rotated, and now it is the forearm's turn. (c) The forearm has been rotated, and now it is the upper arm's turn. (d) The upper arm has been rotated, and now it is the hand's turn.

G. For this, the rotation angle and axis are required. Let O_h denote the origin of the hand's bone space. Then, $\overrightarrow{O_h T}$ represents a vector connecting O_h and T, and $\overrightarrow{O_h G}$ is similarly defined. The rotation angle and axis are computed using the dot product and cross product of $\overrightarrow{O_h T}$ and $\overrightarrow{O_h G}$, respectively, as presented in the previous subsection.

Fig. 13.15-(b) shows the result of rotating the hand. T does not reach G, and therefore the CCD algorithm rotates the forearm such that $\overrightarrow{O_f T}$ is aligned with $\overrightarrow{O_f G}$. The rotation angle and axis are computed using the dot product and cross product of $\overrightarrow{O_f T}$ and $\overrightarrow{O_f G}$, respectively. Fig. 13.15-(c) shows the rotation result. T does not yet reach G, and the same process is performed for the upper arm, leading to the configuration in Fig. 13.15-(d). As the goal is not fulfilled, the next iteration starts from the end effector, hand. The iterations through the chain are repeated until either the goal is achieved, i.e., until T is equal or close enough to G, or the pre-defined number of iterations is reached.

Fig. 13.16: IK enables the character's hand to reach the flying ball. Dynamic gazing is also applied to the head bone.

Using IK is a distinguished step many of the contemporary games have taken to accomplish realistic character animations. In a soccer game, for example, IK is solved in real time to make the player's foot reach a flying ball. Fig. 13.16 shows a series of snapshots of the IK-based animation, where the character extends his arm to the flying ball. IK has many other uses. In order to have a character gaze at a randomly moving target, IK is applied to the head bone. Fig. 13.16 uses IK not only for the arm's motion but also for such dynamic gazing. IK is also widely used in shooting games to have a soldier aim a gun at the enemies.

Exercises

1. Shown below is the bone hierarchy augmented with the transforms for the default pose.

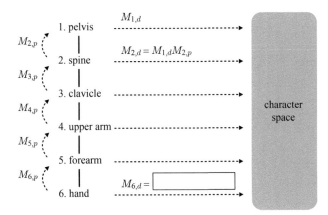

(a) Describe what $M_{2,p}$ does.

(b) Describe what $M_{2,d}$ does.

(c) Fill in the blank for $M_{6,d}$.

(d) Shown below is the inverse process. Fill in the boxes.

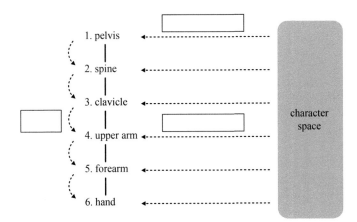

2. Shown on the left is the default pose. Let us take the bone space of the upper arm as the character space. The bone-space origins of the forearm and hand are (12,0) and (22,0), respectively, with respect to the character space. From the default pose, the forearm is rotated by $90°$, and the hand is rotated by $-90°$, to define the animated pose.

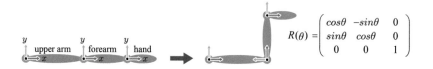

$$R(\theta) = \begin{pmatrix} cos\theta & -sin\theta & 0 \\ sin\theta & cos\theta & 0 \\ 0 & 0 & 1 \end{pmatrix}$$

(a) In the default pose, compute the to-parent matrices of the forearm and hand ($M_{f,p}$ and $M_{h,p}$).

(b) Using $M_{f,p}$ and $M_{h,p}$, compute the matrices, $M_{f,d}$ and $M_{h,d}$, which respectively transform the vertices of the forearm and hand into the character space.

(c) Compute $M_{f,d}^{-1}$ and $M_{h,d}^{-1}$.

(d) Compute the local transform matrices of the forearm and hand ($M_{f,l}$ and $M_{h,l}$).

(e) Compute the matrix, $M_{f,a}$, which animates the vertices of the forearm and transforms them back to the character space.

(f) Compute the matrix, $M_{h,a}$, which animates the vertices of the hand and transforms them back to the character space.

(g) Consider a vertex v whose coordinates in the forearm's bone space are (8,0). It is affected by two bones, the forearm and hand, which have the same blend weights. Using the skinning algorithm, compute the character-space position of v in the animated pose.

3. Consider the same arm as in Problem 2. The forearm is rotated by $-90°$, and the hand is rotated by $90°$, to define the animated pose shown below. Answer the same questions as (a) through (g) of Problem 2.

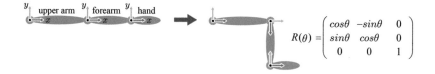

$$R(\theta) = \begin{pmatrix} cos\theta & -sin\theta & 0 \\ sin\theta & cos\theta & 0 \\ 0 & 0 & 1 \end{pmatrix}$$

4. From the default pose shown on the left, the forearm is rotated by $-90°$, and the hand is rotated by $90°$, to define the animated pose. Suppose that v is affected by both forearm and hand.

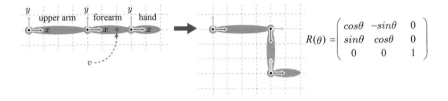

$$R(\theta) = \begin{pmatrix} cos\theta & -sin\theta & 0 \\ sin\theta & cos\theta & 0 \\ 0 & 0 & 1 \end{pmatrix}$$

(a) What are v's coordinates in the bone space of the forearm?

(b) Using two matrices, show the process of computing the coordinates of "v rotated by the forearm" in the bone space of the upper arm.

(c) What are v's coordinates in the bone space of the hand?

(d) Using four matrices, show the process of computing the coordinates of "v rotated by the hand" in the bone space of the upper arm.

(e) The forearm and hand have the blend weights of 80% and 20%, respectively, on v. Compute the coordinates of v in the bone space of the upper arm.

5. Shown below is the pseudocode for combining skinning and keyframe animation for a human character.

```
 1: for each bone // default pose
 2:     compute Md-
 3:
 4: for each frame
 5:     for each bone i // animated pose
 6:         interpolate key data
 7:         compute Ma
 8:         combine Ma with Md- to define Mi
 9:         store Mi in the matrix palette
10:     invoke vertex shader for skinning
```

(a) At line 6, what kinds of key data are interpolated?

(b) The vertex shader invoked at line 10 will perform texturing and lighting in addition to skinning. List all data stored in the vertex array.

6. The figure shown below depicts how skinning is implemented.

(a) How many bones does the character have?

(b) How many bones affect a vertex?

(c) Fill in the blank at the upper-right corner.

(d) In the matrix palette, M_i is a combination of two matrices: one remains fixed throughout the entire animation whereas the other is updated for every frame. What are the matrices? What do they do?

7. In Fig. 13.16, dynamic gazing is implemented. Involved in dynamic gazing is the 3-DOF joint connecting the head and neck. Describe an analytic solution for dynamic gazing.

Chapter 14

Normal Mapping

Many real-world objects such as brick walls and paved grounds have bumpy surfaces. Fig. 14.1-(a) shows a high-frequency polygon mesh for a paved ground. It is textured with the image in Fig. 14.1-(b) to produce the result in Fig. 14.1-(c). Illustrated in Fig. 14.1-(d) is a closeup view of the bumpy surface with three points, a, b, and c. The diffuse reflection at a surface point is determined by the angle between the normal, n, and the light vector, l, which connects the point to the light source. In Fig. 14.1-(d), b receives more light than a and c. Consequently b reflects more light and appears lighter. The surface normals irregularly change across the bumpy surface, and so do the intensities of the lit surface, making the bumpy features clearly visible in the rendered result. Unfortunately it is not cheap to process the high-resolution mesh in Fig. 14.1-(a).

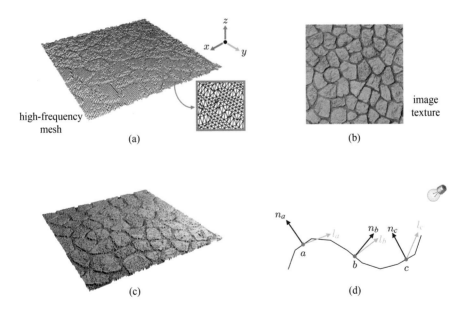

Fig. 14.1: Bumpy surface rendering: The irregular change in shading is made by the high-frequency surface normals.

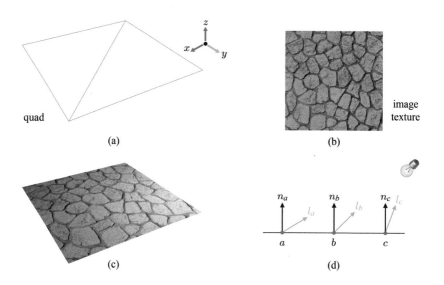

Fig. 14.2: Flat surface rendering: The quad has a uniform normal across its surface, and therefore the bumpy features are not properly demonstrated.

Fig. 14.2 uses a simple quad composed of two triangles. It is cheap to process such a low-resolution mesh. However, the quad does not properly expose the bumpy features even though it is textured with the paved-ground image. As illustrated in Fig. 14.2-(d), the quad has a uniform normal across its surface. When we move from a to b and then to c, the angle between n and l keeps decreasing and the points are more lit. Consequently, there is smooth change in shading across the surface. If the viewpoint gets closer to the quad, the lack of geometric detail will be more clearly noticeable.

A way out of the dilemma presented in Fig. 14.1 and Fig. 14.2 is to pre-compute the normals of the high-frequency mesh and store them in a special texture named the *normal map*. Then, at run time, we use the simple quad and fetch the normals from the normal map to light it. This technique of mimicking the surface bumpiness is called *bump mapping* or *normal mapping*.

14.1 Height Map

The high-frequency surface given in Fig. 14.1-(a) can be described as a *height field*. It is a function $h(x, y)$, which takes (x, y) coordinates and returns a height value. Fig. 14.3-(a) shows a height field sampled at regularly spaced

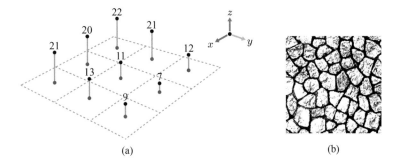

(a) (b)

Fig. 14.3: Height map: (a) Height values are stored at regularly sampled (x, y) coordinates. (b) A height map is often visualized as a gray-scale image.

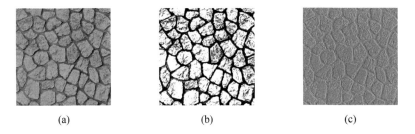

(a) (b) (c)

Fig. 14.4: Creation of a height map and a normal map: (a) Image texture. (b) The height map is semiautomatically constructed from the image texture. (c) The normal map is automatically constructed from the height map.

(x, y) coordinates. The 2D array of sampled height values is stored in a special texture, named the *height map*.

The height map is often visualized in gray scale. If the height is in the integer range $[0, 255]$, the lowest height 0 is colored in black, and the highest 255 is colored in white. Fig. 14.3-(b) visualizes the height map that represents the high-frequency mesh in Fig. 14.1-(a). A smoothly shaded part on the gray-scale image represents a smooth surface whereas an unevenly colored part represents an uneven surface.

Height maps can be created from image textures. Consider the paved-ground image in Fig. 14.4-(a). Using 2D graphics packages, the RGB colors are converted into gray scale[1], and the gray-scale image is often edited by hand to produce the height map in Fig. 14.4-(b). Then, the height map has the same resolution as the image texture.

---

[1]The simplest method is to take the mean of RGB components as the gray-scale value.

[Note: Height map and terrain rendering]

This chapter presents the use of height map for normal mapping. Note that, however, the height map is the most popular representation of terrain and is also frequently used for representing fluid or water surfaces. Fig. 14.5-(a) and -(b) respectively show the height map (visualized in a gray-scale image) and the image texture for a mountainous area. It is straightforward to generate a triangle mesh from a height map. Fig. 14.5-(c) shows the triangle mesh generated from the height map of Fig. 14.3-(a), and Fig. 14.5-(d) shows a part of the triangle mesh generated from the height map of Fig. 14.5-(a). The triangle mesh can be textured, as shown in Fig. 14.5-(e).

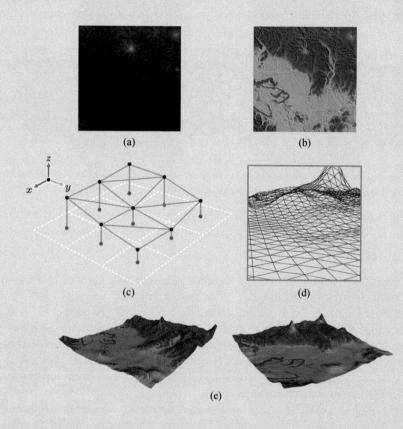

Fig. 14.5: Terrain rendering using a height map and an image texture. (The data were originally from the United States Geological Survey (USGS) and were processed by the authors of the paper [7].)

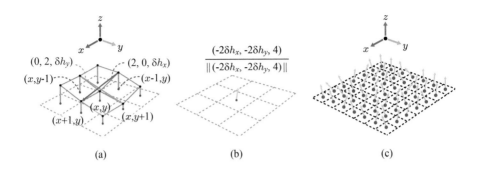

Fig. 14.6: The normal at a sampled point of the height map is computed using the heights of its neighbors. (a) The surface normal at $(x, y, h(x, y))$ is defined by the cross product of the red and green vectors. (b) The surface normal at $(x, y, h(x, y))$ is stored at (x, y). (c) A normal map stores vectors, all of which are considered as the perturbed instances of $(0, 0, 1)$.

14.2 Normal Map

A popular method to create a normal map is to use a height map. The height map of Fig. 14.3-(a) is redrawn in Fig. 14.6-(a). The quad mesh represents the surface reconstructed from the height map's texels. Let us compute the surface normal at $(x, y, h(x, y))$, where $h(x, y)$ represents the height at (x, y). The red vector connects $(x - 1, y, h(x - 1, y))$ and $(x + 1, y, h(x + 1, y))$. It is denoted by $(2, 0, \delta h_x)$, where $\delta h_x = h(x + 1, y) - h(x - 1, y)$. Similarly, the green vector connecting $(x, y - 1, h(x, y - 1))$ and $(x, y + 1, h(x, y + 1))$ is denoted by $(0, 2, \delta h_y)$, where $\delta h_y = h(x, y + 1) - h(x, y - 1)$. We take $(2, 0, \delta h_x)$ and $(0, 2, \delta h_y)$ as the *tangent vectors* at $(x, y, h(x, y))$. Then, their cross product, $(-2\delta h_x, -2\delta h_y, 4)$, is taken as the surface normal. It is normalized and stored in the normal map. See Fig. 14.6-(b). Such a normal is pointing away from the height-field surface and reflects the slopes of the nearby areas. Fig. 14.6-(c) gives a conceptual illustration of a normal map. Note that a normal map has the same resolution as the height map.

Presented above is the simplest algorithm for normal map creation. More elaborate algorithms are available, which consider more neighbors for computing the surface normal at a point of the height field. Many 2D graphics packages such as Photoshop provide well-developed plug-ins that automatically convert a height map to a normal map.

Each component of a normal (n_x, n_y, n_z) is a floating-point value in the range of $[-1, 1]$. In order to store the normal in a texture, where each RGB

component is in the range of $[0, 1]$, we need a *range conversion*:

$$R = (n_x + 1)/2$$
$$G = (n_y + 1)/2 \qquad (14.1)$$
$$B = (n_z + 1)/2$$

Note that, as can be found in Fig. 14.6-(c), a normal pointing away from the height field surface is generally a *perturbed* instance of $(0, 0, 1)$, and therefore its x- and y-coordinates are usually much smaller than its z-coordinate. Then, the dominant color channel of the normal map in the RGB format is blue. Fig. 14.4-(c) displays the normal map as an image texture.

14.3   Shaders for Normal Mapping

The low-resolution mesh used for normal mapping, such as the quad in Fig. 14.2-(a), is named the *base surface*. It is rasterized and each fragment is passed to the fragment shader, which will fetch a normal from the normal map to light the fragment.

Sample code 14-1 Vertex shader for normal mapping

```
 1: #version 300 es
 2:
 3: uniform mat4 worldMat, viewMat, projMat;
 4: uniform vec3 eyePos;
 5:
 6: layout(location = 0) in vec3 position;
 7: layout(location = 2) in vec2 texCoord;
 8:
 9: out vec3 v_view;
10: out vec2 v_texCoord;
11:
12: void main() {
13:     vec3 worldPos = (worldMat * vec4(position, 1.0)).xyz;
14:     v_view = normalize(eyePos - worldPos);
15:     v_texCoord = texCoord;
16:     gl_Position = projMat * viewMat * vec4(worldPos, 1.0);
17: }
```

Sample code 14-1 shows the vertex shader for normal mapping. It has been slightly modified from Sample code 9-1 presented in Section 9.2. Observe that there is no vertex normal input. In contrast, **texCoord** is copied to **v_texCoord** as usual, and each fragment will be given the interpolated texture coordinates, with which the normal map is accessed to return the normal for that fragment.

Sample code 14-2 Fragment shader for normal mapping

```
1: #version 300 es
2:
3: precision mediump float;
4:
5: uniform sampler2D colorMap, normalMap;
6: uniform vec3 matSpec; // Ms
7: uniform float matSh; // shininess
8: uniform vec3 srcDiff, srcSpec, srcAmbi; // Sd, Ss, Sa
9: uniform vec3 lightDir; // directional light
10:
11: in vec3 v_view;
12: in vec2 v_texCoord;
13:
14: layout(location = 0) out vec4 fragColor;
15:
16: void main() {
17:     // normal map filtering
18:     vec3 normal = normalize(2.0 * texture(normalMap, v_texCoord).xyz
               - 1.0);
19:
20:     vec3 light = normalize(lightDir);
21:     vec3 view = normalize(v_view);
22:
23:     // diffuse term
24:     vec3 matDiff = texture(colorMap, v_texCoord).rgb;
25:     vec3 diff = max(dot(normal, light), 0.0) * srcDiff * matDiff;
26:
27:     // specular term
28:     vec3 refl = 2.0 * normal * dot(normal, light) - light;
29:     vec3 spec = pow(max(dot(refl, view), 0.0), matSh) * srcSpec * matSpec;
30:
31:     fragColor = vec4(diff + spec, 1.0);
32: }
```

Sample code 14-2 shows the fragment shader. It has been modified from Sample code 9-2 in Section 9.2, which implemented the Phong lighting. In addition to the image texture (`colorMap`), the normal map (`normalMap`) is defined at line 5. It is filtered using `v_texCoord` at line 18. The built-in function `texture` returns an RGB color, each component in the range of $[0, 1]$. We need a range conversion into $[-1, 1]$, which is the inverse of Equation (14.1):

$$n_x = 2R - 1$$
$$n_y = 2G - 1 \qquad (14.2)$$
$$n_z = 2B - 1$$

If the normal map is filtered by bilinear interpolation, (n_x, n_y, n_z) are not necessarily a unit vector. Therefore, the built-in function `normalize` is invoked at line 18. The result, `normal`, is used to compute the diffuse term (line 25) and the reflection vector of the specular term (line 28).

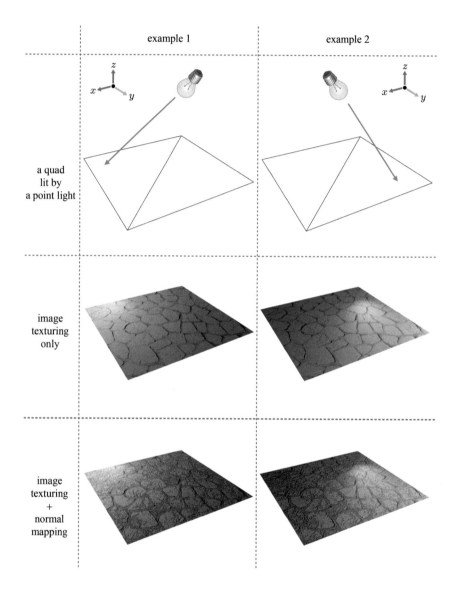

Fig. 14.7: Comparison of "image texturing only" and "image texturing + normal mapping."

Fig. 14.7 compares a quad rendered with only an image texture and the same quad rendered with both an image texture and a normal map. Without normal mapping, the surface normal of the quad is fixed to the z-axis unit vector $(0,0,1)$ at every fragment. With normal mapping, the normal of each fragment is obtained from the normal map. Even for adjacent fragments, the normals may have significantly different directions, and thus the shading on the flat surface may change rapidly and irregularly.

Normal mapping gives the *illusion* of high-frequency surface detail in that it is achieved without adding or processing more geometry. Unlike the high frequency mesh in Fig. 14.1, the normal-mapped quad in Fig. 14.7 exposes its linear edges. It is unavoidable since normal mapping does not alter the shape of the base surface at all but simply perturbs its normals during lighting.

[Note: Discussion on normal mapping]

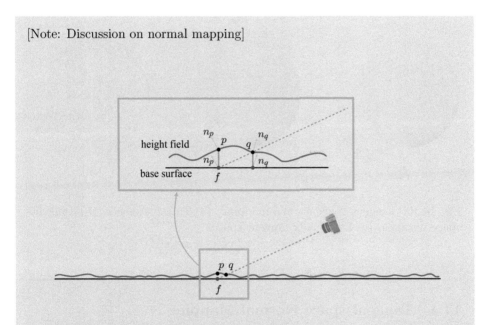

Fig. 14.8: Height field processing and its approximation (modified from [8]).

Fig. 14.8 illustrates the height field in a cross section. Consider the fragment f of the base surface. For lighting f, we use the normal n_p computed at p. If the height-field surface itself were used for rendering, however, the surface point actually visible from the camera would be q and therefore n_q should be used for lighting f. Normal mapping implicitly assumes that, compared to the extent of the base surface, the altitude of the height field is negligibly small. Then, the visible point q is approximated to p and its normal n_p is taken for lighting.

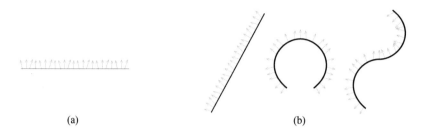

(a)   (b)

Fig. 14.9: Normal mapping: (a) A normal map visualized in a cross section. (b) The normal map can be pasted to any kind of surface.

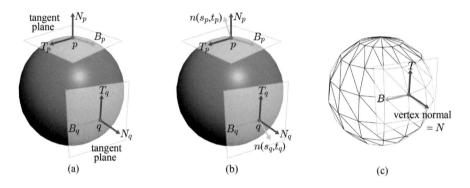

(a)   (b)   (c)

Fig. 14.10: Tangent-space normal mapping: (a) Tangent spaces. (b) Tangent-space normals. (c) Per-vertex tangent space.

14.4   Tangent-space Normal Mapping

Texturing is described as 'pasting' a texture on an object surface. Fig. 14.9-(a) visualizes a normal map in a cross section. We should be able to paste it to various surfaces, as illustrated in Fig. 14.9-(b). For this, we need an additional process, which is not performed during image texturing.

14.4.1   Tangent-space Normals

Let N denote the normal of a surface point. In the *tangent plane* perpendicular to N, consider two orthonormal vectors denoted by T (for *tangent*) and B (for *bitangent*). Fig. 14.10-(a) shows two instances of $\{T, B, N\}$ for the surface points p and q. The coordinate system defined by a surface point and $\{T, B, N\}$ is named the *tangent space*.

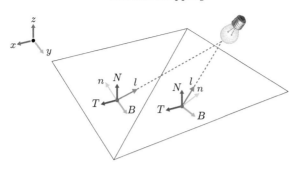

Fig. 14.11: The tangent-space basis, $\{T, B, N\}$, at every base-surface point is identical to the world-space basis. Obviously this is a special case.

In Fig. 14.10-(b), $n(s_p, t_p)$ is the normal fetched from the normal map using p's texture coordinates, (s_p, t_p). Without normal mapping, N_p would be used for lighting. In normal mapping, however, $n(s_p, t_p)$ replaces N_p, which is $(0, 0, 1)$ in the tangent space of p. This implies that, as a 'perturbed' instance of $(0, 0, 1)$, $n(s_p, t_p)$ can be considered to be defined in the tangent space of p. The same discussion is made for q, and $n(s_q, t_q)$ is defined in the tangent space of q. Note that the tangent spaces vary across the object's surface. Whatever surface point is normal-mapped, the normal fetched from the normal map is considered to be defined in the tangent space of that point.

14.4.2 Shaders for Tangent-space Normal Mapping

The fragment shader in Sample code 14-2 invoked `dot(normal, light)` at line 25. However, it does not work in general because `normal` is a tangent-space vector but `light` is a world-space vector. Two vectors defined in different spaces may not be combined through dot product. In the paved-ground example of Fig. 14.7, `dot(normal, light)` worked because the basis of the world space was identical to that of the tangent space for every point of the base surface, the quad. It is illustrated in Fig. 14.11. If the quad is tilted, for example, the tangent-space bases are no longer identical to the world-space basis and `dot(normal, light)` may return an unexpected result.

We have two options to resolve the inconsistency between the tangent-space vector, `normal`, and the world-space vector, `light`: (1) transform `normal` into the world space, or (2) transform `light` into the tangent space. We will take the second option.

The transform to the tangent space will be distinct for each surface point because the tangent spaces vary across the object's surface. Recall that each vertex of a polygon mesh is assigned a normal at the modeling step. Taking it as N and adding T and B to it, the tangent-space basis, $\{T, B, N\}$, is defined *per vertex*. Fig. 14.10-(c) shows an example. There are many utility functions

---

Sample code 14-3 Vertex shader for tangent-space normal mapping

---

```
 1: #version 300 es
 2:
 3: uniform mat4 worldMat, viewMat, projMat;
 4: uniform vec3 eyePos, lightDir;
 5:
 6: layout(location = 0) in vec3 position;
 7: layout(location = 1) in vec3 normal;
 8: layout(location = 2) in vec2 texCoord;
 9: layout(location = 3) in vec3 tangent;
10:
11: out vec3 v_lightTS, v_viewTS;
12: out vec2 v_texCoord;
13:
14: void main() {
15:     vec3 worldPos = (worldMat * vec4(position, 1.0)).xyz;
16:
17:     vec3 Nor = normalize(transpose(inverse(mat3(worldMat))) * normal);
18:     vec3 Tan = normalize(transpose(inverse(mat3(worldMat))) * tangent);
19:     vec3 Bin = cross(Nor, Tan);
20:     mat3 tbnMat = transpose(mat3(Tan, Bin, Nor)); // row major
21:
22:     v_lightTS = tbnMat * normalize(lightDir);
23:     v_viewTS = tbnMat * normalize(eyePos - worldPos);
24:
25:     v_texCoord = texCoord;
26:     gl_Position = projMat * viewMat * vec4(worldPos, 1.0);
27: }
```

---

that compute T and B on each vertex of a polygon mesh, and an algorithm will be presented in Section 14.4.3.

The per-vertex tangent-space basis, $\{T, B, N\}$, is stored in the vertex array and passed to the vertex shader. The basis vectors are all defined in the object space, and the vertex shader transforms them into the world space. Then, a 3×3 matrix is constructed with the world-space vectors, T, B, and N:

$$M_{TBN} = \begin{pmatrix} T_x & T_y & T_z \\ B_x & B_y & B_z \\ N_x & N_y & N_z \end{pmatrix} \tag{14.3}$$

This is the *basis-change* matrix that converts the world-space light vector into the tangent space.

Shown in Sample code 14-3 is the vertex shader for tangent-space normal mapping. In addition to **normal** (for N), a new attribute, **tangent** (for T), is provided (line 9). In the main function, they are transformed into the world space (lines 17 and 18). We could provide B as another attribute, but it would lead to a larger vertex array. The memory bandwidth can be reduced by not including B in the vertex array but having the vertex shader compute

Sample code 14-4 Fragment shader for tangent-space normal mapping

```
1: #version 300 es
2:
3: precision mediump float;
4:
5: uniform sampler2D colorMap, normalMap;
6: uniform vec3 matSpec; // Ms
7: uniform float matSh; // shininess
8: uniform vec3 srcDiff, srcSpec, srcAmbi; // Sd, Ss, Sa
9:
10: in vec3 v_lightTS, v_viewTS;
11: in vec2 v_texCoord;
12:
13: layout(location = 0) out vec4 fragColor;
14:
15: void main() {
16:     vec3 normal = normalize(2.0 * texture(normalMap, v_texCoord).xyz
                - 1.0);
17:
18:     vec3 light = normalize(v_lightTS);
19:     vec3 view = normalize(v_viewTS);
20:
21:     vec3 matDiff = texture(colorMap, v_texCoord).rgb;
22:     vec3 diff = max(dot(normal, light), 0.0) * srcDiff * matDiff;
23:
24:     vec3 refl = 2.0 * normal * dot(normal, light) - light;
25:     vec3 spec = pow(max(dot(refl, view), 0.0), matSh) * srcSpec * matSpec;
26:
27:     fragColor = vec4(diff + spec, 1.0);
28: }
```

it by taking the cross product of N and T (line 19). The cross product is implemented by the built-in function, `cross`.

Then, the matrix in Equation (14.3) is defined (line 20)[2]. It transforms the world-space light vector, `lightDir` given as a uniform, into the tangent-space light vector, `v_lightTS` (line 22). Note that not only the normal and light vector but also the view vector is involved in lighting. It is also transformed into the tangent space: `v_viewTS` at line 23. Observe that `normal` at line 7 is used only to define the transform to the tangent space and is not output to the rasterizer. In contrast, `v_lightTS` and `v_viewTS` are output so as to be interpolated by the rasterizer.

The fragment shader in Sample code 14-4 has been slightly changed from Sample code 14-2. It accepts new input variables, `v_lightTS` and `v_viewTS`,

---

[2]In GL, a matrix constructor such as `mat3` fills the matrix *column by column*. In this example, `Tan`, `Bin`, and `Nor` fill the first, second, and third columns, respectively. Such a matrix is often called a *column major* matrix. It is the transpose of the matrix in Equation (14.3) and therefore we invoke the built-in function `transpose` at line 20.

Fig. 14.12: A single pair of image texture and normal map is applied to the faces of a sphere, a cylinder, and a torus.

and normalizes them into `light` and `view`, respectively. They are tangent-space vectors and therefore can be combined with `normal` for lighting. As shown in Fig. 14.12, a single pair of the paved-ground image texture (in Fig. 14.4-(a)) and normal map (in Fig. 14.4-(c)) can be applied to a variety of objects with arbitrary geometries.

14.4.3 Computing Tangent Spaces*

As discussed in the previous subsection, the tangent spaces vary across an object's surface and it is necessary to define a tangent space *per vertex* in the polygon mesh. Given the vertex normal, N, we need to compute T and B.

Fig. 14.13-(a) shows a triangle, $\langle p_0, p_1, p_2 \rangle$, of a polygon mesh. Fig. 14.13-(b) shows its vertices and texture coordinates *projected* into the image texture. Note that the texture coordinates are used for both image texturing and normal mapping. Using the fact that the image-texture axis s is aligned with the normal-map axis T and similarly the t-axis is aligned with the B-axis, we can compute T and B.

Fig. 14.13-(c) shows the triangle together with unknown T and B at p_0. The vector connecting p_0 and p_1 is denoted by q_1, and the vector connecting p_0 and p_2 is q_2. Then, q_1 and q_2 are defined as follows:

$$q_1 = (s_1 - s_0)T + (t_1 - t_0)B$$
$$q_2 = (s_2 - s_0)T + (t_2 - t_0)B \tag{14.4}$$

If we abbreviate $(s_1 - s_0)$ to s_{10}, and $(t_1 - t_0)$, $(s_2 - s_0)$, and $(t_2 - t_0)$ are similarly abbreviated, Equation (14.4) is rewritten as follows:

$$q_1 = s_{10}T + t_{10}B$$
$$q_2 = s_{20}T + t_{20}B \tag{14.5}$$

Note that q_1, q_2, T, and B are all 3D vectors. As we have six equations and six unknowns, we can compute T and B.

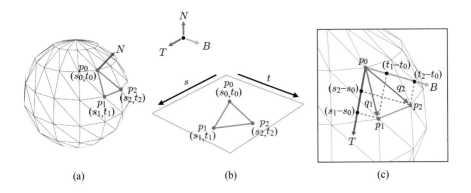

(a) (b) (c)

Fig. 14.13: Computing the per-vertex tangent space: (a) Each vertex in the polygon mesh is associated with texture coordinates (s_i, t_i). (b) The texture coordinate s_i of each vertex is defined with respect to the s- and T-axes, which are identical to each other. Similarly, t_i is defined with respect to the t- and B-axes, which are identical to each other. (c) Analysis of (s_i, t_i) unveils the directions of the T- and B-axes.

In Fig. 14.13, T and B at p_0 are computed using the texture coordinates associated with the triangle $\langle p_0, p_1, p_2 \rangle$. As p_0 is shared by multiple triangles, T and B are computed for each triangle. We denote the sum of all tangent vectors by T', and the sum of all bitangent vectors by B'. T' and B' are neither normalized nor necessarily orthogonal to each other. Furthermore, they are not necessarily orthogonal to N, the normal vector at p_0. We use the Gram-Schmidt algorithm to convert $\{T', B', N\}$ into an orthonormal basis. (See any linear algebra book for the Gram-Schmidt algorithm.) The orthonormal basis is taken as the tangent-space basis at p_0.

14.5 Authoring Normal Maps

Normal maps for planar or low-curvature surfaces can be created using 2D graphics packages, as presented in Section 14.2. However, the 2D packages are not appropriate for creating a normal map for a complex surface. Instead, digital sculpting tools, such as ZBrush developed by Pixologic, are used. Above all, they allow digital sculptors to make global or local changes to a polygon mesh. See Fig. 14.14 for a sculpting process.

The original low-resolution model in Fig. 14.14-(a) is taken as the *base surface*, and the high-frequency model in Fig. 14.14-(e) is taken as the *reference*

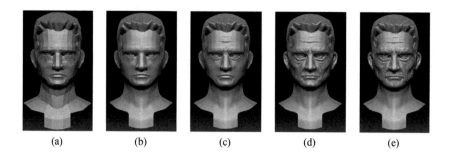

(a)   (b)   (c)   (d)   (e)

Fig. 14.14: Sculpting using ZBrush: (a) shows the input low-resolution model, (b) shows a high-resolution 'smooth' model obtained by automatically refining the low-resolution model in (a), and the rest show the manual sculpting operations to convert the high-resolution model in (b) to the high-frequency model in (e).

surface. Fig. 14.15-(a) shows the reference surface overlapped with the base surface. (The reference surface is drawn as a purple-colored wireframe.) Using these surfaces, ZBrush automatically creates a normal map, which will be pasted on the base surface at run time.

Let us see how the normal map is created by ZBrush. First, the base surface is *parameterized* such that each vertex is assigned normalized coordinates, (s, t). Suppose that we want to create a normal map of resolution $r_x \times r_y$. Then, s and t are multiplied by r_x and r_y, respectively, to define the new coordinates $(r_x s, r_y t)$. Fig. 14.15-(b) shows the parameterized base surface, where each vertex has the coordinates, $(r_x s, r_y t)$. Then, every triangle of the parameterized base surface is *rasterized* into a set of texels, to each of which a normal will be assigned.

In Fig. 14.15-(b), the magnified box shows a triangle $\langle v_0, v_1, v_2 \rangle$ and a texel, T. The original base surface is a 3D polygon mesh, and therefore each vertex is associated with a normal. During rasterization, the vertex normals (denoted as n_0, n_1, and n_2) are interpolated to define the temporary normal at T, which we denote by n_T.

Fig. 14.15-(c) illustrates the base and reference surfaces in cross section. They are depicted as if they were separated. In reality, however, they usually intersect. The bold triangle in the base surface corresponds to $\langle v_0, v_1, v_2 \rangle$, and p corresponds to texel T. The 3D coordinates of p are computed using the *barycentric coordinates* of T with respect to $\langle v_0, v_1, v_2 \rangle$. Then, a ray is cast along n_T (the temporary normal) from p. The intersection between the ray and a triangle of the reference surface (henceforth, reference triangle) is computed. The barycentric coordinates of the intersection point with respect

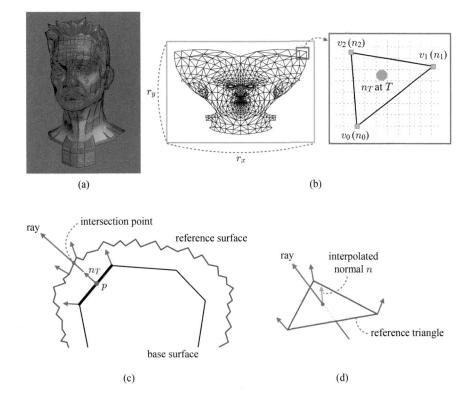

Fig. 14.15: Normal map creation: (a) Base and reference surfaces. (b) Parameterized base surface and rasterization. (c) Ray casting. (d) Normal interpolation.

to the reference triangle are used to interpolate the vertex normals of the reference triangle, as shown in Fig. 14.15-(d). The interpolated normal, n, is stored at T in the normal map such that it can later be fetched using the texture coordinates (s, t).

The normal computed through the above procedure is an object-space vector. The texture that stores such normals is called an *object-space normal map*. It is visualized in Fig. 14.15-(e). The object-space normal map does not have a dominant color because the surface normals of the reference surface usually have diverse directions.

It is not difficult to convert an object-space normal into a tangent-space normal. In Fig. 14.15-(c), consider the base surface's triangle where p lies. For each vertex of the triangle, a tangent space can be computed using the method presented in Section 14.4.3. The per-vertex *TBN*-bases are interpolated at p using its barycentric coordinates. Then, the *TBN* vectors at p are used

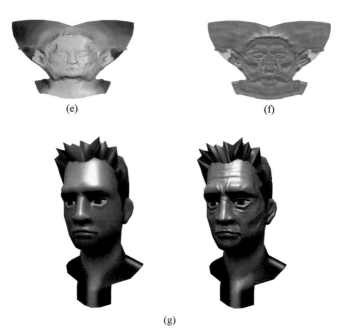

(e)   (f)

(g)

Fig. 14.15: Normal map creation (*continued*): (e) Object-space normal map. (f) Tangent-space normal map. (g) Rendering without and with normal mapping.

to define the rotation matrix presented in Equation (14.3). It converts the object-space normal, n, into the tangent space. Fig. 14.15-(f) visualizes the tangent-space normal map. The dominant color is blue, as is the case in most tangent-space normal maps. Fig. 14.15-(g) compares the rendered results without and with normal mapping.

[Note: Polygon mesh editing]
This section showed that a high-frequency model can be generated from a low-resolution model using ZBrush. Having a wide spectrum of functionalities, ZBrush can be used also for the reverse direction, i.e., for simplifying a high-frequency model to the extent that it becomes appropriate for real-time applications.

The shape of a real-world object is often captured by *3D scanning*, which samples the object's surface with a non-contact technology and creates a set of points often called *point clouds*. The points are connected to define a polygon mesh of the object. Fig. 14.16-(a) shows the mesh of a 3D-scanned face.

The polygon mesh produced via 3D scanning usually has quite a high resolution, which is inappropriate for real-time rendering and also makes it hard to edit the mesh. The face model in Fig. 14.16-(a) has about 100,000 triangles. ZBrush is often used to reduce the resolution. Fig. 14.16-(b) shows the result of semiautomatic simplification made with ZBrush. It is relatively easy to edit such a low-resolution model. Fig. 14.16-(c) shows the result of editing the eyes with 3ds Max, and Fig. 14.16-(d) shows the textured model.

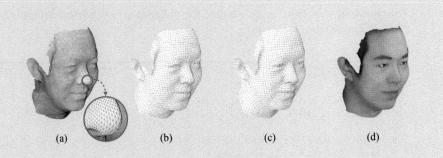

(a)   (b)   (c)   (d)

Fig. 14.16: Mesh simplification and editing: (a) A high-resolution mesh built upon 3D point clouds. (b) Semiautomatically simplified mesh. (c) Manual editing of the low resolution mesh. (d) Textured mesh.

Exercises

1. Vertex array data.

    (a) In order to apply tangent-space normal mapping to a character, what data does the vertex array store?

    (b) In addition, the character is going to be skin-animated. What data does the vertex array store?

2. Shown below is the vertex shader for tangent-space normal mapping. Fill in the boxes.

```
 1: #version 300 es
 2:
 3: uniform mat4 worldMat, viewMat, projMat;
 4: uniform vec3 eyePos, lightDir;
 5:
 6: layout(location = 0) in vec3 position;
 7: layout(location = 1) in vec3 normal;
 8: layout(location = 2) in vec2 texCoord;
 9: layout(location = 3) in vec3 tangent;
10:
11: out vec3 v_lightTS, v_viewTS;
12: out vec2 v_texCoord;
13:
14: void main() {
15:     vec3 worldPos = (worldMat * vec4(position, 1.0)).xyz;
16:     vec3 Nor = normalize(transpose(inverse(mat3(worldMat))) * normal);
17:     vec3 Tan = [                                               ];
18:     vec3 [                                    ];
19:     mat3 tbnMat = transpose(mat3(Tan, Bin, Nor)); // row major
20:
21:     v_lightTS = tbnMat * normalize(lightDir);
22:     v_viewTS = [                                  ];
23:
24:     v_texCoord = texCoord;
25:     gl_Position = projMat * viewMat * vec4(worldPos, 1.0);
26: }
```

3. Suppose that the per-vertex tangent-space basis, $\{T, B, N\}$, is stored in the vertex array and passed to the vertex shader. Write the matrix that converts a tangent-space normal vector into the world space.

4. In Fig. 14.6, we use the finite difference method to compute the normal at a height-field point. Describe another method that computes the normal using the surface normals of the triangles sharing the point.

5. Shown below is the fragment shader for tangent-space normal mapping. Fill in the boxes.

```
 1: #version 300 es
 2:
 3: precision mediump float;
 4:
 5: uniform sampler2D colorMap, normalMap;
 6: uniform vec3 srcDiff; // Sd
 7:
 8: in vec3 v_lightTS;
 9: in vec2 v_texCoord;
10:
11: layout(location = 0) out vec4 fragColor;
12:
13: void main() {
14:     // normal map access
15:     vec3 normal = [                        ];
16:
17:     vec3 light = [                ];
18:
19:     // diffuse term
20:     vec3 matDiff = [                        ];
21:     vec3 diff = max(dot(normal, light), 0.0) * srcDiff * matDiff;
22:
23:     fragColor = vec4(diff, 1.0);
24: }
```

6. Consider a cylinder and its parameterization shown below. Suppose that the cylinder axis equals the y-axis of the coordinate system. Normal mapping is to be applied to its surface. Describe how you can compute a tangent space for each vertex (x, y, z). (Do not use any information from other vertices but use only (x, y, z) of the vertex.)

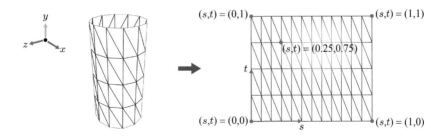

Chapter 15

Shadow Mapping

Virtually all scenes in the real world have shadows, and therefore shadow generation is an indispensable component in computer graphics. Shadows also help us understand the spatial relationships among objects in a scene. In Fig. 15.1-(a), the relative pose of the character against the ground is not clear. In contrast, given the successive snapshots in Fig. 15.1-(b), we can easily recognize a character landing on the ground.

Numerous shadow algorithms have been proposed over the past decades. The most dominant among them is the *shadow mapping* algorithm, which was originally proposed by L. Williams [9]. This chapter presents the essential ingredients of the shadow mapping algorithm.

15.1 Two-pass Algorithm

The shadow mapping algorithm is implemented in two passes. The goal of the first pass is to construct a special texture, i.e., the *shadow map*. In Fig. 15.2-(a), the surfaces lit by the light source are colored in cyan. The lit surfaces are regularly sampled, and for each sampled point p, the distance to the light source, which we denote by z, is stored in the shadow map. The distance represents a scene *depth* measured "from the viewpoint of the light source," and the shadow map is therefore a type of *depth map*.

(a)   (b)

Fig. 15.1: Shadows: (a) Little information is provided about the spatial relationship between the character and the ground. (b) The shadows enable us to perceive the character landing on the ground.

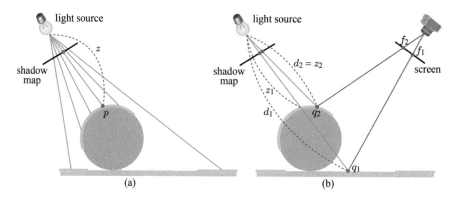

Fig. 15.2: Two-pass algorithm for shadow mapping: (a) The first pass constructs a shadow map. (b) The second pass uses the shadow map to test whether a scene point is to be fully lit or shadowed.

The second pass performs rendering "from the viewpoint of the camera" and uses the shadow map to create shadows. In Fig. 15.2-(b), consider fragment f_1 and its scene point q_1. The distance d_1 between q_1 and the light source is compared with z_1 stored in the shadow map. It is found that $d_1 > z_1$, which implies that something occludes q_1 from the light source, and therefore q_1 is determined to be shadowed. In contrast, consider fragment f_2 and its scene point q_2. It is found that d_2 equals z_2, i.e., nothing occludes q_2 from the light source. Therefore, q_2 is determined to be fully lit.

The shadow mapping algorithm is conceptually simple, but its brute-force implementation reveals several problems. Fig. 15.3-(a) shows a scene configuration, and Fig. 15.3-(b) shows the rendered result. The entire scene is decomposed into a number of fractional areas: some are fully lit whereas others are shadowed. This artifact is called *surface acne*.

To see why we have such an artifact, consider f_2 in Fig. 15.2-(b). Its scene point q_2 was assumed to have been sampled in the first pass. Unfortunately, this kind of situation rarely happens in reality. The scene points sampled in the second pass are usually different from those sampled in the first pass. Fig. 15.3-(c) shows an example. The scene point q_1 (for fragment f_1) does not coincide with any surface point sampled in the first pass.

The shadow map is nothing more than a texture and therefore its filtering method needs to be specified. Suppose that it is filtered by *nearest point sampling*. Then, for q_1 in Fig. 15.3-(c), z_1 will be retrieved from the shadow map. As $d_1 > z_1$, q_1 will be determined to be shadowed. It is incorrect. On the other hand, consider fragment f_2 that is adjacent to f_1. For its scene point q_2, z_2 will be retrieved from the shadow map, making q_2 fully lit. It is correct. Such a coexistence of shadowed and fully lit pixels leads to the surface acne artifact in Fig. 15.3-(b).

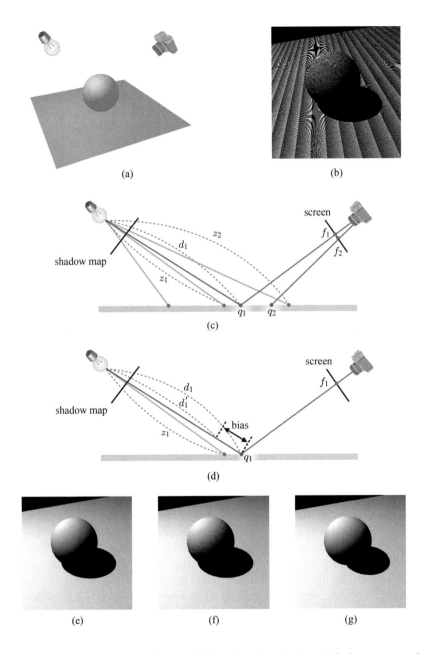

Fig. 15.3: Surface acne artifact and bias-based solution: (a) A scene configuration. (b) Surface acne artifact. (c) Surface point q_1 is shadowed whereas q_2 is fully lit. (d) Bias is subtracted from the distance to the light source. (e) Biased shadow mapping. (f) Too small a bias. (g) Too large a bias.

This artifact can be eliminated simply by moving the surface geometry toward the light source by a small amount, i.e., by subtracting a *bias* from the computed distance, d, to the light source. In Fig. 15.3-(d), a bias value is subtracted from d_1 to return d'_1. Then, $z_1 > d'_1$, and so q_1 will be fully lit. Fig. 15.3-(e) shows the result of biased shadow mapping.

It is important to appropriately determine the bias. If the bias value is too small, the surface acne artifact is not completely eliminated. In the example of Fig. 15.3-(f), the sphere still suffers from the surface acne artifact. In contrast, too large a bias also leads to incorrect shadows, as shown in Fig. 15.3-(g). Some areas that should be shadowed are erroneously taken as fully lit, and consequently the shadow appears smaller than desired. Typically the bias value is determined through a few trials.

15.2 Shadow Map Filtering

In Fig. 15.4-(a), consider the scene points, q_1 and q_2, projected between p_1 and p_2 in the texture space. If we use nearest point sampling, q_1 is compared with p_1 and is shadowed whereas q_2 is compared with p_2 and is fully lit. A fragment can be either fully lit or shadowed. It has no other option. Then, the shadow boundary usually has a jagged appearance. See Fig. 15.4-(b). This is an *aliasing* artifact.

Hoping to remove the artifact, you might think of replacing nearest point sampling by bilinear interpolation. However, it does not help. Fig. 15.4-(c) presents an example, where a scene point q is projected into the shadow map and is surrounded by four texels. The values attached to the texels denote the depths stored in the shadow map[1]. When they are bilinearly interpolated, the result is 64. Suppose that q's depth is 80. Then, q would be determined to be shadowed. Again, a fragment is either fully lit or shadowed and the shadow quality is not improved by choosing bilinear interpolation.

A solution to this problem is to first determine the *visibilities* of a fragment with respect to its surrounding texels and then interpolate them. See Fig. 15.4-(d). The visibility of q with respect to the upper-left texel is 0, i.e., q is invisible from the light source, because q is deeper than the texel. In contrast, the visibilities with respect to the other three texels are 1, i.e., q is visible from the light source. The four visibility values are bilinearly interpolated, and q's visibility is set to the interpolated, 0.58 in the example. By doing so, q is not restricted to either "fully lit (1)" or "shadowed (0)." Instead, its reflection color computed through lighting is multiplied by the visibility in the range of

---

[1]By default, the shadow map texels are in the range of $[0, 1]$, as will be presented in the next section, but the current example shows integer depths just for presentation purposes.

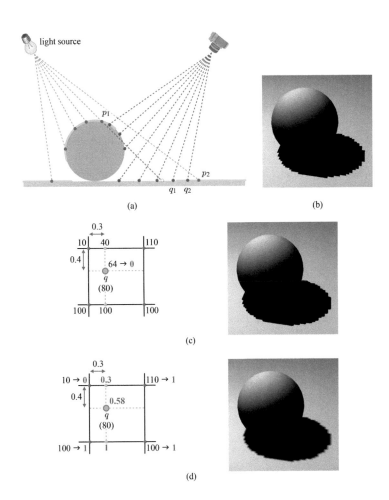

Fig. 15.4: Shadow map filtering: (a) Scene points q_1 and q_2 are projected between p_1 and p_2 in the texture space of the shadow map. (b) Jagged edge produced by nearest point sampling. (c) Bilinear interpolation does not make a meaningful difference from nearest point sampling. (d) The visibility is computed for each texel, and the visibilities are bilinearly interpolated.

$[0, 1]$. As a result, the jagged edge of the shadow can be smoothed to some extent, as shown in Fig. 15.4-(d).

In general, the technique of taking multiple texels from the shadow map and blending the visibilities is named the *percentage closer filtering* (PCF). Note that PCF works differently from traditional bilinear interpolation. Therefore, it requires special handling. This will be presented in the next section.

15.3   GL Program and Shaders for Shadow Mapping*

During the first pass, the surfaces *visible* from the light source are sampled to create the shadow map. For this, the scene is rendered from the light source's viewpoint, i.e., with the camera placed at the light source position. Neither lighting nor texturing is done, but the resulting z-buffer is taken as the shadow map. During the second pass, the scene is rendered normally with the real position of the camera.

This section presents a pair of vertex and fragment shaders for each pass. The shaders might not be easy to understand. If you are not interested in programming, you might want to skip this section.

15.3.1   First-pass Shaders

The view matrix is defined with **EYE** placed at the light source position. It transforms the world-space vertex into a space, which is different from the conventional camera space. It is named the *light space*. Then, as illustrated on the left of Fig. 15.5, the view frustum is specified in the light space.

Sample code 15-1 First-pass vertex shader for shadow mapping

```
 1: #version 300 es
 2:
 3: uniform mat4 worldMat;
 4: uniform mat4 lightViewMat, lightProjMat;
 5:
 6: layout(location = 0) in vec3 position;
 7:
 8: void main() {
 9:     // generate shadow map
10:     gl_Position = lightProjMat * lightViewMat * worldMat
                  * vec4(position, 1.0);
11: }
```

The vertex shader in Sample code 15-1 takes new uniforms, `lightViewMat` and `lightProjMat`. After `lightViewMat` transforms the world-space vertex into the light space, `lightProjMat` transforms the light-space vertex into "the clip space related to the light source." It is stored in `gl_Position`. The vertex shader does not output anything else. The clip-space vertex in `gl_Position` will then go through *perspective division*. In Fig. 15.5, the point p visible from the light source has been transformed into the 2×2×2 cube in NDC.

The cube in NDC is transformed into the screen-space viewport shown on the right of Fig. 15.5. The screen-space objects are rasterized into fragments,

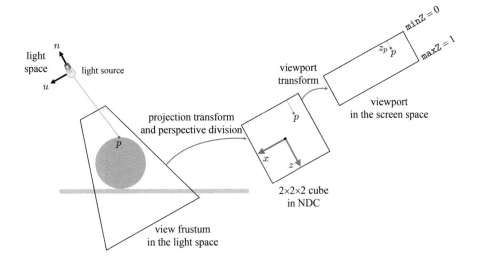

Fig. 15.5: **EYE**, **AT**, and **UP** are specified with respect to the light source, and then $\{u, v, n\}$ is computed. (Only the u- and n-axes are presented in the cross-section illustration.) **EYE** and $\{u, v, n\}$ define the light space. The view frustum is specified in the light space. The sampled point p is projection-transformed into the clip space. The perspective division defines p in NDC, i.e., within the 2×2×2 cube, and the viewport transform computes z_p in $[0, 1]$.

but there are no attributes to interpolate because the vertex shader outputs nothing except `gl_Position`. Shown in Sample code 15-2 is the fragment shader. Not surprisingly, it takes nothing as input, and its main function is empty because the task of the first-pass fragment shader is not to determine the fragment's color.

Even though the fragment shader does not return the color of a fragment, the screen-space coordinates of the fragment are passed to the output merger, as always, so that it goes through z-buffering. Consequently, the z-buffer is updated so as to finally contain the depth values of the surfaces visible from the light source. It is taken as the shadow map. In Fig. 15.5, z_p denotes the depth of the visible point p.

Sample code 15-2 First-pass fragment shader for shadow mapping

```
1: #version 300 es
2:
3: void main() {}
```

If the viewport's depth range, $[\texttt{minZ}, \texttt{maxZ}]$, is set to the default, $[0, 1]$, each texel of the shadow map stores a depth value normalized in that range. Note that, in the conceptual presentation of Fig. 15.2, the shadow map contains the world-space distances from the light source, however, in the actual implementation, it stores normalized depth values in the screen space.

15.3.2 Render-to-Texture and Framebuffer Object

Sample code 15-3 GL program for framebuffer object

```
 1: #define SHADOW_MAP_SIZE 1024
 2:
 3: GLuint texture;
 4: glGenTextures(1, &texture);
 5: glBindTexture(GL_TEXTURE_2D, texture);
 6: glTexImage2D(GL_TEXTURE_2D, 0, GL_DEPTH_COMPONENT16,
          SHADOW_MAP_SIZE, SHADOW_MAP_SIZE, 0,
          GL_DEPTH_COMPONENT, GL_UNSIGNED_SHORT, NULL);
 7: glTexParameteri(GL_TEXTURE_2D, GL_TEXTURE_MIN_FILTER, GL_LINEAR);
 8: glTexParameteri(GL_TEXTURE_2D, GL_TEXTURE_MAG_FILTER, GL_LINEAR);
 9: glTexParameteri(GL_TEXTURE_2D, GL_TEXTURE_WRAP_S, GL_CLAMP_TO_EDGE);
10: glTexParameteri(GL_TEXTURE_2D, GL_TEXTURE_WRAP_T, GL_CLAMP_TO_EDGE);
11: glTexParameteri(GL_TEXTURE_2D, GL_TEXTURE_COMPARE_MODE,
          GL_COMPARE_REF_TO_TEXTURE);
12: glTexParameteri(GL_TEXTURE_2D, GL_TEXTURE_COMPARE_FUNC, GL_LEQUAL);
13:
14: GLuint fbo;
15: glGenFramebuffers(1, &fbo);
16: glBindFramebuffer(GL_FRAMEBUFFER, fbo);
17: glFramebufferTexture2D(GL_FRAMEBUFFER,
          GL_DEPTH_ATTACHMENT, GL_TEXTURE_2D, texture, 0);
```

The first pass of shadow mapping implements *off-screen rendering* to produce a shadow map. It is generally called *render-to-texture*. For this, the GL program has to reserve a texture for the shadow map before making the drawcall. See Sample code 15-3. Lines 3 through 6 follow the routine of generating, binding, and specifying a texture, as was done in Sample code 8-1. The third argument of **glTexImage2D** (at line 6) is **GL_DEPTH_COMPONENT16**, which declares that the depth is represented in 16 bits; the fourth and fifth arguments define the resolution of the shadow map. Lines 7 and 8 specify the shadow map filtering method. For both minification and magnification, **GL_LINEAR** is selected, but it works differently from image texturing, as will be presented in Section 15.3.3. Lines 9 and 10 specify the texture wrapping mode. Lines 11 and 12 will be discussed in Section 15.3.3.

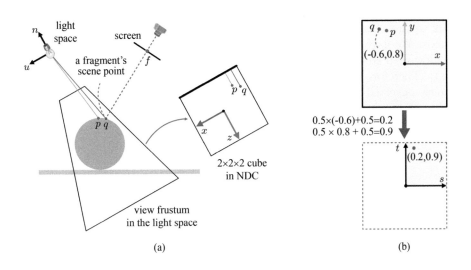

Fig. 15.6: Depth comparison: (a) The scene point q goes through the same transforms applied to the scene point p sampled in the first pass. (b) The coordinates of q are range-converted. Suppose that q's coordinates are $(-0.6, 0.8)$. The *relative* location of q within the 2×2 square is the same as that of the texture coordinates, $(0.2, 0.9)$, within the unit-square parameter space.

In GL, off-screen rendering or render-to-texture is supported under the name of *framebuffer object* (FBO). Section 10.1 introduced three components of the frame buffer: color, depth, and stencil buffers. Similarly, an FBO has color, depth, and stencil *attachments*. The texture reserved for the shadow map should be attached to the "depth attachment point" of the FBO. Then, the first-pass rendering is made with the attached texture. The last four lines in Sample code 15-3 generate, bind, and specify an FBO. At line 17, the arguments of `glFramebufferTexture2D` assert that `texture` (defined at line 3) is attached to the FBO.

15.3.3 Second-pass Shaders

The second pass renders the scene from the camera's viewpoint. In Fig. 15.6-(a), q represents the scene point for a fragment. Suppose that its depth is going to be compared with that of p sampled in the first pass. For the comparison, we retrace the path we took for p. We transform q into "the clip space related to the light source" and then perform perspective division. Fig. 15.6-(a) shows q transformed into the 2×2×2 cube. The depth of q is in the range $[-1, 1]$ whereas that of p, denoted as z_p in Fig. 15.5, is in $[0, 1]$. We need range conversion from $[-1, 1]$ to $[0, 1]$. We denote the resulting depth of q by d_q.

Consider the bold boundary of the 2×2×2 cube in Fig. 15.6-(a). It is a 2×2 square. Shown on the top of Fig. 15.6-(b) is the square seen along the z-axis. We have to compare the depth values of p and q, i.e., z_p and d_q. The shadow map storing z_p is accessed by (s, t) and both s and t are in the range $[0, 1]$. Therefore, the x- and y-coordinates of q, currently in $[-1, 1]$, should be range-converted to $[0, 1]$, as illustrated in Fig. 15.6-(b).

Let us summarize the procedure. Suppose that q is transformed into the clip space to have the homogeneous coordinates, (x, y, z, w). The subsequent operations on the coordinates are presented as follows:

$$\begin{pmatrix} x \\ y \\ z \\ w \end{pmatrix} \rightarrow \begin{pmatrix} x/w \\ y/w \\ z/w \end{pmatrix} \rightarrow \begin{pmatrix} 0.5x/w + 0.5 \\ 0.5y/w + 0.5 \\ 0.5z/w + 0.5 \end{pmatrix} = \begin{pmatrix} s \\ t \\ d_q \end{pmatrix} \tag{15.1}$$

The first arrow represents the perspective division and the second represents the range conversion applied uniformly to all coordinates. Then, the first two coordinates, (s, t), are used to access the shadow map and fetch z_p, which is then compared with the last coordinate, d_q.

The vertex and fragment shaders can be implemented more efficiently if we derive (s, t, d_q) in a way different from Equation (15.1):

$$\begin{pmatrix} x \\ y \\ z \\ w \end{pmatrix} \rightarrow \begin{pmatrix} 0.5x + 0.5w \\ 0.5y + 0.5w \\ 0.5z + 0.5w \\ w \end{pmatrix} \rightarrow \begin{pmatrix} 0.5x/w + 0.5 \\ 0.5y/w + 0.5 \\ 0.5z/w + 0.5 \end{pmatrix} = \begin{pmatrix} s \\ t \\ d_q \end{pmatrix} \tag{15.2}$$

The first step will be done by the vertex shader. The second step divides the homogeneous coordinates by the w-coordinate. This is generally called *projection*, as presented in Fig. 4.3, and will be done by the fragment shader.

Shown in Sample code 15-4 is the second-pass vertex shader. See line 29. The world-space vertex (`worldPos`) is transformed by `lightViewMat` and `lightProjMat` to define the homogeneous clip-space coordinates, (x, y, z, w), which are then multiplied by a special matrix, `tMat`. The first step in Equation (15.2) is implemented by `tMat`[2]:

$$\begin{pmatrix} 0.5 & 0 & 0 & 0.5 \\ 0 & 0.5 & 0 & 0.5 \\ 0 & 0 & 0.5 & 0.5 \\ 0 & 0 & 0 & 1 \end{pmatrix} \begin{pmatrix} x \\ y \\ z \\ w \end{pmatrix} = \begin{pmatrix} 0.5x + 0.5w \\ 0.5y + 0.5w \\ 0.5z + 0.5w \\ w \end{pmatrix} \tag{15.3}$$

This 4D vector is output as `v_shadowCoord`. The last statement of the main function returns `gl_Position`, which will go through the conventional pipeline to contribute to the image rendered on the screen.

---

[2]In the same manner as `mat3` presented in Sample code 14-3 of Section 14.4.2, `mat4` constructs a column-major matrix.

Sample code 15-4 Second-pass vertex shader for shadow mapping

```
1: #version 300 es
2:
3: uniform mat4 worldMat, viewMat, projMat;
4: uniform mat4 lightViewMat, lightProjMat;
5: uniform vec3 lightPos;
6:
7: layout(location = 0) in vec3 position;
8: layout(location = 1) in vec3 normal;
9: layout(location = 2) in vec2 texCoord;
10:
11: out vec3 v_normal, v_light;
12: out vec2 v_texCoord;
13: out vec4 v_shadowCoord;
14:
15: const mat4 tMat = mat4(
16:        0.5, 0.0, 0.0, 0.0,
17:        0.0, 0.5, 0.0, 0.0,
18:        0.0, 0.0, 0.5, 0.0,
19:        0.5, 0.5, 0.5, 1.0
20: );
21:
22: void main() {
23:        v_normal = normalize(transpose(inverse(mat3(worldMat))) * normal);
24:        vec3 worldPos = (worldMat * vec4(position, 1.0)).xyz;
25:        v_light = normalize(lightPos - worldPos);
26:        v_texCoord = texCoord;
27:
28:        // for shadow map access and depth comparison
29:        v_shadowCoord = tMat * lightProjMat * lightViewMat
                  * vec4(worldPos, 1.0);
30:        gl_Position = projMat * viewMat * vec4(worldPos, 1.0);
31: }
```

Sample code 15-5 is the fragment shader. For the sake of simplicity, it implements only the diffuse reflection term of the Phong model. Observe that, in addition to the image texture (colorMap), the shadow map (shadowMap) is provided as a uniform at line 7. Its type is sampler2DShadow, which distinguishes the shadow map from other texture types.

At line 24, shadowMap is accessed by a new built-in function, textureProj. It performs a texture lookup "with projection." If the first argument of textureProj is a shadow map, the second argument must be a 4D vector. In our fragment shader, it is v_shadowCoord, which was output by the vertex shader. It is first *projected*, i.e., it is divided by its last component, and then the first two components are used as the texture coordinates, (s, t), to access the shadow map and fetch z_p whereas the third component, d_q, is used for depth comparison.

The way z_p and d_q are compared is specified in Sample code 15-3. First of all, GL_COMPARE_REF_TO_TEXTURE at line 11 enables depth comparison between

Sample code 15-5 Second-pass fragment shader for shadow mapping

```
 1: #version 300 es
 2:
 3: precision mediump float;
 4: precision mediump sampler2DShadow;
 5:
 6: uniform sampler2D colorMap;
 7: uniform sampler2DShadow shadowMap;
 8: uniform vec3 srcDiff;
 9:
10: in vec3 v_normal, v_light;
11: in vec2 v_texCoord;
12: in vec4 v_shadowCoord;
13:
14: layout(location = 0) out vec4 fragColor;
15:
16: void main() {
17:     vec3 normal = normalize(v_normal);
18:     vec3 light = normalize(v_light);
19:
20:     // diffuse term
21:     vec3 matDiff = texture(colorMap, v_texCoord).rgb;
22:     vec3 diff = max(dot(normal, light), 0.0) * srcDiff * matDiff;
23:
24:     float visibility = textureProj(shadowMap, v_shadowCoord);
25:
26:     fragColor = vec4(visibility * diff, 1.0);
27: }
```

a fragment (REF) and a texel (TEXTURE). Then, GL_LEQUAL is specified for GL_TEXTURE_COMPARE_FUNC at line 12: If the fragment's depth is less than or equal to the texel's, one is returned, which implies 'visible.' Otherwise, zero is returned, which implies 'invisible.' Together with lines 7 and 8 which specify GL_LINEAR, lines 11 and 12 enable textureProj to implement PCF, i.e., the comparison results (each of which is either one or zero) are bilinearly interpolated to define visibility at line 24 in Sample code 15-5. Finally, visibility is multiplied with the diffuse color, diff, at line 26.

The fragment shader in Sample code 15-5 does not handle the surface acne artifact. The solution proposed in Section 15.1 adds a bias to the fragment's depth. Sample code 15-6 extends Sample code 15-5. See lines 16, 27, and 28.

15.4　Hard Shadow versus Soft Shadow

A point light source generates *hard shadows*. See Fig. 15.7. The planar surface is clearly partitioned into two regions: (1) the region where the light

Sample code 15-6 Second-pass fragment shader for 'biased' shadow mapping

```
1: #version 300 es
2:
3: precision mediump float;
4: precision mediump sampler2DShadow;
5:
6: uniform sampler2D colorMap;
7: uniform sampler2DShadow shadowMap;
8: uniform vec3 srcDiff;
9:
10: in vec3 v_normal, v_light;
11: in vec2 v_texCoord;
12: in vec4 v_shadowCoord;
13:
14: layout(location = 0) out vec4 fragColor;
15:
16: const float offset = 0.005;
17:
18: void main() {
19:     vec3 normal = normalize(v_normal);
20:     vec3 light = normalize(v_light);
21:
22:     // diffuse term
23:     vec3 matDiff = texture(colorMap, v_texCoord).rgb;
24:     vec3 diff = max(dot(normal, light), 0.0) * srcDiff * matDiff;
25:
26:     // visibility + bias
27:     vec4 offsetVec = vec4(0.0, 0.0, offset * v_shadowCoord.w, 0.0);
28:     float visibility = textureProj(shadowMap, v_shadowCoord - offsetVec);
29:
30:     fragColor = vec4(visibility * diff, 1.0);
31: }
```

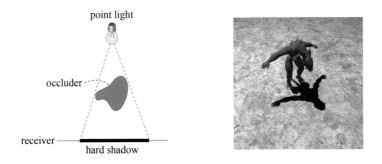

Fig. 15.7: Point light source and hard shadow.

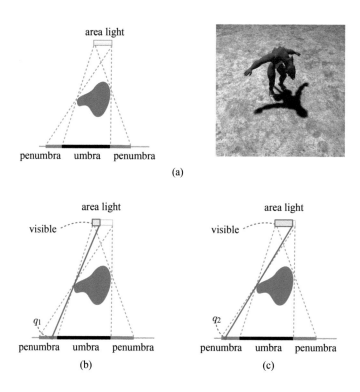

Fig. 15.8: Soft shadows: (a) Area light source and soft shadow. (b) The part of the area light source visible from q_1 is small, and therefore q_1 is not much lit. (c) A larger part of the light source is visible from q_2, and therefore q_2 is more lit.

source is visible, and (2) the region where it is invisible. The latter forms the hard shadow. In contrast, an *area* or *volumetric* light source generates *soft shadows*. See Fig. 15.8-(a). The planar surface is partitioned into three regions: (1) the fully-lit region where the light source is fully visible, (2) the fully-shadowed region named the *umbra* where the light source is completely invisible, and (3) the *penumbra* where the light source is partially visible. The shadows are described as soft due to the penumbra that is located between the umbra and the fully-lit region.

For each surface point in the penumbra, the "degree of illumination" can be computed by measuring how much of the area/volumetric light source is visible from the point. For example, q_1 in Fig. 15.8-(b) sees only a small portion of the area light source whereas q_2 in Fig. 15.8-(c) sees a larger portion. Consequently, q_2 will be assigned a larger degree.

The classical shadow mapping algorithm has been extended along many directions so as to generate soft shadows in real time [10]. In principle, the extended algorithms compute how much of the light source is visible from each surface point in the penumbra.

The shadow's edge shown in Fig. 15.4-(d) might appear *soft*. However, it is not a soft shadow but an *anti-aliased* hard shadow. Note that soft shadows are formed by area or volumetric light sources. The PCF algorithm presented in this chapter assumes a point light source.

Exercises

1. Shadow map filtering.

    (a) In the figure shown on the left, the red and blue dots represent the points sampled in the first and second passes, respectively. Assume that nearest point sampling is used for shadow map filtering and biasing is not adopted. For each of five fragments, f_1 through f_5, determine if it will be shadowed or fully lit.

    (b) In the figure shown on the right, q is a fragment projected into the shadow map. Its depth is 0.5. The values attached to the texels denote the depths stored in the shadow map. What is the fragment's visibility returned by the PCF algorithm?

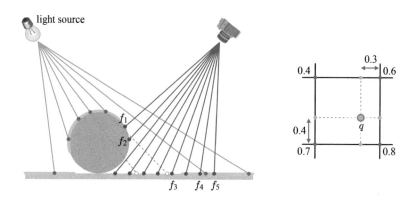

2. Shown below is the first-pass vertex shader for shadow mapping, where lightViewMat and lightProjMat respectively represent the view and projection matrices with respect to the light source. Fill in the box.

```
 1: #version 300 es
 2:
 3: uniform mat4 worldMat;
 4: uniform mat4 lightViewMat, lightProjMat;
 5:
 6: layout(location = 0) in vec3 position;
 7:
 8: void main() {
 9:     gl_Position = [                              ];
10: }
```

3. A problem that could be encountered in shadow mapping is called *Peter Panning*. Suppose that a sphere is placed on a planar surface. In the rendered image, the shadow generated in the planar surface may appear to be disconnected from the sphere that casts the shadow to the surface. The sphere looks as if it were floating above the shadow. When would you encounter this problem?

4. Shown below is the second-pass vertex shader for shadow mapping. It converts the clip-space homogeneous coordinates (x, y, z, w) into $(0.5x + 0.5w, 0.5y + 0.5w, 0.5z + 0.5w, w)$ and stores them into v_shadowCoord. Fill in the boxes.

```
 1: #version 300 es
 2:
 3: uniform mat4 worldMat, viewMat, projMat;
 4: uniform mat4 lightViewMat, lightProjMat;
 5: uniform vec3 lightPos;
 6:
 7: layout(location = 0) in vec3 position;
 8: layout(location = 1) in vec3 normal;
 9: layout(location = 2) in vec2 texCoord;
10:
11: out vec3 v_normal, v_light;
12: out vec2 v_texCoord;
13: out vec4 v_shadowCoord;
14:
15: const mat4 tMat = mat4(
16:         0.5, 0.0, 0.0, 0.0,
17:         [                    ]
18:         [                    ]
19:         [                    ]
20: );
21:
22: void main() {
23:     v_normal = normalize(transpose(inverse(mat3(worldMat))) * normal);
24:     vec3 worldPos = (worldMat * vec4(position, 1.0)).xyz;
25:     v_light = normalize(lightPos - worldPos);
26:     v_texCoord = texCoord;
27:
28:     // for shadow map access and depth comparison
29:     v_shadowCoord = [                                      ];
30:     gl_Position = [                                        ];
31: }
```

5. Shown below is the second-pass fragment shader for 'biased' shadow mapping. Fill in the boxes.

```
 1: #version 300 es
 2:
 3: precision mediump float;
 4: precision mediump sampler2DShadow;
 5:
 6: uniform sampler2D colorMap;
 7: uniform sampler2DShadow shadowMap;
 8: uniform vec3 srcDiff;
 9:
10: in vec3 v_normal, v_light;
11: in vec2 v_texCoord;
12: in vec4 v_shadowCoord;
13:
14: layout(location = 0) out vec4 fragColor;
15:
16: const float offset = 0.005;
17:
18: void main() {
19:     vec3 normal = normalize(v_normal);
20:     vec3 light = normalize(v_light);
21:
22:     // diffuse term
23:     vec3 matDiff = texture(colorMap, v_texCoord).rgb;
24:     vec3 diff = max(dot(normal, light), 0.0) * srcDiff * matDiff;
25:
26:     vec4 offsetVec = [                                        ];
27:     float visibility = textureProj(shadowMap, [                    ]);
28:
29:     fragColor = vec4(visibility * diff, 1.0);
30: }
```

Chapter 16

Texturing toward Global Illumination

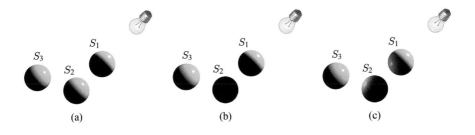

Fig. 16.1: Local illumination versus global illumination: (a) From the perspective of the light source, S_1 hides S_2, but the Phong model does not consider this. (b) S_2 is not lit at all. (c) Even though S_2 is completely hidden from the light source, it receives indirect light from the other objects.

Lighting or illumination models are divided into two categories: *local illumination* and *global illumination*. The Phong model is the representative of local illumination models, where the illumination of an object depends solely on the properties of the object and the light sources. No information about other objects in the scene is considered. The Phong model is physically incorrect. In Fig. 16.1-(a), the light source and two spheres, S_1 and S_2, are linearly aligned. S_1 completely hides S_2 from the light source. However, S_1 is not considered when lighting S_2. Consequently, S_2 is lit as if S_1 did not exist.

On the other hand, if S_2 were not lit at all, as shown in Fig. 16.1-(b), it would also be incorrect. Even though light sources are invisible from a particular point in the scene, light can still be transferred *indirectly* to the point through reflections from other object surfaces. The ambient term of the Phong model accounts for such indirect lighting but it is overly simplified.

The global illumination (GI) model considers the scene objects as potential indirect light sources. In Fig. 16.1-(c), S_2 receives indirect light from S_1 and S_3. Its surface is shaded non-uniformly. For example, the left side of S_2 appears lighter due to the reflections from S_3. Similarly, the bottom of

S_1 is dimly lit even though it does not receive direct light. GI has been widely used for generating photorealistic images in films. Unfortunately, the computational cost for GI is too high to permit interactivity. Complicated GI algorithms may often take several minutes or even hours to generate an image.

Due to the everlasting demand for high-quality images, many attempts have been made to extend the Phong model to the extent that images generated at real time have more and more of a GI look. The trend in real-time graphics is to *approximate* the GI effects or to *pre-compute* GI and use the resulting illumination at run time. In the algorithms developed along the trend, textures play key roles. This chapter first introduces two standard GI algorithms and then presents three texture-based techniques toward GI.

16.1   Global Illumination

In the history of computer graphics, *ray tracing* [11] and *radiosity* [12] were the first algorithms proposed for GI and have been continuously enhanced. This section briefly outlines the original algorithms. Readers interested in advanced topics are referred to the standard textbooks [13, 14].

16.1.1   Ray Tracing

Recall that the view frustum is taken as a pencil of projection lines converging on the camera. If we set the number of projection lines to the resolution of the final image, the color of a pixel will be determined by a projection line. Fig. 16.2-(a) shows an example of an 8×6-resolution image. In the ray tracing algorithm, a ray is fired from the camera toward each pixel to determine the color brought by the projection line. This ray is called the *primary ray*.

When the primary ray intersects an object, whether the intersection point is in shadow is tested. For this, a *secondary ray* named the *shadow ray* is cast toward each light source. In Fig. 16.2-(b), the primary ray hits the green sphere at p_1 and the shadow ray s_1 is fired from p_1. If s_1 hits another object on the way to the light source, p_1 is determined to be in shadow, and the direct contributions of the light source on p_1 are ignored. This is the case in Fig. 16.2-(b). If s_1 hit the light source, however, direct lighting would be computed at p_1, e.g., with the Phong model.

In addition to the shadow ray, two more secondary rays are fired from p_1. Firstly, the primary ray incident on p_1 is reflected with respect to p_1's normal n_1 such that the reflection angle equals the incident angle. The *reflection ray* is denoted as r_1 and its direction is computed as

$$I_1 - 2n_1(n_1 \cdot I_1) \tag{16.1}$$

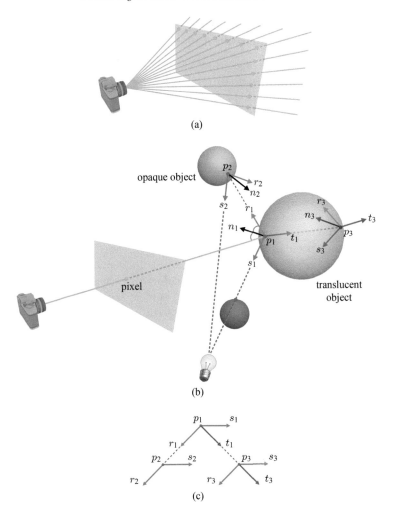

Fig. 16.2: Recursive ray tracing: (a) The projection lines converging on the camera determine the pixel colors. (Only the projection lines at the upper and right edges are illustrated.) (b) For a primary ray, up to three secondary rays are spawned. (c) The recursive rays are structured in a tree.

where I_1 is the primary ray incident on p_1[1]. Secondly, a *transmitted ray*, which is also called a *refraction ray*, is spawned if the object hit by the primary ray

---

[1]Equation (9.8) in Section 9.1.2 presented the reflection of the light vector l. It was $2n(n \cdot l) - l$. Note that I_1 in Equation (16.1) is incident on the surface whereas l in Equation (9.8) leaves the surface.

is not opaque. The transmitted ray spawned at p_1 is denoted as t_1. [Note: Transmitted ray] presents how to calculate the transmitted ray.

Ray tracing is a recursive algorithm, and r_1 and t_1 are traced as if they were the primary rays. In Fig. 16.2-(b), r_1 hits p_2 of an opaque object. Then, a shadow ray (s_2) and a reflection ray (r_2) are fired from p_2, but no transmitted ray is spawned. As s_2 hits the light source, direct lighting is computed at p_2. Simultaneously, r_2 is traced in the same manner as r_1.

The transmitted ray t_1 hits p_3 which is translucent. Then, three secondary rays (s_3, r_3, and t_3) are spawned and traced. The recursive structure of the ray tracing algorithm conceptually generates a *ray tree* shown in Fig. 16.2-(c). The ray tree is expanded until the reflection/transmitted rays leave the scene without hitting any object or a pre-determined recursion level is reached. For each node of the tree, the color computed through the reflection ray is multiplied with the specular reflectance coefficient of the surface. Similarly, the color computed through the transmitted ray is multiplied with the material-specific transmission coefficient. Those colors are then added to the color computed through the shadow ray. The sum is transferred to the parent node, and then we can eventually determine the color of the root node, which is the surface point hit by the primary ray, i.e., p_1 in Fig. 16.2. Fig. 16.3 shows a photorealistic image created by ray tracing.

Fig. 16.3: A ray-tracing image. (Gilles Tran, http://commons.wikimedia.org)

[Note: Transmitted ray]

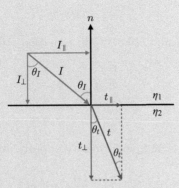

Fig. 16.4: Computing the transmitted vector using Snell's law.

Fig. 16.4 shows light passing through the boundary between two media. The *refractive indices* of the media are denoted by η_1 and η_2. For example, the index is 1.0 for a vacuum and 1.33 for water. The incident vector I makes the incident angle, θ_I, with the normal vector n. Similarly, the transmitted vector t makes the refraction angle, θ_t. Calculating the transmitted ray starts with Snell's law:

$$\eta_1 \sin \theta_I = \eta_2 \sin \theta_t \tag{16.2}$$

The incident vector I is decomposed into a tangential component $I_\parallel$ and a normal component $I_\perp$:

$$I = I_\parallel + I_\perp \tag{16.3}$$

A similar decomposition is made for the transmitted vector:

$$t = t_\parallel + t_\perp \tag{16.4}$$

Assuming that I, t, and n are unit vectors, we obtain the following:

$$\begin{aligned}
\sin \theta_I &= \frac{\|I_\parallel\|}{\|I\|} = \|I_\parallel\| \\
\sin \theta_t &= \frac{\|t_\parallel\|}{\|t\|} = \|t_\parallel\|
\end{aligned} \tag{16.5}$$

Equation (16.2) can be rephrased using Equation (16.5):

$$\|t_\parallel\| = \frac{\eta_1}{\eta_2} \|I_\parallel\| \tag{16.6}$$

Because the directions of $t_\parallel$ and $I_\parallel$ are identical, Equation (16.6) leads to

$$t_\parallel = \frac{\eta_1}{\eta_2} I_\parallel \tag{16.7}$$

$I_\perp$ and n have opposite directions, and their relation is described as follows:

$$I_\perp = -n \cos \theta_I \tag{16.8}$$

Using Equations (16.3) and (16.8), $t_\parallel$ in Equation (16.7) is rephrased as follows:

$$\begin{aligned}
t_\parallel &= \frac{\eta_1}{\eta_2} I_\parallel \\
&= \frac{\eta_1}{\eta_2}(I - I_\perp) \\
&= \frac{\eta_1}{\eta_2}(I + n \cos \theta_I) \\
&= \frac{\eta_1}{\eta_2}(I - n(n \cdot I))
\end{aligned} \tag{16.9}$$

Now let us compute $t_\perp$. As $t_\perp$ and n have opposite directions, their relation is described as follows:

$$\begin{aligned}
t_\perp &= -n \cos \theta_t \\
&= -n\sqrt{1 - \sin^2 \theta_t}
\end{aligned} \tag{16.10}$$

Snell's law presented in Equation (16.2) leads to the following:

$$\begin{aligned}
\sin^2 \theta_t &= (\tfrac{\eta_1}{\eta_2})^2 \sin^2 \theta_I \\
&= (\tfrac{\eta_1}{\eta_2})^2 (1 - \cos^2 \theta_I) \\
&= (\tfrac{\eta_1}{\eta_2})^2 (1 - (n \cdot I)^2)
\end{aligned} \tag{16.11}$$

Equation (16.10) can be rephrased using Equation (16.11):

$$\begin{aligned}
t_\perp &= -n\sqrt{1 - \sin^2 \theta_t} \\
&= -n\sqrt{1 - (\tfrac{\eta_1}{\eta_2})^2(1 - (n \cdot I)^2)}
\end{aligned} \tag{16.12}$$

The transmitted vector t is obtained by summing $t_\parallel$ and $t_\perp$:

$$\begin{aligned}
t &= t_\parallel + t_\perp \\
&= \frac{\eta_1}{\eta_2}(I - n(n \cdot I)) - n\sqrt{1 - (\tfrac{\eta_1}{\eta_2})^2(1 - (n \cdot I)^2)} \\
&= \frac{\eta_1}{\eta_2}I - n(\frac{\eta_1}{\eta_2}(n \cdot I) + \sqrt{1 - (\tfrac{\eta_1}{\eta_2})^2(1 - (n \cdot I)^2)})
\end{aligned} \tag{16.13}$$

16.1.2 Radiosity*

The radiosity algorithm simulates light bouncing between *diffuse* or *Lambertian surfaces*. Light hitting a surface is reflected back to the environment, and each surface of the environment works as a light source. The radiosity algorithm does not distinguish light sources from the objects to be lit.

For the radiosity algorithm, all surfaces of the scene are subdivided into small *patches*. Then, the *form factors* among all patches are computed. The form factor between two patches describes how much they are visible to each

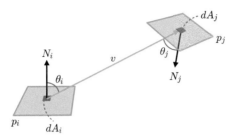

Fig. 16.5: The fraction of energy leaving one surface and arriving at another is described by the form factor.

other. It depends on the distance and relative orientation between the patches. If they are far away or angled obliquely from each other, the form factor will be small.

The radiosity of a patch represents the rate at which light leaves the patch. It is defined to be the sum of the rate at which the patch itself emits light and the rate at which it reflects light:

$$B_i = E_i + r_i \sum_{j=1}^{n} f_{i,j} B_j \tag{16.14}$$

where B_i and B_j are the radiosities of patches p_i and p_j, respectively, E_i is the initial radiosity of p_i, r_i is the reflectance of p_i, and $f_{i,j}$ is the form factor. E_i is non-zero only for light sources. Note that $\sum_{j=1}^{n} f_{i,j} B_j$ describes the *irradiance*, i.e., incoming light. Equation (16.14) is rearranged as follows:

$$B_i - r_i \sum_{j=1}^{n} f_{i,j} B_j = E_i \tag{16.15}$$

Equation (16.15) applies to every patch in the scene, and we obtain the following:

$$\begin{pmatrix} 1 - r_1 f_{1,1} & -r_1 f_{1,2} & \cdots & -r_1 f_{1,n} \\ -r_2 f_{2,1} & 1 - r_2 f_{2,2} & \cdots & -r_2 f_{2,n} \\ \vdots & \vdots & \ddots & \vdots \\ -r_n f_{n,1} & -r_n f_{n,2} & \cdots & 1 - r_n f_{n,n} \end{pmatrix} \begin{pmatrix} B_1 \\ B_2 \\ \vdots \\ B_n \end{pmatrix} = \begin{pmatrix} E_1 \\ E_2 \\ \vdots \\ E_n \end{pmatrix} \tag{16.16}$$

By solving this linear system, the radiosity of each patch is obtained.

Consider two patches in Fig. 16.5, each with the *differential* area dA and the surface normal N. The vector connecting dA_i and dA_j is denoted as v.

Then, θ_i is the angle between N_i and v, and θ_j is the angle between N_j and $-v$. The form factor between dA_i and dA_j is defined as follows:

$$f_{dA_i, dA_j} = \alpha \frac{cos\theta_i cos\theta_j}{\pi v^2} \qquad (16.17)$$

where α denotes the visibility between dA_i and dA_j. If dA_i and dA_j are visible to each other, α is one. Otherwise, it is zero.

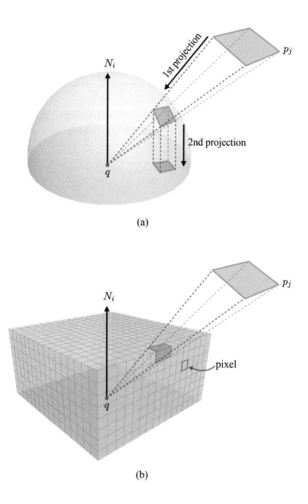

Fig. 16.6: The form factors depend solely on the geometry of the scene. For a static scene, they are computed only once, and can be reused, for example, as the lighting and material attributes are altered. (a) Nusselt analog using a hemisphere. (b) Rasterization using a hemicube.

Equation (16.17) represents a point-to-point form factor. In principle, it should be integrated in order to compute the form factor between the patches in Fig. 16.5. If we assume that the radiosities are constant over the extent of a patch, computing the patch-to-patch form factor is reduced to computing a point-to-patch form factor. Consider a representative point, q, on the patch p_i. It would be the center of the patch. The form factor between q and patch p_j can be calculated using the *hemisphere* placed at q, as shown in Fig. 16.6-(a). Its axis N_i is identical to the surface normal at q. Suppose that p_j is fully visible from q. It is projected onto the hemisphere's surface and then projected onto the base of the hemisphere. The form factor is defined to be the area projected onto the hemisphere's base divided by the base's area. This process was proposed by a German engineer Wilhelm Nusselt and is called the Nusselt analog.

Presented so far is the classic radiosity algorithm. A variety of optimization techniques have been developed. Fig. 16.6-(b) shows an old example, where the hemisphere is replaced by a *hemicube*, each face of which is an array of square pixels. The form factor between q and a pixel depends on the pixel's location in the hemicube. For example, the pixel located at the corner of the hemicube has a smaller form factor than the pixel centered on the top face. Such per-pixel form factors are pre-computed. Then, p_j is *projected* onto the faces of the hemicube. The form factor between q and p_j is the sum of the form factors of the pixels covered by the projection of p_j. The hemicube enables the form factors to be calculated using the ordinary rendering algorithm and further the visibility of p_j to be handled using z-buffering. (Section 16.3 will present how the environment is rendered onto the hemicube.) Fig. 16.7 shows an image generated by the radiosity algorithm.

Fig. 16.7: A radiosity image. (Jlpons, http://commons.wikimedia.org)

The radiosity algorithm is too expensive to be implemented in real time. It is often run at the preprocessing stage, and the irradiance values, $\sum_{j=1}^{n} f_{i,j} B_j$ in Equation (16.14), are stored in a texture to be used at run time. The texture is named the *light map*. It will be presented in Section 16.2.

16.2   Light Mapping

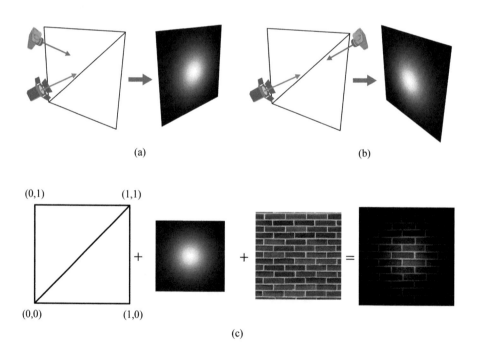

Fig. 16.8: Light mapping: (a) Both the object and the light source are static. The diffuse reflections on the object's surface are captured from a viewpoint. (b) The viewpoint has moved. However, the diffuse reflections captured from the viewpoint are not changed. (c) The light map is combined with an image texture at run time.

Suppose that we navigate a static environment illuminated by static light sources. Fig. 16.8-(a) and -(b) show a simple example. Whereas a spotlight source[2] is fixed in front of a quad, the camera moves from left to right. Assume that the quad is a white Lambertian surface. If the light source is also white, the images captured by the camera would appear in gray scale, as shown in the figure. The gray-scale images represent the *diffuse reflections*. Observe that the diffuse reflections remain constant over the quad independently of the camera position.

For now, consider the diffuse reflection term, $max(n \cdot l, 0)s_d \otimes m_d$, of the Phong model. When the scene and light sources are static, we can pre-compute $max(n \cdot l, 0)s_d$, which represents the incoming light named the *irradiance*. In contrast, the diffuse reflectance, m_d, will be read from an image texture at run time. The pre-computed irradiance is stored in a texture, named the *light map*, and is looked up at run time to be combined with m_d. This technique is called *light mapping*. It increases the run-time performance. Fig. 16.8-(c) illustrates the procedure. Typically, the light map is made smaller than the image texture because diffuse reflection varies over a surface at a lower frequency.

When the irradiance values are pre-computed, there is no real-time constraint. Therefore, we can use an expensive global illumination model. In most cases, we use the radiosity algorithm presented in Section 16.1.2. Consequently, light-mapped scenes show higher quality than the ones locally illuminated.

The method for creating a light map is similar to the one for creating a normal map presented in Section 14.5. The surface to be light-mapped is parameterized and rasterized in a texture. For each sampled surface point corresponding to a texel, irradiance is computed, as presented in Section 16.1.2. The irradiance values are stored in the texture. It is the light map.

16.3 Environment Mapping

Fig. 16.9 shows a shiny object reflecting its surrounding environment. It is rendered with *environment mapping*. This technique uses a special texture, named the *environment map*, where the surrounding environment is captured.

---

[2]A spotlight is an extension of the point light, which emits a cone of light. It is defined by a set of parameters including the light source position, the spot direction, and the cutoff angle. Light is emitted from the light source position in directions whose angles with respect to the spot direction are less than the cutoff angle. In addition, the intensity of the light is attenuated as the angles increase.

Fig. 16.9: The teapot surface reflects its surrounding environment.

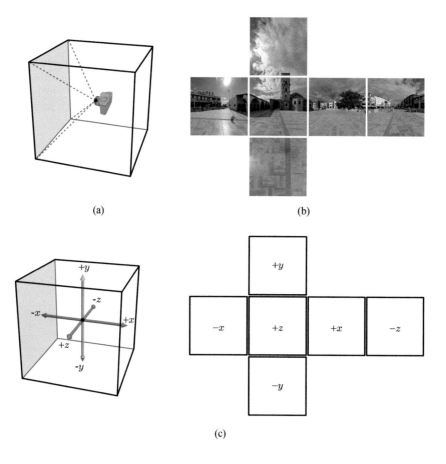

Fig. 16.10: Cube map: (a) The environment is captured along six view directions. (b) Six images in a cube map. (Image courtesy of Emil Persson: http://humus.name) (c) Each face of the cube map is assigned a name.

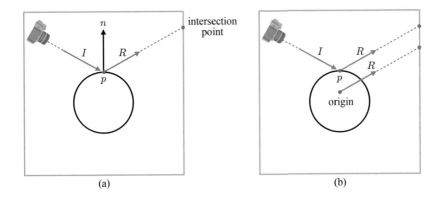

Fig. 16.11: Cube mapping: (a) The cube map (illustrated as a box) surrounds an object. A ray fired from the viewpoint is traced to determine the color reflected at p. (b) The cube map should be referenced by the ray starting from p, but the cube mapping algorithm uses the vector starting from the origin. Only when the environment is infinitely far away will they return the same texture color.

16.3.1 Cube Mapping

The most popularly used environment map is the *cube map*. Fig. 16.10-(a) shows an imaginary cube, at the center of which a camera is located. The environment can be captured onto the six faces of the cube such that each face covers a 90° field of view both vertically and horizontally. Fig. 16.10-(b) shows an unfolded cube map composed of six square images.

It is simple to implement cube mapping. Fig. 16.11-(a) illustrates a spherical object and the cube map in a cross section. Conceptually, the cube map surrounds the sphere. Consider a point, p, on the sphere, which is to reflect the environment. In order to determine the reflected color at p, a ray denoted by I is fired from the viewpoint toward p. It is reflected with respect to the surface normal n. The reflection vector R is computed as follows:

$$R = I - 2n(n \cdot I) \qquad (16.18)$$

This is identical to Equation (16.1) used in ray tracing. R intersects a face of the cube map. Then, the texture associated with that face is filtered, e.g., the texels around the intersection point are bilinearly interpolated. The texture color is used to determine the color reflected at p. Environment mapping is often called a simplified ray tracing in the sense that only the *one-bounce* reflection vector, R, is traced.

16.3.2 GL Program and Shaders for Cube Mapping

Sample code 16-1 GL program for cube map creation

```
 1: TexData texData;
 2:
 3: GLuint texture;
 4: glGenTextures(1, &texture);
 5: glBindTexture(GL_TEXTURE_CUBE_MAP, texture);
 6: for (unsigned int i = 0; i < 6; i++)
 7:     glTexImage2D(GL_TEXTURE_CUBE_MAP_POSITIVE_X + i, 0, GL_RGBA,
                texData.width, texData.height, 0, GL_RGBA, GL_UNSIGNED_BYTE,
                texData.texels.data() + texData.texels.size() * i / 6);
 8:
 9: glTexParameteri(GL_TEXTURE_CUBE_MAP, GL_TEXTURE_MIN_FILTER, GL_LINEAR);
10: glTexParameteri(GL_TEXTURE_CUBE_MAP, GL_TEXTURE_MAG_FILTER, GL_LINEAR);
```

Cube mapping is widely used in real-time graphics and is supported in GL. Sample code 16-1 shows how a cube map is created. Assume that the six image textures shown in Fig. 16.10-(b) have been loaded into the GL program to fill `texData` of `struct TexData` defined in Sample code 8-1. Its elements are `texels`, `width`, and `height`: `texels` stores all texels of the six textures, and `width`×`height` represents the resolution of each texture. Because every face of a cube map is square, `width` equals `height`.

The cube map is a sort of texture, and therefore `glGenTextures` (line 4) and `glBindTexture` (line 5) are invoked as usual. Note that the first argument of `glBindTexture` is GL_TEXTURE_CUBE_MAP. Then, `glTexImage2D` will be invoked to provide the texture object with six textures stored in `texData`.

Each face of the cube map is named after the axis pointing toward that face. For example, the cyan face in Fig. 16.10-(c) is pointed to by the -x axis and is named -x. In GL, the symbolic constants for the six faces of a cube map are reserved as GL_TEXTURE_CUBE_MAP_*, where * is POSITIVE_X, NEGATIVE_X, POSITIVE_Y, NEGATIVE_Y, POSITIVE_Z, or NEGATIVE_Z. They are unsigned integer IDs. In Sample code 16-1, `glTexImage2D` is invoked six times. Its first argument is GL_TEXTURE_CUBE_MAP_POSITIVE_X for the first invocation. The other faces are accessed by adding one to it in succession. Specifically, GL_TEXTURE_CUBE_MAP_NEGATIVE_X = GL_TEXTURE_CUBE_MAP_POSITIVE_X + 1, GL_TEXTURE_CUBE_MAP_POSITIVE_Y = GL_TEXTURE_CUBE_MAP_NEGATIVE_X + 1, and so forth.

Shown in Sample code 16-2 is the vertex shader. It outputs `v_normal` and `v_view`. Sample code 16-3 is the fragment shader. It declares a uniform, `cubeMap`, of type `samplerCube` that represents a cube map. The fragment shader normalizes `v_normal` and `v_view` into `normal` and `view`, respectively. Note that the direction of `view` is opposite to that of I presented in Fig. 16.11-

(a), i.e., $I = -$view, and line 14 of the fragment shader implements Equation (16.18) to return R that is named refl in the code[3]. Finally, the built-in function texture takes a cube map and a 3D reflection vector as input and returns an RGB color.

Sample code 16-2 Vertex shader for cube mapping

```
 1: #version 300 es
 2:
 3: uniform mat4 worldMat, viewMat, projMat;
 4: uniform vec3 eyePos;
 5:
 6: layout(location = 0) in vec3 position;
 7: layout(location = 1) in vec3 normal;
 8:
 9: out vec3 v_normal, v_view;
10:
11: void main() {
12:     v_normal = normalize(transpose(inverse(mat3(worldMat))) * normal);
13:     vec3 worldPos = (worldMat * vec4(position, 1.0)).xyz;
14:     v_view = normalize(eyePos - worldPos);
15:     gl_Position = projMat * viewMat * vec4(worldPos, 1.0);
16: }
```

Sample code 16-3 Fragment shader for cube mapping

```
 1: #version 300 es
 2:
 3: precision mediump float;
 4:
 5: uniform samplerCube cubeMap;
 6:
 7: in vec3 v_normal, v_view;
 8:
 9: layout(location = 0) out vec4 fragColor;
10:
11: void main() {
12:     vec3 normal = normalize(v_normal);
13:     vec3 view = normalize(v_view);
14:     vec3 refl = 2.0 * normal * dot(normal, view) - view;
15:     fragColor = texture(cubeMap, refl);
16: }
```

---

[3]GLSL provides a built-in function, reflect, and line 14 can be changed to vec3 refl = reflect(-view, normal).

Notice that R in Equation (16.18) is not a *ray* but a *vector* with an irrelevant start point. Consequently, as compared in Fig. 16.11-(b), the cube map is accessed by "the reflection vector starting from the origin of the coordinate system," not by "the reflection ray starting from p." The scene points hit by them are captured at an identical texel of the cube map only when the environment is infinitely far away. Fortunately, people are usually oblivious to the incorrectness that results even though the environment is not sufficiently far away.

It has been shown that implementing environment mapping is simple and the result is fairly pleasing. Environment mapping is often taken as an effort toward global illumination, and in fact it adds a global illumination look to the images generated by a local illumination model. However, it is just a small step out of local illumination and does not sufficiently overcome its limitations. For example, a concave object does not reflect itself. In Fig. 16.9, the teapot surface does not reflect its mouth.

16.4 Ambient Occlusion

In the Phong lighting model, the ambient term, $s_a \otimes m_a$, accounts for indirect lighting. It assumes that the ambient light randomly bounces in the scene and arrives at a surface point from *all* directions. In reality, however, some of the directions may be occluded. Fig. 16.12-(a) shows two surface points, p_1 and p_2. Whereas the ambient light incident on p_1 is not occluded at all, that on p_2 is partly occluded. The *ambient occlusion* algorithm estimates how much of the ambient light is occluded, which we call the *occlusion degree*. It is used to modulate the ambient term. In Fig. 16.12-(a), the occlusion degree at p_2 will be larger than that of p_1, and therefore the ambient reflection at p_2 will be accordingly reduced.

Fig. 16.12-(b) shows a hemisphere placed at p_2. It is oriented around p_2's surface normal. In order to compute the occlusion degree, the hemisphere surface is evenly sampled and then rays are cast from p_2 toward the sampled points. The percentage of the rays intersecting the scene geometry is taken as the occlusion degree. In the example of Fig. 16.12-(b), half of the rays intersect the scene geometry, and therefore the occlusion degree will be set to 0.5, implying that 50% of ambient light is occluded.

Unfortunately, ray casting is expensive. Consider an alternative. Fig. 16.12-(c) shows that the hemisphere centered at p_2 is partitioned into 'occupied' and 'empty' spaces. The occlusion degree may be approximated as the ratio between the occupied space and the entire hemisphere space. Measuring the ratio is again approximated by using a set of sample points distributed within the hemisphere. The blue dots in Fig. 16.12-(d) represent the samples.

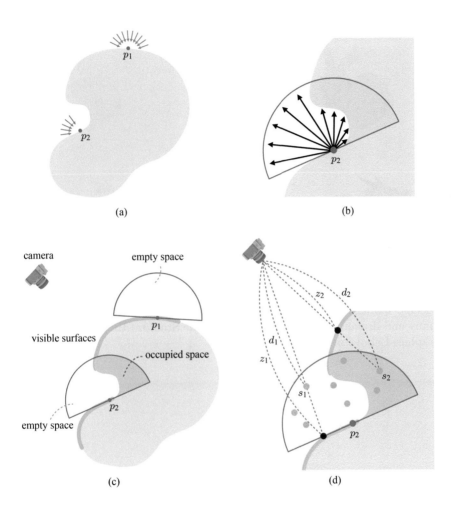

Fig. 16.12: Computing ambient occlusion: (a) The ambient light incident on a surface point can be occluded. This is the case for p_2. In contrast, no ambient light incident on p_1 is occluded. (b) Ray casting could be used to compute the occlusion degree. (c) The occlusion degree could be defined as the percentage of the occupied space. (d) Computing the percentage is approximated by the depth test using the depth map and the points sampled in the hemisphere.

In Fig. 16.12-(c) and -(d), the gold bold curves represent the surfaces *visible* from the camera. They are regularly sampled. For each visible point, its *screen-space depth*, denoted as z, is stored in the *depth map*. Now consider two samples in the hemisphere, s_1 and s_2, in Fig. 16.12-(d). Each sample's depth, denoted as d, is compared with the z-value stored in the depth map.

Fig. 16.13: Each row shows (from left to right) a polygon model, the ambient-reflected model, and the same model shaded using ambient occlusion. (The bunny and dragon models are provided by the Stanford University Computer Graphics Laboratory.)

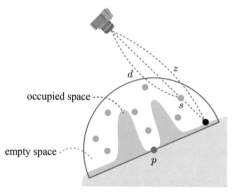

Fig. 16.14: The depth, d, of sample s is smaller than z stored in the depth map, and therefore s is found to be in the empty space. In this contrived example, the occlusion degree of p will be determined to be zero. In reality, however, the occlusion degree should be much higher.

Note that s_1 is determined to be in the empty space because $d_1 < z_1$. In contrast, s_2 is determined to be in the occupied space because $d_2 > z_2$. This is similar to the depth comparison performed in shadow mapping.

In Fig. 16.12-(d), the occlusion degree of p_2 would be 3/8 because three out of eight samples lose the depth test against the depth map. It is different from 0.5, which was estimated in Fig. 16.12-(b). This is a natural discrepancy brought by different sampling methods. On the other hand, consider p_1 shown in Fig. 16.12-(c). No sample would lose the depth test, and therefore the occlusion degree would be zero. In the ambient term, $s_a \otimes m_a$, s_a is modulated using the occlusion degree.

Fig. 16.13 compares the models shaded with only the traditional ambient reflection and those with ambient occlusion. Lighting augmented with ambient occlusion usually produces pleasing images. However, ambient occlusion is an approximate algorithm, and it does not consider the scene geometry that is located outside of the view frustum. Consequently, ambient occlusion is prone to errors. Fig. 16.14 illustrates another problem of ambient occlusion's sampling method. Nonetheless, the artifacts caused by those errors are rarely perceived by the average users, and ambient occlusion is widely accepted in games.

Exercises

1. In the specular term of the Phong model, the reflection vector is defined to be $2n(n \cdot l) - l$, where n is the surface normal and l is the light vector. In ray tracing, the reflection ray's direction is defined to be $I - 2n(n \cdot I)$, where I is the primary ray's direction. What causes this difference?

2. Consider applying ray tracing to a sphere of radius 2, which is centered at the origin of the coordinate system.

    (a) A ray is fired from $(10, 1, 0)$ with the direction vector $(-1, 0, 0)$. Represent the ray in a parametric equation of t.

    (b) Using the implicit equation of the sphere, $x^2 + y^2 + z^2 - 2^2 = 0$, and the parametric equation of the ray, compute the intersection point between the sphere and the ray.

    (c) In order to compute the reflection ray, the surface normal, n, at the intersection is needed. How would you compute n in this specific example?

    (d) The reflection ray's direction is defined to be $I - 2n(n \cdot I)$, where I represents the primary ray's. Compute $I - 2n(n \cdot I)$.

3. Light mapping is usually combined with image texturing at run time to determine the diffuse reflection.

    (a) The light map can store the diffuse reflection, instead of the irradiance, so as to avoid the run-time combination of irradiance and diffuse reflectance. This would lead to an improved run-time performance but has a disadvantage. What is it?

    (b) Light mapping is often called *dark mapping* because the pixel lit by the light map is darker than the unlit texel of the image texture. Why does this happen? How would you resolve this problem?

4. Consider capturing six images for a cube map. Each image is generated using the view and projection transforms.

    (a) Is each image generated using a different view transform? Discuss why it is or is not.

    (b) Is each image generated using a different projection transform? Discuss why it is or is not.

5. Shown in the next page is the unfolded cube map of six faces. Suppose that a reflection ray is computed and its direction is along $(0.5, 0.4, -0.2)$.

    (a) Which face of the cube map does the reflection ray hit?

(b) What are the 2D coordinates of the intersection point between the reflection ray and the face?

(c) Compute the texture coordinates corresponding to the intersection point.

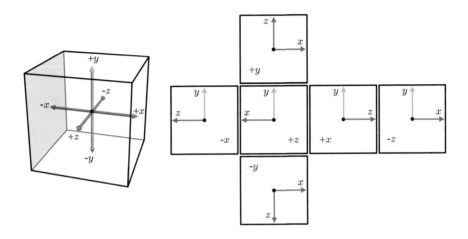

6. Shown below is the process of computing the texture coordinates, (s, t), for cube mapping, which is done automatically by the GPU. Suppose that the reflection ray hits face -x at $(-1.0, 0.8, 0.4)$. Write the coordinates of A and B.

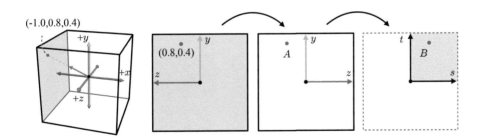

Chapter 17

Parametric Curves and Surfaces

The representation of 3D surfaces that we have considered so far is limited to the polygon mesh. As discussed in Chapter 3, however, it is not an accurate representation but an approximation of a smooth surface. In general, a smooth surface is defined as a continuous function of parameters. Such *parametric surfaces* were developed in areas of computer-aided design and manufacturing but are increasingly garnering attention in the interactive graphics field especially because the GPU began to accept them. (The GPU support for parametric surfaces will be presented in Chapter 18.)

There exist many representations for parametric surfaces[1]. This chapter presents the simplest among them, the *Bézier surface*, which was named after Pierre Bézier, a French engineer at Renault. The *Bézier curve* forms the foundation of the Bézier surface and therefore this chapter introduces it first.

17.1 Parametric Curves

A line is a special instance of a curve. Section 17.1.1 starts by presenting a parameterized line and extends it into quadratic and cubic Bézier curves. Section 17.1.2 presents another type of parametric curve, the Hermite curve.

17.1.1 Bézier Curves

Fig. 17.1 shows a line segment between p_0 and p_1. As presented in Section 2.5, it is described as *linear interpolation* of p_0 and p_1:

$$p(t) = (1 - t)p_0 + tp_1 \qquad (17.1)$$

where t represents the parameter in the range of $[0, 1]$. We take $(1 - t)$ and t as the *weights* for p_0 and p_1, respectively. In Fig. 17.1, consider a specific value of t, e.g., 0.35, which reduces $p(t)$ to a point. Then, the line segment can be thought of as being divided into two parts by the point. The weight

---

[1] An excellent introductory book of parametric curves and surfaces is [15].

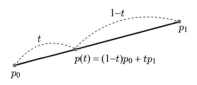

Fig. 17.1: A line segment connecting two end points is represented as the linear interpolation of the two points.

for an end point is proportional to the length of the part "on the opposite side."

Whereas a line segment is defined by two points, we need three or more points in order to define a curve. A well-known technique for constructing a parametric curve based on a series of points is the *de Casteljau algorithm*, named after its inventor Paul de Casteljau, a French mathematician at Citroën. It is an algorithm consisting of iterative linear interpolations. Given three points, p_0, p_1, and p_2, the consecutive pairs are linearly interpolated:

$$p_0^1 = (1 - t)p_0 + tp_1 \qquad (17.2)$$

$$p_1^1 = (1 - t)p_1 + tp_2 \qquad (17.3)$$

where superscript 1 denotes the first level of iteration. Then, p_0^1 and p_1^1 are linearly interpolated:

$$p_0^2 = (1 - t)p_0^1 + tp_1^1 \qquad (17.4)$$

Superscript 2 denotes the second level of iteration. The process of iterative interpolations is illustrated in Fig. 17.2-(a).

When we insert Equations (17.2) and (17.3) into Equation (17.4), we obtain the equation of the quadratic (degree-2) Bézier curve:

$$p_0^2 = p(t) = (1 - t)^2 p_0 + 2t(1 - t)p_1 + t^2 p_2 \qquad (17.5)$$

As shown in Fig. 17.2-(b), the curve starts from p_0 (when $t = 0$) and ends at p_2 (when $t = 1$). The curve is pulled toward p_1 but does not pass through it. Fig. 17.2-(c) shows two more examples of a quadratic Bézier curve. The points, p_0, p_1, and p_2, control the shape of the curve and are called the *control points*. Observe that a quadratic Bézier curve has at most one inflection point.

The de Casteljau algorithm can be used for constructing higher-degree Bézier curves. Fig. 17.3-(a) illustrates iterative linear interpolations for constructing a cubic (degree-3) Bézier curve with four control points. The equation of the cubic Bézier curve is derived as follows:

$$p(t) = (1 - t)^3 p_0 + 3t(1 - t)^2 p_1 + 3t^2(1 - t)p_2 + t^3 p_3 \qquad (17.6)$$

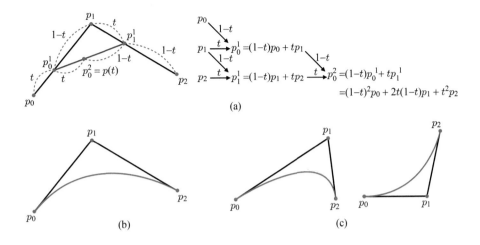

(a)

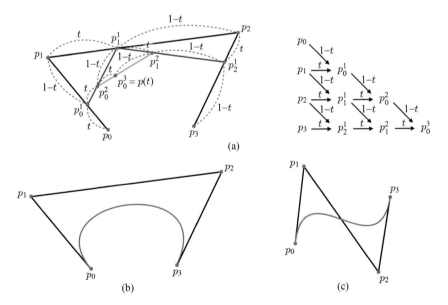

Fig. 17.2: Quadratic Bézier curves: (a) Iterative linear interpolations. (b) A quadratic Bézier curve is defined by three control points. (c) The control points determine the shape of the curve.

Fig. 17.3: Cubic Bézier curves: (a) Iterative linear interpolations. (b) A cubic Bézier curve is defined by four control points. (c) The control points determine the shape of the curve.

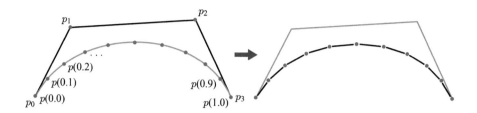

Fig. 17.4: A Bézier curve can be displayed through tessellation.

As illustrated in Fig. 17.3-(b), the curve starts from p_0 (when $t = 0$) and ends at p_3 (when $t = 1$). The curve is pulled toward p_1 and p_2 but does not pass through them. Fig. 17.3-(c) shows another example of a cubic Bézier curve. Observe that a cubic Bézier curve has at most two inflection points.

A degree-n Bézier curve requires $n+1$ control points. As shown in Equations (17.1), (17.5), and (17.6), the coefficient for a control point is a polynomial of t. The coefficients are named the *Bernstein polynomials*. The Bernstein polynomial for p_i in the degree-n Bézier curve is defined as follows:

$$B_i^n(t) = {}_nC_i t^i (1 - t)^{n-i} \tag{17.7}$$

Then, the Bézier curve is described as a weighted sum of the control points:

$$p(t) = \sum_{i=0}^{n} B_i^n(t) p_i \tag{17.8}$$

The typical method to display a Bézier curve on the screen is to approximate it using a series of tiny line segments. This process is often called *tessellation*. It *evaluates* the curve at a fixed set of parameter values and joins the evaluated points with line segments. Fig. 17.4 shows an example of uniform tessellation, where the curve is evaluated at 11 evenly spaced values of parameter t and is approximated by 10 line segments[2].

The Bézier curve has many interesting properties, and one of them is its *affine invariance*. Suppose that a Bézier curve, C, needs to be affine-transformed and displayed. Then, we would have two options. One option is to evaluate C into a set of points P and then affine-transform P. Fig. 17.5-(a) shows an example for rotation. The other option is to affine-transform the control points of C and then evaluate the curve defined by the transformed control points. See Fig. 17.5-(b). The results are the same, but the latter is usually preferred because we transform a smaller number of points.

---

[2]Non-uniform tessellation methods are usually preferred. An example is adaptive tessellation, which adapts the tessellation factor based on the curvature.

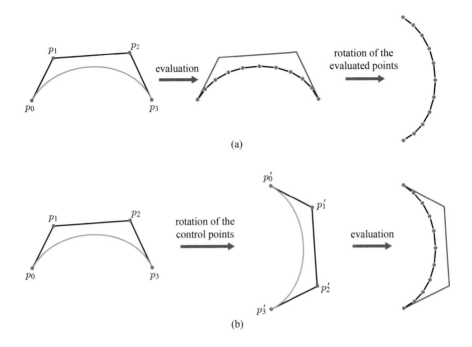

(a)

(b)

Fig. 17.5: Affine invariance: (a) Evaluation and then rotation of the evaluated points. (b) Rotation of the control points and then evaluation.

You may consider a curve that has a degree higher than three. For example, a quartic (degree-4) Bézier curve can be constructed using five control points. Unfortunately, such higher-degree curves are expensive to evaluate and often reveal undesired wiggles. Therefore, cubic curves are most popularly used in the graphics field. A complex curve, e.g., with more than two inflection points, is defined by concatenating multiple cubic curves. It is presented in the next subsection.

17.1.2 Hermite Curve and Catmull-Rom Spline

Consider the first-order derivative of the cubic Bézier curve:

$$\dot{p}(t) = \frac{d}{dt}[(1-t)^3 p_0 + 3t(1-t)^2 p_1 + 3t^2(1-t)p_2 + t^3 p_3]$$
$$= -3(1-t)^2 p_0 + [3(1-t)^2 - 6t(1-t)]p_1 + [6t(1-t) - 3t^2]p_2 + 3t^2 p_3$$
$$(17.9)$$

This represents the *tangent vectors* along the curve. The end tangent vectors, v_0 at p_0 and v_3 at p_3, are obtained by setting the parameter t in Equa-

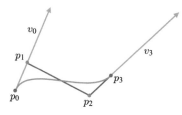

Fig. 17.6: The tangent vectors, v_0 and v_3, at the end points are defined as $3(p_1 - p_0)$ and $3(p_3 - p_2)$, respectively. Then, the Bézier curve built upon $\{p_0, p_1, p_2, p_3\}$ is redefined as the Hermite curve built upon $\{p_0, v_0, p_3, v_3\}$.

tion (17.9) to 0 and 1, respectively:

$$v_0 = \dot{p}(0) = 3(p_1 - p_0) \tag{17.10}$$

$$v_3 = \dot{p}(1) = 3(p_3 - p_2) \tag{17.11}$$

They are illustrated in Fig. 17.6. Equations (17.10) and (17.11) are rewritten as follows:

$$p_1 = p_0 + \frac{1}{3}v_0 \tag{17.12}$$

$$p_2 = p_3 - \frac{1}{3}v_3 \tag{17.13}$$

Using Equations (17.12) and (17.13), the cubic Bézier curve defined in Equation (17.6) is rewritten as follows:

$$
\begin{aligned}
p(t) &= (1-t)^3 p_0 + 3t(1-t)^2 p_1 + 3t^2(1-t)p_2 + t^3 p_3 \\
&= (1-t)^3 p_0 + 3t(1-t)^2 (p_0 + \tfrac{1}{3}v_0) + 3t^2(1-t)(p_3 - \tfrac{1}{3}v_3) + t^3 p_3 \\
&= (1 - 3t^2 + 2t^3)p_0 + t(1-t)^2 v_0 + (3t^2 - 2t^3)p_3 - t^2(1-t)v_3
\end{aligned}
\tag{17.14}
$$

Now, the curve is defined in terms of $\{p_0, v_0, p_3, v_3\}$, i.e., two end points and their tangent vectors. The curve has the same geometry as the Bézier curve defined in terms of $\{p_0, p_1, p_2, p_3\}$. This new representation is called the *Hermite curve* that was named in honor of Charles Hermite, a French mathematician.

Consider constructing a curve that passes through a series of points. Shown in Fig. 17.7-(a) is an example with five points, $\{q_0, q_1, q_2, q_3, q_4\}$. Such a complex curve can be constructed by defining a parametric curve for each pair of consecutive points. This piecewise curve is generally named the *spline*. Suppose that the spline in Fig. 17.7-(a) is composed of four Hermite curves. For the spline to be globally continuous, two adjacent Hermite curves should share the tangent vector at their junction. For example, C_1 and C_2 should

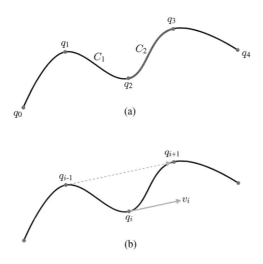

Fig. 17.7: Catmull-Rom spline: (a) A spline composed of Hermite curves passes through the given points. (b) The tangent vector at q_i is made to be parallel to the vector connecting q_{i-1} and q_{i+1}.

share the tangent vector at q_2. The *Catmull-Rom spline* [16] uses q_{i-1} and q_{i+1} to define the tangent vector v_i at q_i:

$$v_i = \tau(q_{i+1} - q_{i-1}) \qquad (17.15)$$

where τ controls how sharply the curve bends at q_i and is often set to $1/2$. See Fig. 17.7-(b). The Catmull-Rom spline is popularly used in games, mainly for being relatively easy to compute.

17.1.3 Application: Camera Path

The parametric curve has many applications. For example, it is often used to define a path along which the camera moves, as shown in Fig. 17.8-(a). Such a path is often defined by the Catmull-Rom spline. For simplicity, assume that the camera path in Fig. 17.8-(a) is composed of a single Hermite curve $p(t)$. In a simple implementation, a step size Δt may be adopted such that **EYE** continuously moves from $p(t)$ to $p(t + \Delta t)$ for a pre-defined time interval. In Fig. 17.8-(a), Δt is 0.1 and the sub-path from $p(t)$ to $p(t + \Delta t)$ is traversed per second.

Assume that, as shown in Fig. 17.8-(b), **AT** is set to the origin of the world space and **UP** is set to its y-axis. Then, the camera-space basis, $\{u, v, n\}$, is dynamically computed and the moving camera space is defined with $\{u, v, n\}$ and **EYE**, as illustrated in Fig. 17.8-(c). Fig. 17.8-(d) shows the scene captured from three sampled positions along the path.

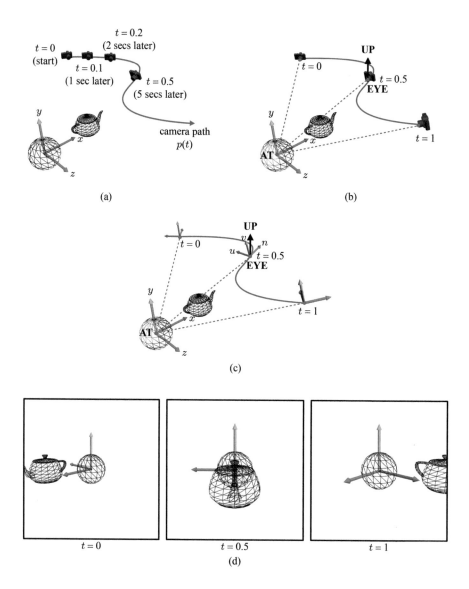

Fig. 17.8: The camera travels along a curved path and captures a static scene. (a) The path is described as a parametric curve, $p(t)$. Each sampled point on the curve defines **EYE**. (b) **AT** and **UP** are fixed to the origin and the y-axis of the world space, respectively. (c) Given **EYE**, **AT**, and **UP**, the camera space is defined. It is moving along the curve. (d) The scene is captured with the moving camera space.

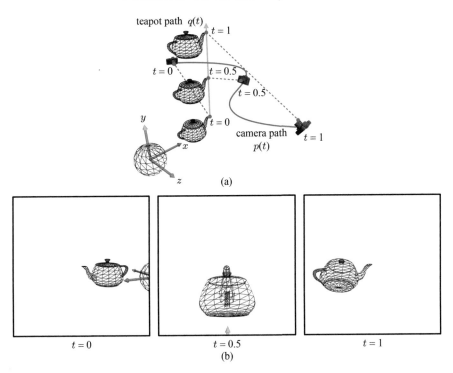

Fig. 17.9: Both **EYE** and **AT** are moving. (a) **EYE** and **AT** are computed by sampling $p(t)$ and $q(t)$, respectively. (b) The scene is captured with the moving camera space.

Suppose that the teapot is translating upward, as shown in Fig. 17.9-(a), and **AT** is set to the position of the teapot's mouth tip. The path of **AT** can be defined by another curve $q(t)$. For a frame, **EYE** and **AT** are computed by sampling $p(t)$ and $q(t)$, respectively. If **UP** is set to the y-axis, we have the rendered results shown in Fig. 17.9-(b) for three sampled values of t.

17.2 Parametric Surfaces

A finite piece of a surface is called a *patch*. This section presents Bézier patches. Bézier curves form the foundations of Bézier patches. To present Bézier curves, we proceeded from the line segment to the quadratic Bézier curve, and then to the cubic Bézier curve. To present Bézier patches, we follow a similar order and start with a bilinear patch.

17.2.1   Bilinear Patch

A bilinear patch is defined by four 3D control points, which are not necessarily in a plane. In Fig. 17.10-(a), they are denoted as p_{00}, p_{01}, p_{10}, and p_{11}. The control points are first interpolated in terms of u. As shown in Fig. 17.10-(b), p_{00} and p_{01} are linearly interpolated to generate p_0^u, and p_{10} and p_{11} are linearly interpolated to generate p_1^u:

$$p_0^u = (1 - u)p_{00} + up_{01} \tag{17.16}$$

$$p_1^u = (1 - u)p_{10} + up_{11} \tag{17.17}$$

Then, p_0^u and p_1^u are linearly interpolated in terms of v:

$$\begin{aligned} p(u, v) &= (1 - v)p_0^u + vp_1^u \\ &= (1 - u)(1 - v)p_{00} + u(1 - v)p_{01} + (1 - u)vp_{10} + uvp_{11} \end{aligned} \tag{17.18}$$

This is *bilinear interpolation*, and therefore $p(u, v)$ is named the bilinear patch.

In Fig. 17.10-(b), p_0^u and p_1^u are connected by a line segment (colored in orange). Conceptually, a bilinear patch can be considered as a set of infinitely many such line segments, as visualized in Fig. 17.10-(c). In the set, a line segment is defined for a distinct value of u and is a linear function of v.

Shown in Fig. 17.10-(d) is the unit-square *domain* of the patch. The 2D coordinates (u, v) in the domain are mapped to a 3D point $p(u, v)$ on the patch. In Equation (17.18), the coefficient for each control point works as a weight. Fig. 17.10-(e) visualizes the weights in the unit-square domain. Consider specific values of u and v, e.g., $u = 0.6$ and $v = 0.7$. They partition the square into four rectangles, and the weight for a control point equals the area of the rectangle "on the opposite side." For example, the weight for p_{00} is the area of the smaller yellow rectangle, $(1 - u)(1 - v)$. This is basically the same observation we made in the linear interpolation of Fig. 17.1, where the weight for p_0 is $(1 - t)$, and that for p_1 is t.

In general, displaying a bilinear patch requires it to be *tessellated* into a triangle mesh, i.e., the bilinear patch is *evaluated* at a number of points, and the evaluated points are connected to form triangles that approximate the patch's surface. For a uniform tessellation, the uv-domain can be sampled using nested `for` loops (one for u, and the other for v). See Sample code 17-1. Simply put, line 3 inserts u and v into Equation (17.18) to obtain a 3D point (x, y, z) on the patch. Fig. 17.10-(f) shows the tessellation result where both u and v are uniformly sampled by 10 steps each.

Sample code 17-1 Bézier patch evaluation for uniform tessellation

```
1: for each u in [0,1]
2:     for each v in [0,1]
3:         evaluate the patch using (u,v) to obtain (x,y,z)
```

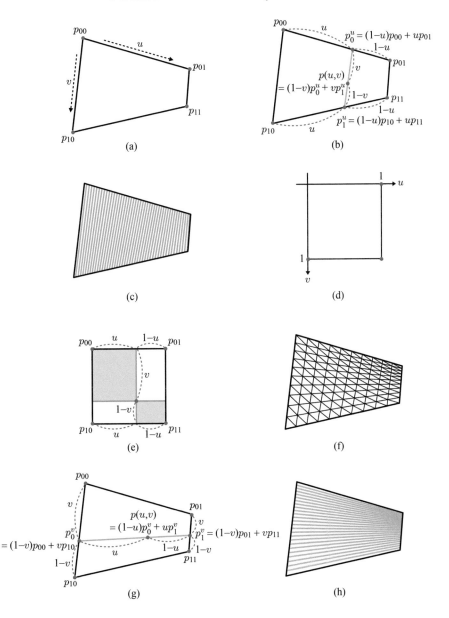

Fig. 17.10: Bilinear patch: (a) 2×2 control points. (b) Bilinear interpolation (u first and then v). (c) A collection of line segments. (d) The unit-square parametric domain. (e) Weights for the control points. (f) Tessellation. (g) Bilinear interpolation (v first and then u). (h) Another collection of line segments.

The bilinear patch in Equation (17.18) can be expressed in a matrix form:

$$
\begin{aligned}
p(u, v) &= \begin{pmatrix} 1 - v & v \end{pmatrix} \begin{pmatrix} p_{00} & p_{01} \\ p_{10} & p_{11} \end{pmatrix} \begin{pmatrix} 1 - u \\ u \end{pmatrix} \\
&= \begin{pmatrix} 1 - v & v \end{pmatrix} \begin{pmatrix} (1 - u)p_{00} + up_{01} \\ (1 - u)p_{10} + up_{11} \end{pmatrix} \\
&= (1 - u)(1 - v)p_{00} + u(1 - v)p_{01} + (1 - u)vp_{10} + uvp_{11}
\end{aligned}
\tag{17.19}
$$

where the 2×2 matrix in the first line corresponds to the 2×2 control points shown in Fig. 17.10-(a). The row and column vectors on either side of the matrix are degree-1 Bernstein polynomials in v and u, respectively. In the second line, the column vector contains p_0^u and p_1^u shown in Fig. 17.10-(b).

In Equation (17.19) and Fig. 17.10-(b), linear interpolations are done with u first and then with v. The order can be reversed:

$$
\begin{aligned}
p(u, v) &= \begin{pmatrix} 1 - v & v \end{pmatrix} \begin{pmatrix} p_{00} & p_{01} \\ p_{10} & p_{11} \end{pmatrix} \begin{pmatrix} 1 - u \\ u \end{pmatrix} \\
&= \begin{pmatrix} (1 - v)p_{00} + vp_{10} & (1 - v)p_{01} + vp_{11} \end{pmatrix} \begin{pmatrix} 1 - u \\ u \end{pmatrix} \\
&= (1 - u)(1 - v)p_{00} + u(1 - v)p_{01} + (1 - u)vp_{10} + uvp_{11}
\end{aligned}
\tag{17.20}
$$

This process is illustrated in Fig. 17.10-(g), where p_0^v and p_1^v are connected by a line segment. In Fig. 17.10-(h), the bilinear patch is visualized as a set of many such line segments. A line segment is defined for a distinct value of v and is a linear function of u. The patches in Fig. 17.10-(c) and -(h) have the same surface geometry. Fig. 17.11 shows another instance of the bilinear patch.

17.2.2 Biquadratic Bézier Patch

The bilinear patch was defined by 2×2 control points. If we extend them to 3×3 control points, we obtain a *biquadratic Bézier patch*. Fig. 17.12-(a) shows 3×3 control points structured in a rectangular net. Fig. 17.12-(b) shows three quadratic Bézier curves defined in u (colored in cyan), each defined by a *row* of three control points in the net.

The matrix form of the biquadratic Bézier patch is obtained by extending that of the bilinear patch presented in Equation (17.19):

$$
\begin{aligned}
p(u, v) &= \begin{pmatrix} (1 - v)^2 & 2v(1 - v) & v^2 \end{pmatrix} \begin{pmatrix} p_{00} & p_{01} & p_{02} \\ p_{10} & p_{11} & p_{12} \\ p_{20} & p_{21} & p_{22} \end{pmatrix} \begin{pmatrix} (1 - u)^2 \\ 2u(1 - u) \\ u^2 \end{pmatrix} \\
&= \begin{pmatrix} (1 - v)^2 & 2v(1 - v) & v^2 \end{pmatrix} \begin{pmatrix} (1 - u)^2 p_{00} + 2u(1 - u)p_{01} + u^2 p_{02} \\ (1 - u)^2 p_{10} + 2u(1 - u)p_{11} + u^2 p_{12} \\ (1 - u)^2 p_{20} + 2u(1 - u)p_{21} + u^2 p_{22} \end{pmatrix}
\end{aligned}
\tag{17.21}
$$

where the 3×3 matrix in the first line corresponds to the 3×3 control points shown in Fig. 17.12-(a). The row and column vectors on either side of the

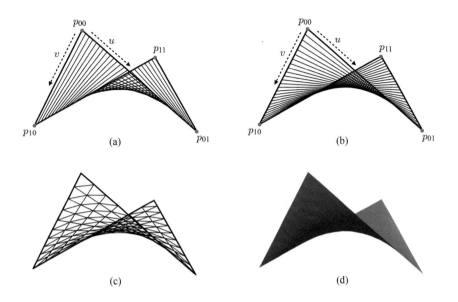

Fig. 17.11: The control points are not necessarily in a plane, and the bilinear patch is not planar in general. (a) Interpolation with u first and then v. (b) Interpolation with v first and then u. (c) Tessellation. (d) Rendered result.

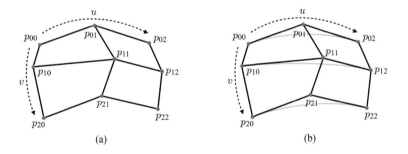

Fig. 17.12: Biquadratic Bézier patch: (a) Control points. (b) Three quadratic Bézier curves (in u).

matrix are degree-2 Bernstein polynomials in v and u, respectively. In the second line of Equation (17.21), the column vector represents the quadratic Bézier curves in Fig. 17.12-(b).

Consider a specific value of u, e.g., 0.65. It reduces each Bézier curve to a point. In Fig. 17.12-(c), the blue dots denote three such points. Taking

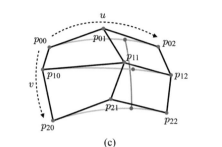 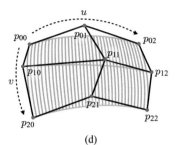

(c)	(d)

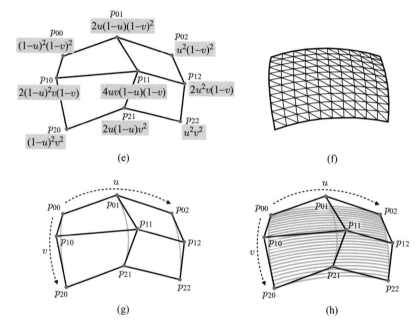

(e)	(f)

(g)	(h)

Fig. 17.12: Biquadratic Bézier patch (*continued*): (c) A quadratic Bézier curve (in v). (d) A biquadratic Bézier patch as a collection of Bézier curves (each defined in v). (e) Weights for the control points. (f) Tessellation. (g) Three quadratic Bézier curves (in v). (h) A biquadratic Bézier patch as a collection of Bézier curves (each defined in u).

them as control points, we can define a quadratic Bézier curve in v. It is colored in orange. Then, a biquadratic Bézier patch is conceptually taken as a set of infinitely many such Bézier curves, as visualized in Fig. 17.12-(d). The left boundary of the patch in Fig. 17.12-(d) is the Bézier curve constructed from $\{p_{00}, p_{10}, p_{20}\}$. Similarly, the right boundary is constructed from $\{p_{02}, p_{12}, p_{22}\}$.

When we complete the matrix multiplications in Equation (17.21), we obtain the equation of the biquadratic Bézier patch:

$$p(u, v) = (1 - u)^2(1 - v)^2 p_{00} + 2u(1 - u)(1 - v)^2 p_{01} + u^2(1 - v)^2 p_{02} +$$
$$2(1 - u)^2 v(1 - v)p_{10} + 4uv(1 - u)(1 - v)p_{11} + 2u^2 v(1 - v)p_{12} +$$
$$(1 - u)^2 v^2 p_{20} + 2u(1 - u)v^2 p_{21} + u^2 v^2 p_{22}$$

(17.22)

The coefficient for a control point is a combination of the Bernstein polynomials in u and v. It works as a weight for the control point. Fig. 17.12-(e) illustrates the weights for all control points.

Displaying a biquadratic Bézier patch requires tessellation, and the same uv-sampling procedure adopted for bilinear patch tessellation can be used. Specifically, line 3 of Sample code 17-1 inserts u and v into Equation (17.22) to obtain a 3D point (x, y, z) on the patch. Fig. 17.12-(f) shows an example of tessellation, where both u and v are uniformly sampled by 10 steps each.

As discussed in the bilinear patch, we can reverse the order of processing u and v. Fig. 17.12-(g) shows three quadratic Bézier curves in v, each defined by a *column* of the 3×3 control point matrix. They will be combined in terms of u. The resulting surface is visualized in Fig. 17.12-(h), which is identical to the surface in Fig. 17.12-(d).

The top boundary of the patch in Fig. 17.12-(h) is the Bézier curve constructed from $\{p_{00}, p_{01}, p_{02}\}$, and the bottom boundary is constructed from $\{p_{20}, p_{21}, p_{22}\}$. The boundaries of a biquadratic Bézier patch are composed of four quadratic Bézier curves, which are constructed from the outer rows and columns of the 3×3 control point matrix. The same applies not only to the bilinear patch but also to the bicubic Bézier patch to be presented later.

In Fig. 17.12, a triple of control points defines a curve in one parameter, and then three such curves are combined in terms of the other parameter. Fig. 17.13 shows a different way of defining a biquadratic Bézier patch. The 3×3 control points are considered as a collection of four nets, each with 2×2 control points. Then, a bilinear interpolation is performed for each net. For example, in Fig. 17.13-(a), bilinear interpolation with $\{p_{00}, p_{01}, p_{10}, p_{11}\}$ produces p_{00}^1. When all nets of 2×2 control points are processed, we obtain four

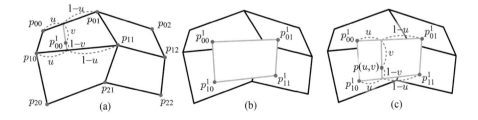

Fig. 17.13: Repeated bilinear interpolations: (a) Bilinear interpolation. (b) 2×2 intermediate points. (c) Another bilinear interpolation.

points shown in Fig. 17.13-(b):

$$
\begin{aligned}
p_{00}^1 &= (1-u)(1-v)p_{00} + u(1-v)p_{01} + (1-u)vp_{10} + uvp_{11} \\
p_{01}^1 &= (1-u)(1-v)p_{01} + u(1-v)p_{02} + (1-u)vp_{11} + uvp_{12} \\
p_{10}^1 &= (1-u)(1-v)p_{10} + u(1-v)p_{11} + (1-u)vp_{20} + uvp_{21} \\
p_{11}^1 &= (1-u)(1-v)p_{11} + u(1-v)p_{12} + (1-u)vp_{21} + uvp_{22}
\end{aligned}
\tag{17.23}
$$

Taking these as new 2×2 control points, we do another step of bilinear interpolation, as illustrated in Fig. 17.13-(c):

$$
\begin{aligned}
p(u,v) &= (1-u)(1-v)p_{00}^1 + u(1-v)p_{01}^1 + (1-u)vp_{10}^1 + uvp_{11}^1 \\
&= (1-u)(1-v)[(1-u)(1-v)p_{00} + u(1-v)p_{01} + (1-u)vp_{10} + uvp_{11}] + \\
&\quad u(1-v)[(1-u)(1-v)p_{01} + u(1-v)p_{02} + (1-u)vp_{11} + uvp_{12}] + \\
&\quad (1-u)v[(1-u)(1-v)p_{10} + u(1-v)p_{11} + (1-u)vp_{20} + uvp_{21}] + \\
&\quad uv[(1-u)(1-v)p_{11} + u(1-v)p_{12} + (1-u)vp_{21} + uvp_{22}] \\
&= (1-u)^2(1-v)^2 p_{00} + 2u(1-u)(1-v)^2 p_{01} + u^2(1-v)^2 p_{02} + \\
&\quad 2(1-u)^2 v(1-v)p_{10} + 4uv(1-u)(1-v)p_{11} + 2u^2 v(1-v)p_{12} + \\
&\quad (1-u)^2 v^2 p_{20} + 2u(1-u)v^2 p_{21} + u^2 v^2 p_{22}
\end{aligned}
\tag{17.24}
$$

We call this new method *repeated bilinear interpolations*. Note that $p(u,v)$ in Equation (17.24) is identical to that in Equation (17.22), i.e., they produce the same biquadratic Bézier patch.

17.2.3   Bicubic Bézier Patch

The biquadratic Bézier patch was defined by 3×3 control points. If we extend them to 4×4 control points, we obtain a *bicubic Bézier patch*. Fig. 17.14-(a) shows 4×4 control points structured in a rectangular net. The matrix form of the bicubic Bézier patch is defined as follows:

$$
p(u,v) = \begin{pmatrix} (1-v)^3 & 3v(1-v)^2 & 3v^2(1-v) & v^3 \end{pmatrix}
\begin{pmatrix} p_{00} & p_{01} & p_{02} & p_{03} \\ p_{10} & p_{11} & p_{12} & p_{13} \\ p_{20} & p_{21} & p_{22} & p_{23} \\ p_{30} & p_{31} & p_{32} & p_{33} \end{pmatrix}
\begin{pmatrix} (1-u)^3 \\ 3u(1-u)^2 \\ 3u^2(1-u) \\ u^3 \end{pmatrix}
\tag{17.25}
$$

The 4×4 matrix represents the 4×4 control points, and the row and column vectors on either side of the matrix are degree-3 Bernstein polynomials.

Fig. 17.14-(b) shows four cubic Bézier curves. As a function of u, each is defined by a row of the 4×4 control point matrix. The curves are then combined in terms of v to define a bicubic Bézier patch. In contrast, Fig. 17.14-(c) illustrates the method of repeated bilinear interpolations. The methods presented in Fig. 17.14-(b) and -(c) produce the same geometry. Fig. 17.14-(d) shows the results of tessellation and shading.

Fig. 17.15 shows that moving a control point in a Bézier patch leads to a substantial change in the surface geometry. It is an advantage of the Bézier patch. In order to obtain the same result by directly manipulating the vertices of a triangle mesh, we would have to individually move many more vertices.

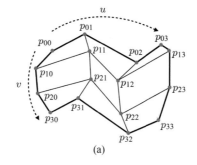

(a)

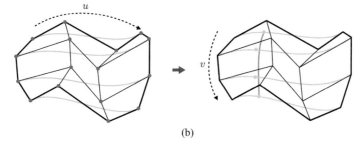

(b)

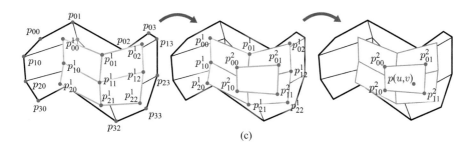

(c)

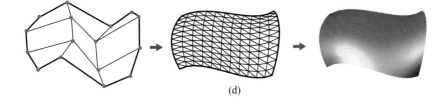

(d)

Fig. 17.14: Bicubic Bézier patch: (a) 4×4 control points. (b) Four cubic Bézier curves (each in u) are combined (in terms of v). (c) Repeated bilinear interpolations. (d) Tessellation and rendered result.

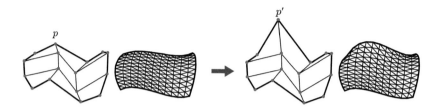

Fig. 17.15: Shape control in a Bézier patch is performed by manipulating the control points. A control point p is moved to p', leading to a significant change in the surface geometry.

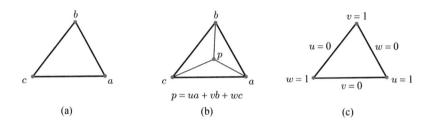

Fig. 17.16: Linear Bézier triangle: (a) Three control points. (b) A point on the Bézier triangle is defined by the barycentric coordinates, (u, v, w). (c) The parameters at the boundaries.

17.2.4 Bézier Triangle

To this point, we have studied the bilinear patch, the biquadratic Bézier patch, and the bicubic Bézier patch. They are all 'rectangular' patches. In contrast, the *Bézier triangle* represents a 'triangular' patch. It is defined by a triangular net of control points. Fig. 17.16-(a) shows the simplest Bézier triangle with three control points. Whereas the control points of a bilinear patch are not necessarily in a plane, the three control points of the Bézier triangle are always in a plane. Therefore, the Bézier triangle with three control points is nothing but a triangle. It is called the *linear Bézier triangle*.

Consider a surface point p on the Bézier triangle $\langle a, b, c \rangle$ shown in Fig. 17.16-(b). It divides the triangle into three sub-triangles. As presented in Section 12.1.5, p is described as a *barycentric combination* of the control points, i.e., $p = ua + vb + wc$, where (u, v, w) are called the *barycentric coordinates*. Observe that the weights (u, v, and w) add up to one and the weight for a control point is proportional to the area of the sub-triangle "on the opposite side." This is the same feature we have found for the linear interpolation (in Fig. 17.1) and the bilinear interpolation (in Fig. 17.10-(e)).

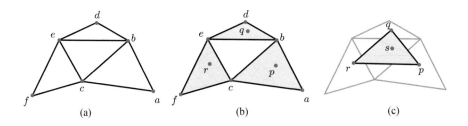

Fig. 17.17: Quadratic Bézier triangle: (a) The triangular net of six control points. (b) Barycentric combinations produce p, q, and r. (c) Another barycentric combination produces s, which represents the equation of the quadratic Bézier triangle.

If a component of the barycentric coordinates, (u, v, w), is one, the other two components are zero because $u + v + w = 1$. Then, p coincides with a control point. If $u = 1$, for example, $p = a$. What if a component of (u, v, w) is zero? If $u = 0$, for example, $v + w = 1$ and therefore $p = ua + vb + wc = (1 - w)b + wc$. It is the line segment connecting b and c. Fig. 17.16-(c) shows the parameters for the three vertices and three edges of the Bézier triangle.

With more control points, a non-planar Bézier triangle can be defined. Fig. 17.17-(a) shows the triangular net of six control points. To construct a surface using the triangular net, we do what we call *repeated barycentric combinations*, which are conceptually the same as the repeated bilinear interpolations presented in Fig. 17.13. In the first-level iterations, a barycentric combination is performed for each of the shaded triangles in Fig. 17.17-(b):

$$p = ua + vb + wc$$
$$q = ub + vd + we \qquad (17.26)$$
$$r = uc + ve + wf$$

In the second-level iteration, a barycentric combination is performed for the triangle $\langle p, q, r \rangle$, as shown in Fig. 17.17-(c):

$$s = up + vq + wr \qquad (17.27)$$

When p, q, and r in Equation (17.26) are inserted into Equation (17.27), we obtain the equation for the *quadratic Bézier triangle*:

$$
\begin{aligned}
s &= up + vq + wr \\
&= u(ua + vb + wc) + v(ub + vd + we) + w(uc + ve + wf) \qquad (17.28) \\
&= u^2 a + 2uvb + 2wuc + v^2 d + 2vwe + w^2 f
\end{aligned}
$$

Note that the coefficients for all control points are degree-2 polynomials. They work as weights, and Fig. 17.17-(d) illustrates the weights for the six control points.

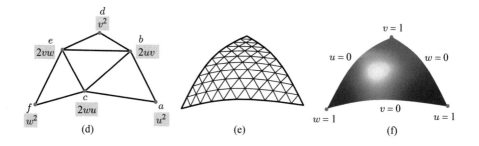

Fig. 17.17: Quadratic Bézier triangle (*continued*): (d) Weights for the control points. (e) Tessellation. (f) Rendered result and boundary features. The corner points are obtained when one of the barycentric coordinates is one, i.e., we obtain a when $u = 1$, d when $v = 1$, and f when $w = 1$. The edges are defined when one of the barycentric coordinates is zero, i.e., the left edge is defined when $u = 0$, the bottom edge when $v = 0$, and the right edge when $w = 0$.

Displaying a Bézier triangle requires tessellation. For this, we slightly modify Sample code 17-1: Line 3 first sets w to $1 - u - v$ and then inserts u, v, and w into Equation (17.28) to obtain a 3D point (x, y, z) on the quadratic Bézier triangle. Using a set of these evaluated points, a triangle mesh can be constructed. Fig. 17.17-(e) shows the tessellation result where both u and v are uniformly sampled by 10 steps each.

Fig. 17.17-(f) shows the result of rendering the Bézier triangle. Its corners and edges are described by the same parameters shown in Fig. 17.16-(c). If $u = 1$, for example, $v = w = 0$ and Equation (17.28) is reduced to a. On the other hand, if $u = 0$, Equation (17.28) is reduced to $v^2 d + 2vwe + w^2 f$. It can be expressed as $(1 - w)^2 d + 2w(1 - w)e + w^2 f$ because $v + w = 1$. It is a quadratic Bézier curve and defines the left edge of the Bézier triangle shown in Fig. 17.17-(f). The left edge is defined solely by d, e, and f. Recall that similar 'boundary' features were observed in the rectangular Bézier patches.

A *cubic Bézier triangle* is defined by 10 control points, as illustrated in Fig. 17.18-(a). Three levels of barycentric combinations are performed to define the equation in Fig. 17.18-(b). Sample code 17-1 would use that equation to construct the mesh shown in Fig. 17.18-(c).

The boundary features presented in Fig. 17.16-(c) and Fig. 17.17-(f) are also found in the cubic Bézier triangle. For example, the right edge in Fig. 17.18-(d) is obtained when $w = 0$. It is a cubic Bézier curve defined by the control points, $\{a, b, d, g\}$. Fig. 17.18-(e) shows the triangular *domain* for all three (linear, quadratic, and cubic) Bézier triangles.

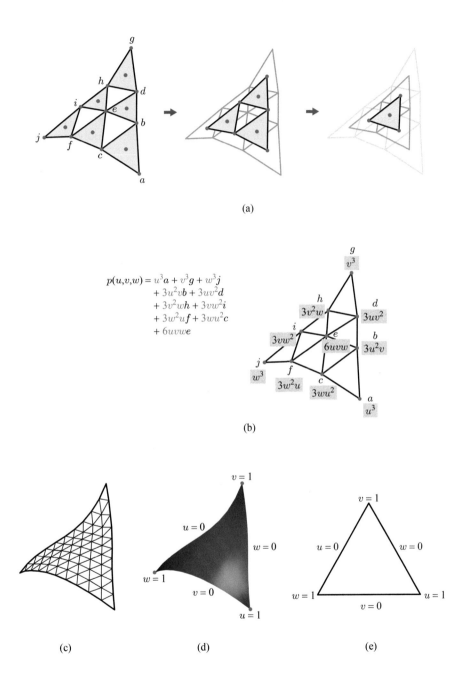

Fig. 17.18: Cubic Bézier triangle: (a) The triangular net of 10 control points and the repeated barycentric combinations. (b) The Bézier triangle's equation and the weights for all control points. (c) Tessellation. (d) Rendered result and boundary features. (e) The parametric domain of all Bézier triangles.

Exercises

1. The *cubic* Bézier curve has the equation, $(1 - t)^3 p_0 + 3t(1 - t)^2 p_1 + 3t^2(1 - t)p_2 + t^3 p_3$. Write the equation of the *quartic* (degree-4) Bézier curve defined by $\{p_0, p_1, p_2, p_3, p_4\}$.

2. Consider a quintic (degree-5) Bézier curve. How many control points are needed? For each control point, write the Bernstein polynomial over t in $[0, 1]$.

3. You are given three 2D points $\{(1, 0), (0, 1), (-1, 0)\}$.

   (a) Assuming that the point at $(0, 1)$ is associated with parameter 0.5, compute the control points of the quadratic Bézier curve that passes through all three points.

   (b) On the Bézier curve, compute the coordinates of the point whose parameter is 0.75.

4. Consider a spline composed of two cubic Bézier curves defined by the control point sets, $\{p_0, p_1, p_2, p_3\}$ and $\{q_0, q_1, q_2, q_3\}$, where $p_3 = q_0$. If they have the same tangent vector at their junction, the spline is called continuous. What is the necessary condition that makes the spline continuous? Describe the condition as an equation of p_2, p_3, q_0, and q_1.

5. In the figure shown below, the camera is moving along the quadratic Bézier curve $p(t)$ defined by the control points, p_1, p_2, and p_3, whereas **AT** is moving along the linear path $q(t)$ connecting the origin and p_4. **UP** is fixed to the y-axis of the world space.

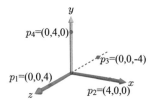

   (a) Both $p(t)$ and $q(t)$ are defined in parameter t in the range $[0, 1]$. Compute the points on $p(t)$ and $q(t)$ when $t = 0.5$.

   (b) Compute the basis of the camera space when $t = 0.5$.

   (c) Compute the 4×4 translation and rotation matrices defining the view matrix when $t = 0.5$.

6. A Bézier patch is defined by the control point matrix shown below. In its domain, the u- and v-axes run horizontally and vertically, respectively.

$$\begin{pmatrix} p_{00} & p_{01} & p_{02} \\ p_{10} & p_{11} & p_{12} \\ p_{20} & p_{21} & p_{22} \end{pmatrix} = \begin{pmatrix} (0,0,6) & (0,3,3) & (0,6,6) \\ (3,0,0) & (3,3,0) & (3,6,0) \\ (6,0,0) & (6,3,0) & (6,6,0) \end{pmatrix}$$

(a) Compute the 3D point when $(u, v) = (1, 0)$.

(b) Using the method of "repeated bilinear interpolations," compute the 3D point when $(u, v) = (0.5, 0.5)$.

7. Consider a Bézier patch, whose degrees in terms of u and v are three and two, respectively. The control point matrix is given as follows:

$$\begin{pmatrix} p_{00} & p_{01} & p_{02} \\ p_{10} & p_{11} & p_{12} \\ p_{20} & p_{21} & p_{22} \\ p_{30} & p_{31} & p_{32} \end{pmatrix} = \begin{pmatrix} (0,0,4) & (0,3,4) & (0,6,4) \\ (3,0,0) & (3,3,0) & (3,6,0) \\ (6,0,0) & (6,3,0) & (6,6,0) \\ (5,0,4) & (5,3,4) & (5,6,4) \end{pmatrix}$$

(a) Compute the surface point when $(u, v) = (0, 1)$.

(b) Compute the surface point when $(u, v) = (0.5, 0.5)$.

8. Given the following quadratic Bézier triangle, compute the surface point when $(u, v) = (1/3, 1/3)$.

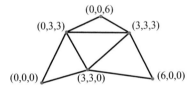

9. Shown below is the triangular net of a quartic (degree-4) Bézier triangle. When $v = 1$, the Bézier triangle is reduced to k. When $w = 1$, it is o. Define the equation of the curve when $u = 0$.

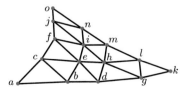

Chapter 18

Surface Tessellation

The most notable feature of OpenGL ES 3.2 is the support for *hardware tessellation*. It enables the GPU to decompose a primitive into a large number of smaller ones. GPU tessellation involves two new programmable stages, the *tessellation control shader* (henceforth, simply control shader) and the *tessellation evaluation shader* (henceforth, evaluation shader), and a new hard-wired stage, the *tessellation primitive generator* (henceforth, tessellator). See Fig. 18.1. Due to hardware tessellation, a variety of complex surfaces can have direct acceleration support. This chapter presents two tessellation examples: displacement mapping in Section 18.1 and PN-triangles in Section 18.2. The PN-triangles are not widely used and Section 18.2 is optional.

Fig. 18.1: For hardware tessellation, two programmable stages and a hard-wired stage are newly added in GL 3.2. (The geometry shader is also new but is less useful. This book does not discuss the geometry shader.)

18.1 Displacement Mapping

In normal mapping, presented in Chapter 14, the underlying geometry of the base surface is not altered. In contrast, *displacement mapping* tessellates the base surface and then displaces the vertices of the tessellated mesh.

18.1.1 GPU Tessellation

In GL 3.2, displacement mapping is implemented jointly by the control shader, the tessellator, and the evaluation shader. Fig. 18.2 presents an im-

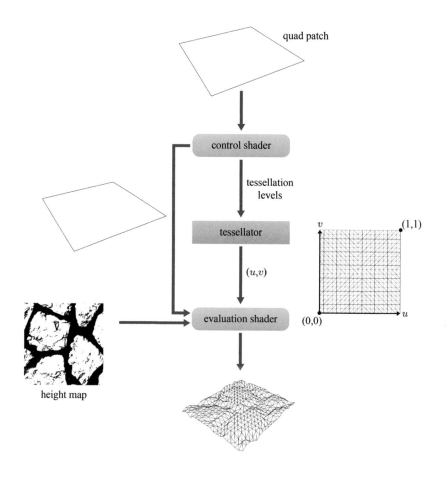

Fig. 18.2: Displacement mapping in GL 3.2.

plementation for a part of the paved ground we used in Chapter 14. The input to the control shader is called a *patch*. It is a new primitive type in GL 3.2 and is either a triangle or a quad. For our paved-ground example, the control shader takes a quad as the base surface and passes it *as is* to the evaluation shader, bypassing the tessellator.

In addition, the control shader determines the *tessellation levels* and passes them to the hard-wired stage, the tessellator, which accordingly tessellates the *domain* of the quad into a 2D triangle mesh. See the example on the right of Fig. 18.2. Each vertex of the mesh is assigned its own (u, v) coordinates. The lower-left corner of the square domain is assigned $(0,0)$, and the upper-right one is $(1,1)$. The (u,v) coordinates vary linearly across the domain.

The evaluation shader runs once for each vertex of the 2D mesh:

- The quad passed from the control shader is taken as a *bilinear patch* defined as a function of two variables, u and v. Then, a point on the quad is evaluated using (u,v) of the vertex input by the tessellator.
- The GL program provides the evaluation shader with a height map. The evaluation shader extracts a height from the height map.
- The point evaluated on the quad is vertically displaced by the height.

When every vertex is processed, a high-frequency mesh is generated, as shown at the bottom of Fig. 18.2. The mesh will then be sent to the subsequent stages of the rendering pipeline, i.e., the geometry shader, or the rasterizer if no geometry shader is present.

Normal mapping gives an *illusion* of high-frequency surface detail without altering the base surface. It is an *image-space algorithm*, which operates on fragments or pixels. In contrast, displacement mapping is an *object-space algorithm*, which alters the object itself, i.e., the base surface. The distinction between them is most clearly perceived at the objects' silhouettes. Unlike the normal mapping examples shown in Fig. 14.7, the edges of the paved ground in Fig. 18.2 are not linear.

18.1.2   Shaders and Tessellator

For displacement mapping, the GL program creates and compiles the *shader objects* for the control and evaluation shaders, as it did for the vertex shader in Section 6.3. For this, `glCreateShader` is invoked with the arguments `GL_TESS_CONTROL_SHADER` and `GL_TESS_EVALUATION_SHADER`. The shader objects are then attached to the program object. In addition, the GL program has to specify the number of vertices that make up a single patch primitive. For displacement mapping, it calls `glPatchParameteri(GL_PATCH_VERTICES, 4)`, where 4 implies a quad patch.

Sample code 18-1 Vertex shader for displacement mapping

```
 1: #version 320 es
 2:
 3: layout(location = 0) in vec3 position;
 4: layout(location = 2) in vec2 texCoord;
 5:
 6: out vec3 v_position;
 7: out vec2 v_texCoord;
 8:
 9: void main() {
10:     v_position = position; // object-space position
11:     v_texCoord = texCoord;
12: }
```

Sample code 18-2 Tessellation control shader for displacement mapping

```
1: #version 320 es
2:
3: layout(vertices = 4) out;
4:
5: uniform float tessLevel;
6:
7: in vec3 v_position[];
8: in vec2 v_texCoord[];
9:
10: out vec3 es_position[];
11: out vec2 es_texCoord[];
12:
13: void main() {
14:     es_position[gl_InvocationID] = v_position[gl_InvocationID];
15:     es_texCoord[gl_InvocationID] = v_texCoord[gl_InvocationID];
16:
17:     // tessellation levels
18:     gl_TessLevelOuter[0] = tessLevel;
19:     gl_TessLevelOuter[1] = tessLevel;
20:     gl_TessLevelOuter[2] = tessLevel;
21:     gl_TessLevelOuter[3] = tessLevel;
22:     gl_TessLevelInner[0] = tessLevel;
23:     gl_TessLevelInner[1] = tessLevel;
24: }
```

Sample code 18-1 is the vertex shader for displacement mapping. The first line declares that it is written in GLSL 3.2. The vertex shader simply copies position and texCoord to v_position and v_texCoord, respectively. The vertex shader is exempt from the duty of computing gl_Position, the clip-space vertex position. It will be done by the evaluation shader.

Shown in Sample code 18-2 is the control shader. By default, multiple control shaders work in parallel on an input patch to emit an output patch, and an invocation of the control shader outputs the variables "of a vertex" in the patch. The number of output vertices is specified using the keyword, vertices, which equivalently specifies how many control shaders are invoked. Line 3 of Sample code 18-2 implies that four control shaders will work in parallel on the input quad.

The patch input to the control shader is an array of vertices with attributes, which correspond to the output variables produced by the vertex shader. They are v_position (line 7) and v_texCoord (line 8) declared with the qualifier in. The first statement of the main function copies v_position to es_position, which is sent to the evaluation shader, bypassing the tessellator. An invocation of the control shader processes a vertex, and the vertex ID is stored in the built-in variable gl_InvocationID. When four control shaders are invoked, gl_InvocationID takes 0 through 3, i.e., the first control shader fills es_position[0], the second control shader fills es_position[1], and so on.

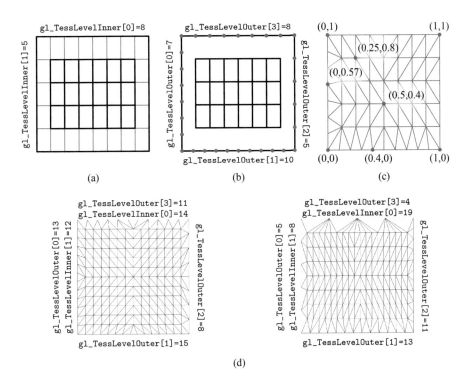

Fig. 18.3: Tessellation levels: (a) Subdivision with `gl_TessLevelInner`. (b) Subdivision with `gl_TessLevelOuter`. (c) Tessellated square domain. (d) Tessellation examples.

The other output variable, `es_texCoord`, is filled in the same manner and sent to the evaluation shader, also bypassing the tessellator.

The rest of the main function specifies the tessellation levels using two built-in *per-patch* arrays, `gl_TessLevelOuter` and `gl_TessLevelInner`. The interior of the quad's domain is first subdivided vertically and horizontally using `gl_TessLevelInner`. In the example shown in Fig. 18.3-(a), the domain is subdivided vertically into eight segments and horizontally into five. Then, the edges are independently subdivided using `gl_TessLevelOuter`, as shown in Fig. 18.3-(b). Using the subdivision results, the entire area of the square domain is filled with a set of non-overlapping smaller triangles. See Fig. 18.3-(c). Each vertex of the triangle mesh is assigned its own (u, v) coordinates. Fig. 18.3-(d) shows two more examples of tessellation[1].

---

[1]The tessellation levels are not limited to integers, but it is beyond the scope of this book to present the floating-point tessellation levels.

Sample code 18-3 Tessellation evaluation shader for displacement mapping

```
1: #version 320 es
2:
3: layout(quads) in;
4:
5: uniform sampler2D heightMap;
6: uniform float dispFactor;
7: uniform mat4 worldMat, viewMat, projMat;
8:
9: in vec3 es_position[];
10: in vec2 es_texCoord[];
11:
12: out vec2 v_texCoord;
13:
14: void main() {
15:     float u = gl_TessCoord.x;
16:     float v = gl_TessCoord.y;
17:
18:     // bilinearly interpolated object-space position
19:     vec3 lowerPos = mix(es_position[0], es_position[1], u);
20:     vec3 upperPos = mix(es_position[2], es_position[3], u);
21:     vec3 position = mix(lowerPos, upperPos, v);
22:
23:     // bilinearly interpolated texture coordinates
24:     vec2 lowerTex = mix(es_texCoord[0], es_texCoord[1], u);
25:     vec2 upperTex = mix(es_texCoord[2], es_texCoord[3], u);
26:     v_texCoord = mix(lowerTex, upperTex, v);
27:
28:     // vertical displacement
29:     float height = texture(heightMap, v_texCoord).z;
30:     position += dispFactor * vec3(0.0, 0.0, height);
31:
32:     // clip-space position
33:     gl_Position = projMat * viewMat * worldMat * vec4(position, 1.0);
34: }
```

In the control shader presented in Sample code 18-2, the inner and outer tessellation levels are made the same for the sake of simplicity. In general, they are different and are often computed internally within the control shader. The tessellation capability of GL 3.2 embodies the *scalability* feature of a parametric surface, which is considered an advantage over a fixed polygon mesh representation. Using the tessellation levels, a parametric surface (the bilinear patch in the example of displacement mapping) can be tessellated into an arbitrary-resolution polygon mesh.

Sample code 18-3 shows the evaluation shader. At line 3, quads implies that the input patches are quads, not triangles. The evaluation shader runs once on each vertex input by the tessellator. Its (u, v) coordinates are stored in the built-in variable gl_TessCoord, and the main function first extracts (u, v) from gl_TessCoord.

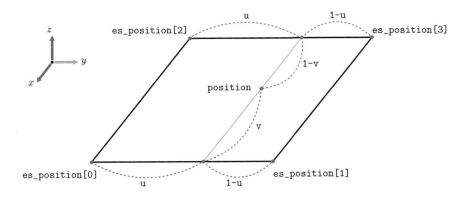

Fig. 18.4: A point on the input quad is evaluated through bilinear interpolation. It is going to be displaced vertically using the height map.

The evaluation shader takes es_position[], passed from the control shader, as the control points of a bilinear patch. Using (u, v), the patch is evaluated to return a 3D point. The evaluation implements a bilinear interpolation. Fig. 18.4 shows the bilinear interpolation implemented in lines 19 through 21 of the main function. The built-in function mix(A,B,u) returns (1-u)A+uB. At line 21, position represents a point on the bilinear patch. The texture coordinates stored in es_texCoord[] are bilinearly interpolated in the same manner so as to produce v_texCoord at line 26.

The evaluation shader has access to samplers. Our example uses a height map (heightMap). It is accessed with v_texCoord to return a height value. Then, position is vertically displaced. (The user-defined variable dispFactor controls how much the entire quad patch is displaced.) Finally, the vertically displaced vertex is transformed into the clip space and stored in the built-in variable, gl_Position. Note that gl_Position is now output by the evaluation shader, not by the vertex shader. However, it behaves identically to the equivalently named vertex shader output, i.e., it is read by subsequent stages of the GPU pipeline as usual.

Fig. 18.5 shows a large paved ground processed by the shaders presented in this section. The base surface is composed of 16 quads. It is represented in a quad mesh, not in a triangle mesh. In the indexed representation of such a quad mesh, the index array will store 64 elements, four elements per quad. A polygon mesh is drawn by making a *drawcall*. Return to Section 6.5 and observe that the first argument of glDrawElements is GL_TRIANGLES for the triangle mesh. In GL 3.2, glDrawElements may take GL_PATCHES instead. We would call glDrawElements(GL_PATCHES, 64, GL_UNSIGNED_SHORT, 0), where 64 is the number of indices to draw.

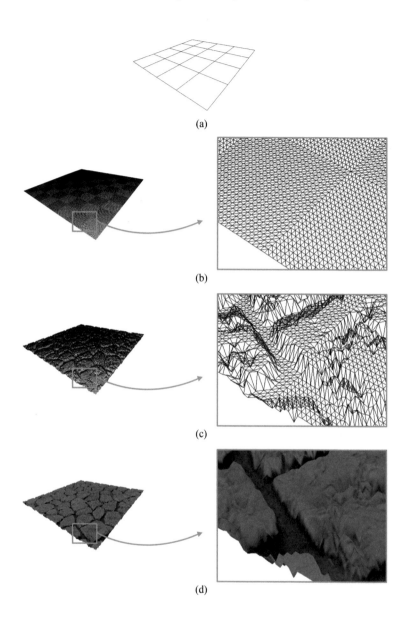

Fig. 18.5: Displacement mapping in GL 3.2: (a) The base surface is composed of 16 quads. (b) In this example, a quad is tessellated into 722 triangles. (c) Using a height map, the vertices of the tessellated mesh are vertically displaced. (d) The high-frequency mesh is shaded.

18.2 PN-triangles*

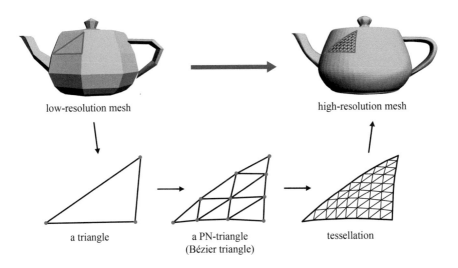

low-resolution mesh   high-resolution mesh

a triangle   a PN-triangle   tessellation
(Bézier triangle)

Fig. 18.6: Using PN-triangles, a low-resolution coarse mesh can be converted into a high-resolution smooth mesh.

A *PN-triangle* (standing for point-normal triangle) refers to a Bézier triangle that is derived from a triangle of a polygon mesh [17]. A PN-triangle can be tessellated into a large number of small triangles such that they replace the original triangle from which the PN-triangle is derived. See Fig. 18.6. When all triangles of the input polygon mesh are converted into PN-triangles, the input mesh can be refined into a higher-resolution smoother mesh.

18.2.1 Computing Control Points

Fig. 18.7-(a) depicts a triangle extracted from a polygon mesh. We describe its vertex attributes as $\{p_i, n_i\}$, where p_i denotes the position and n_i denotes the normal. Let us convert the triangle into the cubic Bézier triangle shown in Fig. 18.7-(b). First of all, the corner control points of the Bézier triangle, p_{300}, p_{030}, and p_{003}, are set to p_1, p_2, and p_3, respectively.

The control points on an outer edge of the triangular net are defined using the vertex attributes of the corresponding edge in the input triangle. For

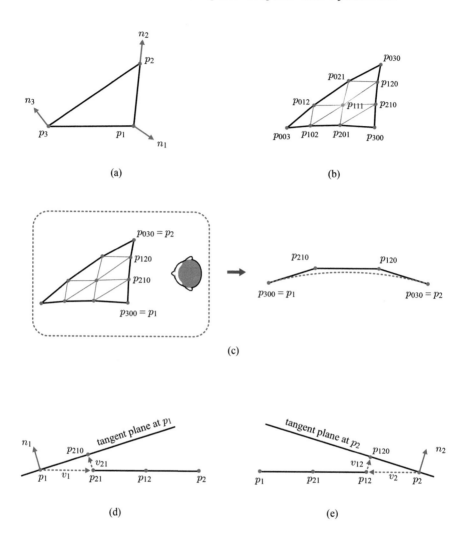

Fig. 18.7: PN-triangle generation: (a) A triangle from a polygon mesh. (b) The control points of a cubic Bézier triangle are computed using the vertex attributes in (a). (c) Control points and surface edge. (d) The temporary point p_{21} is displaced by v_{21} to define p_{210}. (e) Another temporary point p_{12} is displaced by v_{12} to define p_{120}.

example, p_{210} and p_{120} are computed using $\{p_1, n_1\}$ and $\{p_2, n_2\}$. Fig. 18.7-(c) depicts a side view of the Bézier triangle. The dotted curve represents the surface's edge defined by four control points, $\{p_{300}, p_{210}, p_{120}, p_{030}\}$. It is a cubic Bézier curve.

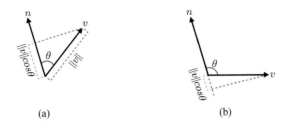

(a) (b)

Fig. 18.8: Projected length: (a) The projected length $\|v\|cos\theta$ is positive. (b) The projected length becomes negative because $cos\theta$ is negative.

In order to define p_{210} and p_{120}, the line segment connecting p_1 and p_2 is divided into three equal parts to produce temporary points, p_{21} and p_{12}, as shown in Fig. 18.7-(d). Then, p_{21} is displaced onto the *tangent plane* at p_1 to define p_{210}. The displacement vector denoted by v_{21} is parallel to n_1. Similarly, Fig. 18.7-(e) shows that p_{120} is obtained by displacing p_{12} onto the tangent plane at p_2.

It is simple to compute p_{21}. We first divide the vector connecting p_1 and p_2 by three:

$$v_1 = \frac{p_2 - p_1}{3} \qquad (18.1)$$

Then, we add v_1 to p_1:

$$p_{21} = p_1 + v_1$$
$$= \frac{2p_1 + p_2}{3} \qquad (18.2)$$

As $p_{210} = p_{21} + v_{21}$, we need v_{21}. We can obtain it using dot product. Consider two vectors, n and v. Their dot product $n{\cdot}v$ is defined as $\|n\|\|v\|cos\theta$, where θ is the angle between n and v. If n is a unit vector, i.e., if $\|n\| = 1$, $n \cdot v$ is reduced to $\|v\|cos\theta$. It is the length of v projected onto n, as shown in Fig. 18.8-(a). The projected length is positive if θ is an acute angle. If θ is an obtuse angle, however, $\|v\|cos\theta$ and equivalently $n \cdot v$ become negative, as shown in Fig. 18.8-(b).

In order to compute v_{21} in Fig. 18.7-(d), we first project v_1 given in Equation (18.1) onto n_1 and compute its length. As n_1 is a unit vector, the length equals the dot product of n_1 and v_1:

$$n_1 \cdot v_1 = n_1 \cdot \frac{p_2 - p_1}{3} \qquad (18.3)$$

This is negative because n_1 and v_1 form an obtuse angle. Equation (18.3) is negated and multiplied with the unit vector n_1 to define v_{21}:

$$v_{21} = -(n_1 \cdot \frac{p_2 - p_1}{3})n_1 \qquad (18.4)$$

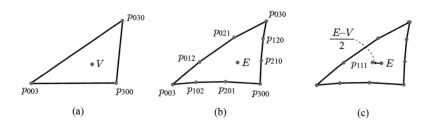

Fig. 18.9: Computing the interior control point: (a) The original vertices define V. (b) The mid-edge control points define E. (c) E is displaced by $\frac{E-V}{2}$ to define p_{111}.

Finally, p_{210} is obtained by adding v_{21} to p_{21}:

$$
\begin{aligned}
p_{210} &= p_{21} + v_{21} \\
&= \tfrac{2p_1+p_2}{3} - (n_1 \cdot \tfrac{p_2-p_1}{3})n_1
\end{aligned}
\tag{18.5}
$$

Fig. 18.7-(e) shows that p_{12} is displaced by v_{12} to define another mid-edge control point p_{120}:

$$
\begin{aligned}
p_{120} &= p_{12} + v_{12} \\
&= \tfrac{p_1+2p_2}{3} - (n_2 \cdot \tfrac{p_1-p_2}{3})n_2
\end{aligned}
\tag{18.6}
$$

The other mid-edge control points, p_{021}, p_{012}, p_{102}, and p_{201}, are computed in the same manner.

Fig. 18.9 shows how to compute the interior control point, p_{111}. The corner control points are averaged to define V:

$$
V = \frac{p_{300} + p_{030} + p_{003}}{3}
\tag{18.7}
$$

The mid-edge control points are averaged to define E:

$$
E = \frac{p_{210} + p_{120} + p_{021} + p_{012} + p_{102} + p_{201}}{6}
\tag{18.8}
$$

Then, E is displaced by $\frac{E-V}{2}$ to define p_{111}:

$$
\begin{aligned}
p_{111} &= E + \tfrac{E-V}{2} \\
&= \tfrac{1}{4}(p_{210} + p_{120} + p_{021} + p_{012} + p_{102} + p_{201}) - \tfrac{1}{6}(p_{300} + p_{030} + p_{003})
\end{aligned}
\tag{18.9}
$$

We have computed 10 control points. Fig. 18.10-(a) presents the equation of the Bézier triangle, $p(u, v, w)$, defined by the control points. The Bézier triangle can be tessellated using a set of barycentric coordinates, (u, v, w), i.e., $p(u, v, w)$ is evaluated with each (u, v, w) to return a surface point (x, y, z), and such evaluated points are connected to generate a polygon mesh.

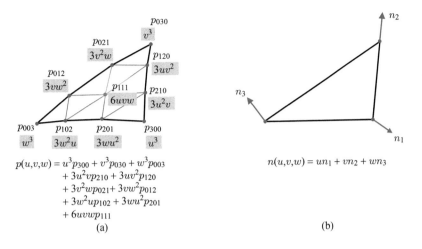

$$p(u,v,w) = u^3 p_{300} + v^3 p_{030} + w^3 p_{003}$$
$$+ 3u^2 v p_{210} + 3uv^2 p_{120}$$
$$+ 3v^2 w p_{021} + 3vw^2 p_{012}$$
$$+ 3w^2 u p_{102} + 3wu^2 p_{201}$$
$$+ 6uvw p_{111}$$

(a)

$$n(u,v,w) = un_1 + vn_2 + wn_3$$

(b)

Fig. 18.10: Control points and normals: (a) The control point net defines $p(u, v, w)$, which maps (u, v, w) to a vertex position (x, y, z). (b) The control normal net defines $n(u, v, w)$, which maps the same (u, v, w) to the vertex normal at (x, y, z).

In order to render the polygon mesh, however, we need additional information, i.e., a *normal* for each evaluated point. The simplest method to compute the normal is to take the barycentric combination of the input vertex normals, i.e., $un_1 + vn_2 + wn_3$, which we denote by $n(u, v, w)$. As shown in Fig. 18.10-(b), $n(u, v, w)$ is nothing but a linear Bézier triangle built upon n_1, n_2, and n_3, which are called *control normals*. Using a single triple, (u, v, w), the position and normal are extracted from $p(u, v, w)$ and $n(u, v, w)$, respectively. As a linear equation, however, $n(u, v, w)$ may often reveal a problem, and Section 18.2.2 will present an alternative.

[Note: Seamless tessellation]
Consider triangles t_1 and t_2 shown in Fig. 18.11. They share the edge connecting p_1 and p_2. Suppose that t_1 and t_2 are converted into PN-triangles. Then, the PN-triangles share the mid-edge control points, p_{210} and p_{120}. It is because p_{210} and p_{120} are computed solely by $\{p_1, n_1\}$ and $\{p_2, n_2\}$, which t_1 and t_2 share. Consequently, the higher-resolution mesh produced by the PN-triangles does not have a gap or crack if both PN-triangles are tessellated with the same sampling rate at the shared boundary. This shows that, if a watertight mesh is converted into a higher-resolution mesh using PN-triangles, the resulting mesh can be also watertight.

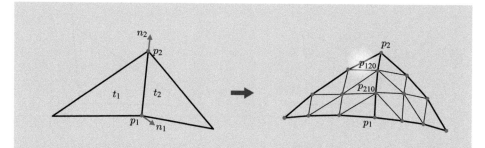

Fig. 18.11: Adjacent triangles t_1 and t_2 are converted into two PN-triangles, and they share the mid-edge control points, p_{210} and p_{120}.

18.2.2 Computing Control Normals

Consider the side view of a Bézier triangle shown in Fig. 18.12-(a). Two end control points, p_1 and p_2, are associated with normals, n_1 and n_2, respectively. Given n_1 and n_2, the underlying surface's edge connecting p_1 and p_2 would be like the dotted curve. Suppose that a point, q, is evaluated in the middle of the edge. Its barycentric coordinates would be $(1/2, 1/2, 0)$. Then, $n(u, v, w)$ presented in Fig. 18.10-(b) returns $\frac{n_1 + n_2}{2}$. It is normalized to define the normal at q. It is likely to be orthogonal to the underlying surface, as illustrated in Fig. 18.12-(a).

Unlike Fig. 18.12-(a), the 'linear' equation $n(u, v, w)$ may often malfunction. Consider the case shown in Fig. 18.12-(b). The vertex normals, n_1 and n_2, point in the same direction, but the tangent planes at p_1 and p_2 are at different levels. Thus, the normals computed through barycentric combinations are not orthogonal to the underlying surface. Instead, the correct normals would be like those illustrated in Fig. 18.12-(c). Such correct normals can be obtained by defining a 'quadratic' equation for $n(u, v, w)$. It is built upon six control normals shown on the right of Fig. 18.12-(d). The control normals located at the corners, i.e., n_{200}, n_{020}, and n_{002}, are set to the input vertex normals, n_1, n_2, and n_3, respectively. We need to define mid-edge control normals, n_{110}, n_{011}, and n_{101}.

Fig. 18.12-(e) illustrates a heuristic for defining n_{110}. Consider a plane P that is orthogonal to the edge connecting p_1 and p_2. P's normal n_P is computed as follows:

$$n_P = \frac{p_1 - p_2}{\|p_1 - p_2\|} \tag{18.10}$$

The end-normals, n_1 and n_2, are summed to make n_{12}. The dot product of n_{12} and n_P is the length of n_{12}'s projection onto n_P. It is multiplied by $-2n_P$ and then added to n_{12} to define n'_{12}, which is the reflection of n_{12} with respect

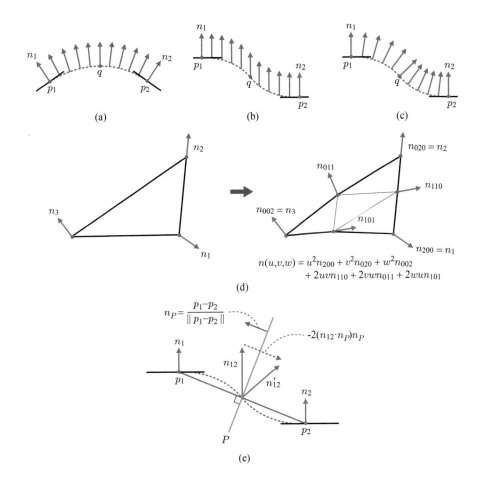

Fig. 18.12: Control normals for PN-triangle: (a) Normals computed though the linear equation of $n(u, v, w)$. (b) Incorrect normals. (c) Correct normals. (d) Six control normals and the quadratic equation of $n(u, v, w)$. (e) Computing a mid-edge control normal.

to P:

$$
\begin{aligned}
n'_{12} &= n_{12} - 2(n_{12} \cdot n_P)n_P \\
&= (n_1 + n_2) - 2\left((n_1 + n_2) \cdot \frac{p_1 - p_2}{\|p_1 - p_2\|}\right)\frac{p_1 - p_2}{\|p_1 - p_2\|} \\
&= (n_1 + n_2) - 2\frac{(n_1 + n_2) \cdot (p_1 - p_2)}{\|p_1 - p_2\|^2}(p_1 - p_2) \\
&= (n_1 + n_2) - 2\frac{(n_1 + n_2) \cdot (p_1 - p_2)}{(p_1 - p_2) \cdot (p_1 - p_2)}(p_1 - p_2)
\end{aligned}
\tag{18.11}
$$

We normalize n'_{12} to define the mid-edge control normal n_{110}. The other mid-edge control normals, n_{011} and n_{101}, are similarly computed.

A single *uvw*-triple extracts a position from the 'cubic' equation of $p(u, v, w)$ and a normal from the 'quadratic' equation of $n(u, v, w)$. You might think of a cubic equation for $n(u, v, w)$, but there seems to be no straightforward method to develop it. Fortunately, the quadratic equation for $n(u, v, w)$ produces satisfactory results in general.

18.2.3   GPU Tessellation

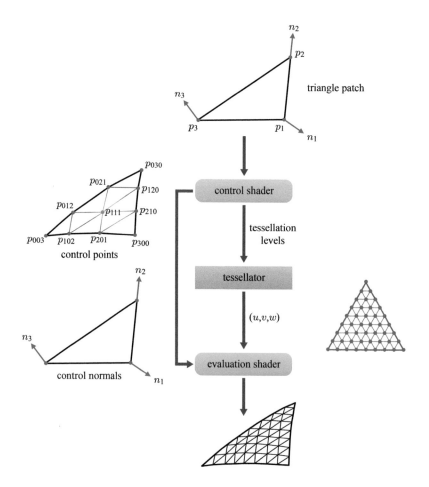

Fig. 18.13: PN-triangle generation and tessellation in GL 3.2.

This subsection presents how a triangle is converted into a PN-triangle and then tessellated. Fig. 18.13 shows an implementation. The triangle patch input to the control shader has been extracted from a triangle mesh, and the vertex attributes include not only positions but also normals. Unlike displacement mapping, where the input patch is passed *as is* to the evaluation shader, the control shader computes the *control points* of a cubic Bézier triangle, as presented in Section 18.2.1. On the other hand, the control shader takes the input vertex normals as the *control normals*[2]. The control points and normals are passed to the evaluation shader.

The control shader also determines the *tessellation levels* and passes them to the tessellator, which accordingly tessellates the triangular domain into a 2D triangle mesh. Shown on the right of Fig. 18.13 is an example, where each vertex is assigned its own *barycentric coordinates*, (u, v, w). In the 2D mesh of Fig. 18.13, the triangles appear completely regular, but tessellation in reality does not produce such regular triangles, as will be presented in Section 18.2.4.

The evaluation shader runs once for each vertex of the 2D triangle mesh generated by the tessellator. Given the control points and normals, the evaluation shader establishes the cubic Bézier triangle, $p(u, v, w)$, presented in Fig. 18.10-(a), and the linear normal equation, $n(u, v, w)$, presented in Fig. 18.10-(b). The barycentric coordinates of the input vertex, (u, v, w), are inserted into $p(u, v, w)$ and $n(u, v, w)$ to determine the vertex position and normal, respectively. When every vertex of the 2D mesh is processed, a high-resolution smooth mesh is obtained, as shown at the bottom of Fig. 18.13.

18.2.4 Shaders and Tessellator

Sample code 18-4 Vertex shader for PN-triangles

```
1: #version 320 es
2:
3: layout(location = 0) in vec3 position;
4: layout(location = 1) in vec3 normal;
5:
6: out vec3 v_position;
7: out vec3 v_normal;
8:
9: void main() {
10:     v_position = position; // object-space position
11:     v_normal = normal;
12: }
```

---

[2]To simplify the presentation, we do not compute the control normals presented in Section 18.2.2.

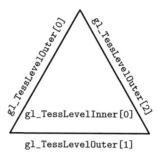

Fig. 18.14: Tessellation levels for a triangle patch.

Sample code 18-4 is the vertex shader for PN-triangles. It simply copies `position` and `normal` to `v_position` and `v_normal`, respectively, and leaves the task of computing `gl_Position` to the evaluation shader.

Shown in Sample code 18-5 is the control shader. Observe that `vertices = 1` at line 3. It implies that the control shader is invoked just once, i.e., the control points and normals are computed through a single invocation of the control shader. For this, a structure named `PNT` is defined at line 10. The first ten elements of `PNT` are the control points and the last three are the control normals. Then, line 16 uses the qualifier, `out patch`, to define the PN-triangle (`pnTri`), which is to be passed to the evaluation shader. The majority of the main function is devoted to filling `pnTri`. It is a straight implementation of the method presented in Section 18.2.1.

In order to tessellate the triangular domain into a 2D triangle mesh, the tessellation levels are specified in `gl_TessLevelOuter` and `gl_TessLevelInner`. See the last four statements of the main function. Fig. 18.14 shows that three elements of `gl_TessLevelOuter` and a single element of `gl_TessLevelInner` need to be specified, i.e., `gl_TessLevelOuter[3]` and `gl_TessLevelInner[1]` are not relevant for a triangle patch.

The interior of the domain is first tessellated using `gl_TessLevelInner[0]`, and then the edges are tessellated independently using the first three elements of `gl_TessLevelOuter`. For interior tessellation, the equilateral triangular domain is subdivided into a collection of concentric *inner triangles*. Suppose that the inner tessellation level (henceforth, inner TL) is two. Then, every edge is temporarily split into two segments, as shown in Fig. 18.15-(a). The lines bisecting the edges are extended to intersect at the triangle's center, i.e., the inner triangle is degenerate. When the inner TL is three, every edge is split into three segments. For each vertex of the triangular domain, two lines are extended from the *nearest* split points, as illustrated in Fig. 18.15-(b). They intersect at a point. We have three such points, and they define the inner triangle.

Sample code 18-5 Tessellation control shader for PN-triangles

```
1: #version 320 es
2:
3: layout(vertices = 1) out;
4:
5: uniform float tessLevel;
6:
7: in vec3 v_position[];
8: in vec3 v_normal[];
9:
10: struct PNT {
11:     vec3 P300, P030, P003; // corner control points
12:     vec3 P210, P120, P021, P012, P102, P201; // mid-edge control points
13:     vec3 P111; // inner control point
14:     vec3 N1, N2, N3; // normals
15: };
16: out patch PNT pnTri;
17:
18: vec3 displace(vec3 p1, vec3 p2, vec3 n1);
19:
20: void main() {
21:     pnTri.N1 = v_normal[0];
22:     pnTri.N2 = v_normal[1];
23:     pnTri.N3 = v_normal[2];
24:
25:     pnTri.P300 = v_position[0];
26:     pnTri.P030 = v_position[1];
27:     pnTri.P003 = v_position[2];
28:
29:     pnTri.P210 = displace(pnTri.P300, pnTri.P030, pnTri.N1);
30:     pnTri.P120 = displace(pnTri.P030, pnTri.P300, pnTri.N2);
31:     pnTri.P021 = displace(pnTri.P030, pnTri.P003, pnTri.N2);
32:     pnTri.P012 = displace(pnTri.P003, pnTri.P030, pnTri.N3);
33:     pnTri.P102 = displace(pnTri.P003, pnTri.P300, pnTri.N3);
34:     pnTri.P201 = displace(pnTri.P300, pnTri.P003, pnTri.N1);
35:
36:     vec3 V = (pnTri.P300 + pnTri.P030 + pnTri.P003) / 3.0;
37:     vec3 E = (pnTri.P210 + pnTri.P120 + pnTri.P021
38:             + pnTri.P012 + pnTri.P102 + pnTri.P201) / 6.0;
38:     pnTri.P111 = E + (E - V) / 2.0;
39:
40:     gl_TessLevelOuter[0] = tessLevel;
41:     gl_TessLevelOuter[1] = tessLevel;
42:     gl_TessLevelOuter[2] = tessLevel;
43:     gl_TessLevelInner[0] = tessLevel;
44: }
45:
46: vec3 displace(vec3 p1, vec3 p2, vec3 n1) {
47:     return (2.0 * p1 + p2) / 3.0 - dot(n1, (p2 - p1) / 3.0) * n1;
48: }
```

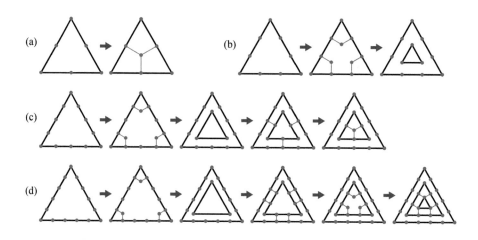

Fig. 18.15: Inner tessellation: (a) Inner TL = 2. (b) Inner TL = 3. (c) Inner TL = 4. (d) Inner TL = 5.

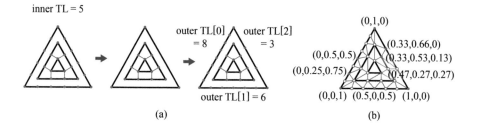

Fig. 18.16: Outer tessellation and triangulation.

Fig. 18.15-(c) shows the steps of inner tessellation when the inner TL is four. Every edge is split into four segments. For each vertex of the triangular domain, two lines are extended from the nearest split points. An inner triangle is defined. Then, from the mid split points on the triangular domain's edges, three lines are extended to intersect the inner triangle. Its state is equal to the initial state of Fig. 18.15-(a), which then directs the subsequent step in Fig. 18.15-(c). Fig. 18.15-(d) shows the case where the inner TL is five.

For the outermost triangle, the edge subdivision was temporary and therefore is discarded. As shown in Fig. 18.16-(a), gl_TessLevelOuter[0] determines how to split the left edge, where $u = 0$; gl_TessLevelOuter[1] splits the bottom edge, where $v = 0$; gl_TessLevelOuter[2] splits the right edge,

Sample code 18-6 Tessellation evaluation shader for PN-triangles

```
1: #version 320 es
2:
3: layout(triangles) in;
4:
5: uniform mat4 worldMat, viewMat, projMat;
6:
7: struct PNT {
8:     vec3 P300, P030, P003; // corner control points
9:     vec3 P210, P120, P021, P012, P102, P201; // mid-edge control points
10:    vec3 P111; // inner control point
11:    vec3 N1, N2, N3; // normals
12: };
13: in patch PNT pnTri;
14:
15: out vec3 v_normal;
16:
17: void main() {
18:     // powers of the parameters
19:     float u1 = gl_TessCoord.x, v1 = gl_TessCoord.y, w1 = gl_TessCoord.z;
20:     float u2 = pow(u1, 2.0), v2 = pow(v1, 2.0), w2 = pow(w1, 2.0);
21:     float u3 = pow(u1, 3.0), v3 = pow(v1, 3.0), w3 = pow(w1, 3.0);
22:
23:     // position evaluation
24:     vec3 position = vec3(0.0);
25:     position += pnTri.P300 * u3 + pnTri.P030 * v3 + pnTri.P003 * w3;
26:     position += pnTri.P210 * 3.0 * u2 * v1 + pnTri.P120 * 3.0 * u1 * v2;
27:     position += pnTri.P021 * 3.0 * v2 * w1 + pnTri.P012 * 3.0 * v1 * w2;
28:     position += pnTri.P102 * 3.0 * w2 * u1 + pnTri.P201 * 3.0 * w1 * u2;
29:     position += pnTri.P111 * 6.0 * u1 * v1 * w1;
30:
31:     // clip-space position
32:     gl_Position = projMat * viewMat * worldMat * vec4(position, 1.0);
33:
34:     // normal evaluation
35:     vec3 normal = pnTri.N1 * u1 + pnTri.N2 * v1 + pnTri.N3 * w1;
36:
37:     // world-space normal
38:     v_normal = normalize(transpose(inverse(mat3(worldMat))) * normal);
39: }
```

where $w = 0$. Finally, the entire area of the triangular domain is filled with a set of non-overlapping smaller triangles, and each vertex of the triangle mesh is assigned its own barycentric coordinates, (u, v, w). Fig. 18.16-(b) shows a few examples of (u, v, w).

Sample code 18-6 shows the evaluation shader. At line 3, `triangles` implies that the input patches are triangles, not quads. The PN-triangle, `pnTri`, passed from the control shader is defined using the qualifier, `in patch`, at line 13. The evaluation shader runs on each vertex input by the tessellator. To compute the position and normal of the vertex, the evaluation shader evaluates

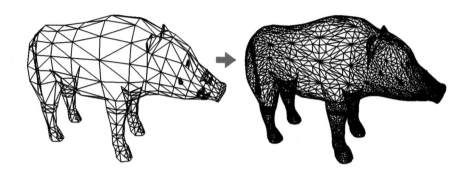

Fig. 18.17: Tessellation using PN-triangles. (© 2016 hilily on CGTrader.com)

pnTri with gl_TessCoord, which is a 3D vector containing the barycentric coordinates, (u, v, w)[3]. Lines 19 through 29 are a straight implementation of $p(u, v, w)$ presented in Fig. 18.10-(a). Line 35 is a barycentric combination of the control normals. The evaluation shader outputs gl_Position, which represents the clip-space vertex position in the tessellated mesh, and v_normal, which represents the world-space normal of the vertex. They are passed to the subsequent stages of the GPU pipeline.

Fig. 18.17 shows an example of tessellation based on PN-triangles. Suppose that a low-resolution polygon mesh enters the rendering pipeline. In the GPU pipeline, the first programmable stage is the vertex shader. It may run various animation and deformation algorithms on the input mesh. Because such algorithms are usually expensive, running the algorithms on a low-resolution mesh may significantly reduce the computational cost. Then, the tessellation-related stages convert the animated/deformed mesh into a high-resolution mesh to enhance the rendering quality. This strategy increases the overall efficiency.

---

[3]For quads, the first and second components of gl_TessCoord store (u, v) and the third is zero.

Exercises

1. Shown below is a tessellated square domain.

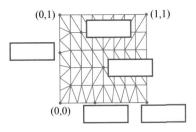

   (a) Each vertex is associated with its own (u, v) coordinates. Fill in the boxes with (u, v) coordinates.

   (b) How many tessellation levels are specified by the control shader? Write the tessellation levels.

2. Shown below is a tessellated triangular domain.

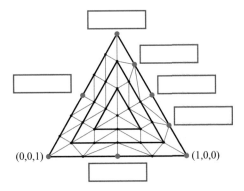

   (a) Each vertex is associated with its own barycentric coordinates. Fill in the boxes with barycentric coordinates.

   (b) How many tessellation levels are specified by the control shader? Write the tessellation levels.

References

[1] Luna, F.D.: Introduction to 3D Game Programming with DirectX 11. Mercury Learning and Information (2012)

[2] Kessenich, J., Sellers, G.: OpenGL Programming Guide: The Official Guide to Learning OpenGL, Version 4.5 with SPIR-V, 9th Edition. Addison-Wesley (2016)

[3] Akenine-Möller, T., Haines, E., Hoffman, N.: Real-Time Rendering, 3rd Edition. A. K. Peters, Ltd. (2008)

[4] Ginsburg, D., Purnomo, B.: OpenGL ES 3.0 Programming Guide. Addison Wesley (2014)

[5] Nicodemus, F.E., Richmond, J.C., Hsia, J.J., Ginsberg, I.W., Limperis, T.: Geometrical Considerations and Nomenclature for Reflectance (NBS Monograph 160). National Bureau of Standards (US) (1977)

[6] Shoemake, K.: Animating rotation with quaternion curves. SIGGRAPH Computer Graphics **19** (1985) 245–254

[7] Lindstrom, P., Pascucci, V.: Visualization of large terrains made easy. In: Proceedings of the Conference on Visualization '01, IEEE Computer Society (2001) 363–371

[8] Szirmay-Kalos, L., Umenhoffer, T.: Displacement mapping on the GPU: State of the art. Computer Graphics Forum **27** (2008) 1567–1592

[9] Williams, L.: Casting curved shadows on curved surfaces. SIGGRAPH Computer Graphics **12** (1978) 270–274

[10] Hasenfratz, J.M., Lapierre, M., Holzschuch, N., Sillion, F.: A survey of real-time soft shadows algorithms. Computer Graphics Forum **22** (2003) 753–774

[11] Whitted, T.: An improved illumination model for shaded display. Communications of the ACM **23** (1980) 343–349

[12] Goral, C.M., Torrance, K.E., Greenberg, D.P., Battaile, B.: Modeling the interaction of light between diffuse surfaces. SIGGRAPH Computer Graphics **18** (1984) 213–222

[13] Dutré, P., Bala, K., Bekaert, P.: Advanced Global Illumination, 2nd Edition. A. K. Peters Ltd. (2006)

[14] Pharr, M., Jakob, W., Humphreys, G.: Physically Based Rendering: From Theory to Implementation, 3rd Edition. Morgan Kaufmann Publishers Inc. (2016)

[15] Farin, G.E., Hansford, D.: The Essentials of CAGD. A. K. Peters, Ltd. (2000)

[16] Catmull, E., Rom, R.: A class of local interpolating splines. In Barnhill, R., Riesenfeld, R., eds.: Computer Aided Geometric Design. Academic Press (1974) 317–326

[17] Vlachos, A., Peters, J., Boyd, C., Mitchell, J.L.: Curved PN triangles. In: Proceedings of the 2001 Symposium on Interactive 3D Graphics, ACM (2001) 159–166

Index